easy
everyday
FAVORITES

easy
everyday
FAVORITES

ALLRECIPES.COM *Seattle, Washington*

AN ALLRECIPES.COM/READERS DIGEST BOOK

ALLRECIPES.COM EDITORIAL
VP, Editor in Chief: JERRY GULLEY
Creative Director: JEFF CUMMINGS
Art Production Manager: KATI CRANE
Designer: IRA GUNAWAN
Senior Designer: BRYCE GIFFORD
Staff Photographer: KIM RODENBAUGH
Senior Recipe Editor: SYD CARTER
Recipe Editors: ITA ARTT, EMILY BRUNE, KRIS ERICKSON, JULIE FAY, RICHARD KOZEL, ELSA WITTE
Culinary Director: CORY VICENS
Managing Editor: FRANCES CROUTER
Deputy Editor: VANESSA GREAVES
Food Editor: CARL HANSON
Assistant Editor: MACKENZIE SCHIECK
Editorial Assistant: ANNA CHOPP

ALLRECIPES.COM CORPORATE
Product Manager, eCommerce and Publishing: LYNN WOLL
Marketing Coordinator: STEPHANIE JONES
VP, New Business Development: JIM KREYENHAGEN
CTO/SVP Product Development: TIM HUNT
CFO: KIRK DICKINSON
SVP, Sales: CARL TRAUTMANN
VP, Marketing: ESMEE WILLIAMS

PHOTO CREDITS
Photographers: CHRISTOPHER CONRAD, TONI DYSERT
Senior Photo Stylist: CHARMAINE NICOLE
Photo Stylist: CHRISTY NORDSTROM

Pictured on front cover: Cajun Chicken Pasta (recipe on page 89)

International Standard Book Number (10) 0-89821-665-6
International Standard Book Number (13) 978-0-89821-665-3
Library of Congress Control Number 2007938811

For other Allrecipes.com books and products, visit www.allrecipes.com
For more Reader's Digest products and information visit www.rd.com (in the United States)
www.rd.ca (in Canada)

Printed in China
1 3 5 7 9 10 8 6 4 2

LETTER FROM THE EDITOR

WHAT'S FOR DINNER?

It's a question that stumps the best of us. Millions of home cooks at Allrecipes.com have been helping one another answer that question for the past 10 years and we've collected the best of their time-saving recipes for you here. You'll find over 250 top-rated recipes—reviewed by the online community at Allrecipes.com—organized by course, to help get you in and out of the kitchen faster than you can say "Eat up!"

Inside you will find starters, main courses and side dishes that can be paired to create easy-to-make (but satisfying) well-balanced meals again and again. You'll also find a grand selection of mouth-watering desserts to finish off your meals. Whether you are preparing an elaborate party, want to make a creative dinner for one, or need to get dinner on the table for your family, you'll find what you're looking for in the following pages. And there are plenty of choices for competent cooks and newbies alike.

I hope you'll enjoy trying and tasting these recipes as much as we enjoyed putting this collection together.

Happy eating,

JERRY GULLEY
Editor- in-Chief, Allrecipes.com

P.S. After you've flipped through these pages, don't forget to visit Allrecipes.com and join our ever-growing community. You'll be able to browse and share recipes, reviews, photos and tips with other home cooks just like you. You can save recipes that you've cooked and rated and collect recipes that you plan to make in the future. You can even save recipes from cookbooks, magazines, and other websites in your private Recipe Box. As a community member, you will decide which recipes deserve five star. Delve into a whole new world of food — and make mealtime fun again.

STARTERS 9

From simple everyday salads to crowd-pleasing party classics, there's something for every taste.

MAIN DISHES 69

A sumptuous selection of trusted and tested main-dish recipes that run the gamut from quick weeknight fare to elegant company-worthy creations.

SIDE DISHES 147

These accompaniments are worthy of star billing on your plate!

DESSERTS 185

Everyone loves dessert. Now they'll have even more ways to enjoy the final course.

STARTERS 9

AS SHOWN IN THE PICTURE

Spicy Three Pepper Hummus

Submitted by: **FLCRACKER**

PREP TIME: 15 MINUTES
READY IN: 8 HOURS 15 MINUTES
SERVING: 24

2 (16 ounce) cans garbanzo beans, drained
2 tablespoons olive oil
1/8 cup lemon juice
2 tablespoons tahini
8 cloves garlic, minced
2 slices jarred jalapeno pepper, chopped
1 teaspoon liquid from the jar of jalapeno peppers
1/2 teaspoon ground black pepper
1 1/2 teaspoons cayenne pepper
1/2 teaspoon ground cumin
3/4 teaspoon dried oregano

In the bowl of a stand mixer, combine the garbanzo beans, olive oil, lemon juice, tahini, garlic, jalapeno, and juice from the jalapeno jar. Season with black pepper, cayenne, cumin and oregano.

Mix using the whisk attachment on low speed until the ingredients start to blend, then turn the speed to medium, and blend to your desired consistency. Cover and refrigerate overnight to allow the flavors to blend. Make sure your container is sealed well, or your fridge will smell like garlic!

I just made this recipe today, and it's wonderful! It has a nice garlicky, spicy bite. I used the pepper, cayenne, and oregano in amounts to suit my taste. I also made mine in a food processor and needed a little more liquid to blend it properly. I had saved the liquid from the beans just in case I needed it, although water would have been fine. This recipe is definitely a keeper.

—JANMART

Just as good as the hummus you buy in the store. I made mine in the food processor and needed to add a little water to help it come together to my desired consistency.

—JENNIFER

Good basic hummus recipe, but don't be afraid to play with the ingredients to make this dish truly yours.

—PHILLYJH

AMOUNT PER SERVING: CALORIES: 65 TOTAL FAT: 2.3g CHOLESTEROL: 0mg SODIUM: 122 mg TOTAL CARBS: 9.4 g DIETARY FIBER: 1.9 g PROTEIN: 2.2 g

Warm Blue Cheese Dip with Garlic and Bacon

Submitted by: **CAROL PALAIKA**

PREP TIME: 30 MINUTES
COOK TIME: 30 MINUTES
READY IN: 1 HOUR
SERVINGS: 14

7 slices bacon
2 cloves garlic, peeled and minced
1 (8 ounce) package cream cheese, softened
1/4 cup half-and-half
4 ounces blue cheese, crumbled
2 tablespoons chopped fresh chives

Place bacon in a large, deep skillet. Cook over medium high heat until evenly browned. Remove bacon from skillet, drain on paper towels and crumble.

Place garlic in hot bacon grease. Cook and stir until soft, about 1 minute. Remove from heat.

Preheat oven to 350°F (175°C). Place cream cheese and half-and-half in a medium bowl. Beat with an electric mixer until blended. Stir in bacon, garlic, blue cheese and chives. Transfer mixture to a medium baking dish.

Bake covered in the preheated oven 30 minutes, or until lightly browned.

AMOUNT PER SERVING: CALORIES: 169   TOTAL FAT: 16.5 g   CHOLESTEROL: 35 mg   SODIUM: 264 mg   TOTAL CARBS: 1 g   DIETARY FIBER: 0 g   PROTEIN: 4.3 g

To Die For Garlic Feta Pate

Submitted by: **DARLENE HINTON**

PREP TIME: 10 MINUTES
READY IN: 10 MINUTES
SERVINGS: 16

2 cloves garlic, minced
4 anchovy fillets, chopped
6 tablespoons butter, softened
1 (8 ounce) package cream cheese, softened
3/4 cup crumbled feta cheese
1/4 cup sour cream
1 tablespoon chopped fresh chives
1 dash hot pepper sauce (e.g. Tabasco™), or to taste
Freshly ground black pepper to taste

Combine the garlic, anchovies, butter, cream cheese, feta cheese, sour cream, chives, hot pepper sauce and pepper in the container of a food processor. Process until smooth. Transfer to a serving bowl, and serve with crackers, bread slices, or pita chips.

I was looking for something different to take to a party and this was it. Everyone loved it! I also doubled the anchovies.

—LPRENTIS

AMOUNT PER SERVING: CALORIES: 129   TOTAL FAT: 12.6 g   CHOLESTEROL: 40 mg   SODIUM: 256 mg
TOTAL CARBS: 1.2 g   DIETARY FIBER: 0 g   PROTEIN: 3.2 g

Salsa Cheese Boule Dip

Submitted by: JULIE

PREP TIME: 5 MINUTES
COOK TIME: 1 HOUR 30 MINUTES
READY IN: 1 HOUR 35 MINUTES
SERVINGS: 9

1 (1 pound) loaf round, crusty Italian bread
1 1/2 cups shredded Cheddar cheese
1 (8 ounce) package cream cheese, softened
1 cup sour cream
1 cup salsa

Preheat oven to 350°F (175°C).

Cut a circle out of the top of the bread and scoop out the inside. Tear the inside into pieces for dipping.

In a medium size mixing bowl, combine salsa, Cheddar cheese, cream cheese, and sour cream. Spoon the mixture into the bread bowl, place the top back on the bread. Wrap the bread in aluminum foil.

Bake for 1 1/2 hours. Serve warm with the reserved bread pieces.

AMOUNT PER SERVING: CALORIES: 362   TOTAL FAT: 22.1 g   CHOLESTEROL: 58 mg   SODIUM: 624 mg
TOTAL CARBS: 29 g   DIETARY FIBER: 1.8 g   PROTEIN: 12.2 g

Fig and Olive Tapenade

Submitted by: ANNE

PREP TIME: 15 MINUTES
COOK TIME: 10 MINUTES
READY IN: 4 HOURS 25 MINUTES
SERVINGS: 6

1 cup chopped dried figs
1/2 cup water
2/3 cup chopped kalamata olives
1 tablespoon olive oil
2 tablespoons balsamic vinegar
2 cloves garlic, minced
1 teaspoon dried rosemary
1 teaspoon dried thyme
1/4 teaspoon cayenne pepper
Salt and pepper to taste
1/3 cup chopped toasted walnuts
1 (8 ounce) package cream cheese

Combine figs and water in a saucepan over medium heat. Bring to a boil, and cook until tender, and liquid has reduced. Remove from heat, and stir in the olive oil, balsamic vinegar, rosemary, thyme, and cayenne. Add olives and garlic, and mix well. Season with salt and pepper to taste. Cover, and refrigerate for 4 hours or overnight to allow flavors to blend.

Unwrap cream cheese block, and place on a serving platter. Spoon tapenade over cheese, and sprinkle with walnuts. Serve with slices of French bread or crackers.

This was a great success and a big hit. I used goat cheese instead of cream cheese and served with small slices of tuscan style green olive bread.

—CHEFMEISTER KIP

AMOUNT PER SERVING: CALORIES: 355   TOTAL FAT: 26.6 g   CHOLESTEROL: 41 mg   SODIUM: 522 mg
TOTAL CARBS: 27.3 g   DIETARY FIBER: 4.9 g   PROTEIN: 5.4 g

AS SHOWN IN THE PICTURE

Hot Artichoke and Spinach Dip

Submitted by: TIFFANY

PREP TIME: 15 MINUTES
COOK TIME: 25 MINUTES
READY IN: 40 MINUTES
SERVINGS: 12

1 (8 ounce) package cream cheese, softened
1/4 cup mayonnaise
1/4 cup grated Parmesan cheese
1/4 cup grated Romano cheese
1 clove garlic, peeled and minced
1/2 teaspoon dried basil
1/4 teaspoon garlic salt
Salt and pepper to taste
1 (14 ounce) can artichoke hearts, drained and chopped
1/2 cup frozen chopped spinach, thawed and drained
1/4 cup shredded mozzarella cheese

Preheat oven to 350°F (175°C). Lightly grease a small baking dish.

In a medium bowl, mix together cream cheese, mayonnaise, Parmesan cheese, Romano cheese, garlic, basil, garlic salt, salt and pepper. Gently stir in artichoke hearts and spinach.

Transfer the mixture to the prepared baking dish. Top with mozzarella cheese. Bake in the preheated oven 25 minutes, until bubbly and lightly browned.

AMOUNT PER SERVING: CALORIES: 143   TOTAL FAT: 11.8 g   CHOLESTEROL: 29 mg   SODIUM: 402 mg
TOTAL CARBS: 4.7 g   DIETARY FIBER: 1.4 g   PROTEIN: 5.1 g

Salsa De Tomatillo

Submitted by: SANDY T.

PREP TIME: 20 MINUTES
COOK TIME: 10 MINUTES
READY IN: 30 MINUTES
SERVINGS: 16

10 tomatillos, husked
1 small onion, chopped
3 cloves garlic, chopped
2 jalapeno peppers, chopped
1/4 cup chopped fresh cilantro
Salt and pepper to taste

Place tomatillos in a nonreactive saucepan with enough water to cover. Bring to a boil. Simmer until tomatillos soften and begin to burst, about 10 minutes.

Drain tomatillos and place in a food processor or blender with onion, garlic, jalapeno peppers, cilantro, salt and pepper. Blend to desired consistency.

This salsa is delicious! I had never used tomatillos before, but they will be a regular on my shopping list. We absolutely love the salsa with chips.

—BEAYUMAN

AMOUNT PER SERVING: CALORIES: 10   TOTAL FAT: 0.2 g   CHOLESTEROL: 0 mg   SODIUM: <1 mg   TOTAL CARBS: 1.9 g
DIETARY FIBER: 0.6 g   PROTEIN: 0.3 g

Best Hot Crab Dip

Submitted by: JOELLE FLYNN

PREP TIME: 20 MINUTES
COOK TIME: 20 MINUTES
READY IN: 40 MINUTES
SERVINGS: 18

2 cups crabmeat

1 cup sour cream

1 (8 ounce) package cream cheese, softened

1 cup buttermilk

1 cup mayonnaise

1 cup shredded Monterey Jack cheese

1 cup white Cheddar cheese

1/2 cup capers, drained

2 (8 ounce) cans artichoke hearts, drained and chopped

2 tablespoons minced garlic

1/2 teaspoon ground black pepper, or to taste

1/2 teaspoon dried dill, or to taste

1/4 cup grated Parmesan cheese

1/2 teaspoon Old Bay Seasoning™

1 (8 ounce) round loaf sourdough bread

Preheat oven to 400°F (200°C). Lightly grease an 8x8 inch square baking pan.

In a large bowl, combine crabmeat, sour cream, cream cheese, buttermilk, mayonnaise, Monterey Jack cheese, Cheddar cheese, capers, artichoke hearts, garlic, black pepper and dill. Stir until well mixed. Spoon dip into prepared baking pan. Sprinkle with Parmesan cheese and Old Bay Seasoning™.

Bake in preheated oven until top is crusty, about 15 to 20 minutes.

Cut the top off the loaf of bread. Hollow out the loaf and cube the top and the removed pieces so that they may be used for dipping. Spoon hot dip into hollow bread loaf. Serve immediately with bread pieces for dipping.

This crab dip is awesome! So delicious & so easy to make! I do, however, have a suggestion. The bread bowl is great but the bread used for dipping is not hard enough to pick up the dip. You may want to toast the bread pieces or use bread sticks instead.

—LSM

I found this recipe a couple of years ago on allrecipes.com and it has become a favorite of our family! I always make it at holidays & when company comes over. Everyone always loves it. I know a lot of people are unsure about putting capers in it, either because they think they wouldn't taste good in it or because they don't know what capers are. I assure you that the capers are a MUST for this recipe. Capers by themselves aren't appetizing, but when added to this recipe, gives it just the right flavor! Trust me!.

—TABITHA HARDER

AMOUNT PER SERVING: CALORIES: 284 TOTAL FAT: 21.8 g CHOLESTEROL: 54 mg SODIUM: 649 mg

TOTAL CARBS: 11.7 g DIETARY FIBER: 1.4 g PROTEIN: 10.8 g

Avocado, Tomato and Mango Salsa

Submitted by: FHIVESHOT

PREP TIME: 15 MINUTES
READY IN: 40 MINUTES
SERVINGS: 6

1 mango - peeled, seeded and diced
1 avocado - peeled, pitted, and diced
4 medium tomatoes, diced
1 jalapeno pepper, seeded and minced
1/2 cup chopped fresh cilantro
3 cloves garlic, minced
1 teaspoon salt
2 tablespoons fresh lime juice
1/4 cup chopped red onion
3 tablespoons olive oil

In a medium bowl, combine the mango, avocado, tomatoes, jalapeno, cilantro, and garlic. Stir in the salt, lime juice, red onion, and olive oil. To blend the flavors, refrigerate for about 30 minutes before serving.

Awesome, easy and ready to go right away. We used this several different ways all in one day - just with chips, on quesadillas and later on some grilled fish.

—KMS1970

AMOUNT PER SERVING: CALORIES: 161   TOTAL FAT: 12.3 g   CHOLESTEROL: 0 mg   SODIUM: 401 mg
TOTAL CARBS: 14 g   DIETARY FIBER: 3.5 g   PROTEIN: 1.8 g

Fresh Salsa

Submitted by: KAYLENE DOW

PREP TIME: 20 MINUTES
COOK TIME: 15 MINUTES
READY IN: 35 MINUTES
SERVINGS: 48

4 jalapeno chile peppers
5 cloves garlic, finely chopped
1 onion, finely chopped
1 tablespoon white sugar
1 teaspoon salt
1/4 teaspoon ground cumin
1 (10 ounce) can diced tomatoes with green chile peppers
1 (28 ounce) can whole peeled tomatoes

Preheat oven to 400°F (200°C).

Place jalapeno chile peppers on a medium baking sheet. Bake in the preheated oven 15 minutes, or until roasted. Remove from heat and chop off stems.

Place jalapeno chile peppers, garlic, onion, white sugar, salt, ground cumin and diced tomatoes with green chile peppers in a blender or food processor. Chop using the pulse setting for a few seconds. Mix in whole peeled tomatoes. Chop using the pulse setting to attain desired consistency. Transfer to a medium bowl. Cover and chill in the refrigerator until serving.

AMOUNT PER SERVING: CALORIES: 7   TOTAL FAT: 0 g   CHOLESTEROL: 0 mg   SODIUM: 74 mg   TOTAL CARBS: 1.6 g
DIETARY FIBER: 0.3 g   PROTEIN: 0.3 g

AS SHOWN IN THE PICTURE

Sun-Dried Tomato Dip

Submitted by: ROBIN C

PREP TIME: 10 MINUTES
READY IN: 1 HOUR 10 MINUTES
SERVINGS: 16

1/4 cup oil-packed sun-dried tomatoes, drained and chopped
8 ounces cream cheese, room temperature
1/2 cup sour cream
1/4 cup mayonnaise
2 cloves garlic, minced
Hot pepper sauce to taste
3/4 teaspoon salt
3/4 teaspoon freshly ground black pepper
1/4 cup fresh basil

In a food processor, mix the sun-dried tomatoes, cream cheese, sour cream, mayonnaise, garlic, hot pepper sauce, salt, and pepper. Process until well-blended. Add basil, and continue processing until smooth. Chill at least 1 hour in the refrigerator before serving.

Loved this one! Very gourmet tasting, but easy too. Great on toasted crostini bread slices, and next time I'll try pita chips. Celery & cucumber would go well, plus try stuffing into cherry tomatoes as a wow appetizer.

—JAMIE47

AMOUNT PER SERVING: CALORIES: 94 TOTAL FAT: 9.4 g CHOLESTEROL: 21 mg SODIUM: 180 mg
TOTAL CARBS. 1.4 g DIETARY FIBER: 0.2 g PROTEIN: 1.5 g

Dill Dip

Submitted by: DIANE

PREP TIME: 20 MINUTES
READY IN: 8 HOURS 20 MINUTES
SERVINGS: 8

2 cups mayonnaise
2 cups sour cream
3 tablespoons chopped onion
1 teaspoon seasoning salt
3 teaspoons dried dill weed
1 tablespoon white sugar

In a medium bowl, mix together mayonnaise, sour cream, chopped onion, seasoning salt, dill weed, and white sugar. Refrigerate for at least 8 hours before serving to blend flavors.

This recipe deserves nothing less than 5 stars! This is the best dip I have ever tasted. It took me 3 minutes to make and tasted wonderful even before refrigeration.

—TREKKERD

AMOUNT PER SERVING: CALORIES: 88 TOTAL FAT: 9.3 g CHOLESTEROL: 10 mg SODIUM: 76 mg TOTAL CARBS: 1 g
DIETARY FIBER: 0 g PROTEIN: 0.4 g

AS SHOWN IN THE PICTURE

Hot Corn Dip

Submitted by: CORINNE DOUBIAGO

PREP TIME: 15 MINUTES
COOK TIME: 30 MINUTES
READY IN: 45 MINUTES
SERVINGS: 48

1 (15 ounce) can white corn, drained
1 (15 ounce) can yellow corn, drained
1 (10 ounce) can diced tomatoes with green chile peppers, drained
1 (8 ounce) package cream cheese, diced and softened
1/2 teaspoon chili powder
1/2 teaspoon garlic powder
Chopped fresh cilantro to taste

Preheat oven to 350°F (175°C).

In a medium baking dish, mix white corn, yellow corn, diced tomatoes with green chile peppers, cream cheese, chili powder, garlic powder and cilantro.

Bake in the preheated oven 30 minutes, or until hot bubbly.

This recipe is easy and very good. A definite pleaser. I like my food spicy so I added more chili powder. I also added cumin and some canned green chiles.

—KRYSTIE K

AMOUNT PER SERVING: CALORIES: 29 TOTAL FAT: 1.7 g CHOLESTEROL: 5 mg SODIUM: 78 mg TOTAL CARBS: 3.3 g
DIETARY FIBER: 0.4 g PROTEIN: 0.8 g

Mexican Layered Dip

Submitted by: RUSTY

PREP TIME: 10 MINUTES
READY IN: 2 HOURS 10 MINUTES
SERVINGS: 10

1 (16 ounce) can refried beans
1 (1.25 ounce) package taco seasoning mix
1 large tomato, seeded and chopped
1 cup guacamole
1 cup sour cream, room temperature
1 cup shredded sharp Cheddar cheese
1/2 cup chopped green onions
1/4 cup chopped black olives

Spread refried beans in the bottom of a (1-quart) shallow edged serving dish (you can use a transparent dish if you'd like). Sprinkle the seasoning packet over the beans. Layer the diced tomatoes over the beans, the sour cream over the tomatoes, and the guacamole over the sour cream. Sprinkle the entire layered dip with cheddar cheese, followed by green onion and finishing it off with a layer of black olives. Cover and refrigerate until ready to serve.

Everybody loved this dip. Instead of tomato I use a fire roasted salsa. I also mixed in a little taco seasoning into the sour cream as suggested. You just can't mess it up!!

—STARKRAZI

AMOUNT PER SERVING: CALORIES: 196 TOTAL FAT: 12.8 g CHOLESTEROL: 28 mg SODIUM: 522 mg
TOTAL CARBS: 13.5 g DIETARY FIBER: 3.7 g PROTEIN: 7.3 g

AS SHOWN IN THE PICTURE
Black Bean Salsa
Submitted by: REBECKAH MACFIE

PREP TIME: 15 MINUTES
READY IN: 8 HOURS 15 MINUTES
SERVINGS: 40

3 (15 ounce) cans black beans, drained and rinsed

1 (11 ounce) can Mexican-style corn, drained

2 (10 ounce) cans diced tomatoes with green chile peppers, partially drained

2 tomatoes, diced

2 bunches green onions, chopped

Cilantro leaves, for garnish

In a large bowl, mix together black beans, Mexican-style corn, diced tomatoes with green chile peppers, tomatoes and green onion stalks. Garnish with desired amount of cilantro leaves. Chill in the refrigerator at least 8 hours, or overnight, before serving.

I made this for my daughter's 2nd birthday party and got rave reviews and many requests for the recipe. I added 2 cloves of garlic, cumin, chopped cilantro, frozen white and yellow corn and green chilies. I chilled it for a day and the flavor was absolutely wonderful. I have used it on salads and also grilled chicken.

—ALICIAB

AMOUNT PER SERVING: CALORIES: 41 TOTAL FAT: 0.2 g CHOLESTEROL: 0 mg SODIUM: 206 mg TOTAL CARBS: 8.2 g
DIETARY FIBER: 2.8 g PROTEIN: 2.4 g

Papaya Bruschetta
Submitted by: LJOLLEY

PREP TIME: 20 MINUTES
READY IN: 20 MINUTES
SERVINGS: 8

1 papaya

5 roma (plum) tomatoes, diced

1/2 red onion, diced

1 red bell pepper, seeded and diced

1/4 cup chopped fresh basil leaves

2 tablespoons white sugar

1/4 cup red wine vinegar

1/4 cup vegetable oil

1/2 teaspoon mustard powder

2 green onions, chopped

1 French baguette, cut into half inch pieces

Cut papaya in half and remove seeds. Reserve 2 tablespoons of seeds for the dressing. Peel and dice the papaya, and place in a medium bowl. Add tomatoes, red onion, red pepper and basil, and set aside.

In a food processor or blender, combine the papaya seeds, sugar, wine vinegar, oil, mustard and green onions. Process until smooth and thick, and most of the seeds have broken up. Pour over the papaya mixture and stir to coat all of the ingredients. Serve with slices of baguette.

This recipe is delicious as a salad also. I simply cut the papaya, tomatoes and red pepper into larger pieces and omit the baguette. One note - it is not always easy to find a ripe papaya, which is very important to the success of this recipe.

—BETSY G.

AMOUNT PER SERVING: CALORIES: 255 TOTAL FAT: 8.8 g CHOLESTEROL: 0 mg SODIUM: 351 mg
TOTAL CARBS: 38.8 g DIETARY FIBER: 3.1 g PROTEIN: 5.8 g

Baked Onion Dip

Submitted by: N O R E E N

PREP TIME: 10 MINUTES
COOK TIME: 45 MINUTES
READY IN: 55 MINUTES
SERVINGS: 24

2 cups sweet onion, peeled and chopped
2 cups mayonnaise
2 cups Parmesan cheese

Preheat oven to 350°F (175°C). Prepare a 2 quart baking dish with cooking spray.

In a large mixing bowl, combine the mayonnaise, onions and cheese. Pour the mixture into the baking dish and bake for approximately 45 minutes, until the top is slightly brown. Serve hot with buttery, round crackers.

This was a great simple recipe. Who would have thought that three simple ingredients would have made such a tasty treat.

—CREATING BEAUTY

AMOUNT PER SERVING: CALORIES: 174   TOTAL FAT: 17.1 g   CHOLESTEROL: 17 mg   SODIUM: 260 mg
TOTAL CARBS: 2 g   DIETARY FIBER: 0.2 g   PROTEIN: 3.8 g

Dip For The Stars

Submitted by: D A N A   C O L E

PREP TIME: 20 MINUTES
READY IN: 1 HOUR 20 MINUTES
SERVINGS: 30

1 cup unsalted butter
3/4 pound feta cheese, crumbled
1 (8 ounce) package cream cheese, softened
2 cloves garlic, minced
1 shallot, minced
3 tablespoons dry vermouth
Ground white pepper, to taste
1/2 cup pine nuts, toasted
1 cup chopped sun-dried tomatoes
3/4 cup pesto sauce

In a food processor, combine the butter, feta cheese, cream cheese, garlic, shallot, vermouth, and white pepper. Process until smooth.

Oil a medium bowl, or gelatin mold, and line with plastic wrap for easy removal. Layer the dip into the mold as follows: Sun-dried tomatoes, pine nuts, pesto, cheese mixture. Repeat. Pat down into the mold, and refrigerate for at least one hour.

Turn the dip out onto a serving plate, and remove plastic wrap. Serve with crackers.

This is a WONDERFUL dip that everyone seems to love. I always put the sun-dried tomatoes in the food processor so that the pieces are smaller. I serve it with the flavored bruschetta pieces you can get at the grocery store - our favorite is garlic parmesan.

—ALLICAT2U

AMOUNT PER SERVING: CALORIES: 162   TOTAL FAT: 15.2 g   CHOLESTEROL: 37 mg   SODIUM: 234 mg
TOTAL CARBS: 2.9 g   DIETARY FIBER: 0.5 g   PROTEIN: 4.2 g

Baked Potato Dip

Submitted by: BRENDA T.

PREP TIME: 5 MINUTES
READY IN: 5 MINUTES
SERVINGS: 32

2 (16 ounce) containers sour cream
1 (3 ounce) can bacon bits
2 cups shredded Cheddar cheese
1 bunch green onions, chopped

In a medium size mixing bowl, combine sour cream, bacon, Cheddar cheese and green onions; stir well. Refrigerate, or serve immediately.

Actually this should be 10 stars!!! I made this (without testing it first) for a baked potato potluck at work. It was inhaled and the next day people were looking for leftovers. Everyone wanted the recipe.

—AUNTPT

AMOUNT PER SERVING: CALORIES: 100   TOTAL FAT: 8.8 g   CHOLESTEROL: 22 mg   SODIUM: 144 mg
TOTAL CARBS: 1.9 g   DIETARY FIBER: 0.2 g   PROTEIN: 3.8 g

Chicken Wing Dip

Submitted by: ASCBRADY

PREP TIME: 10 MINUTES
COOK TIME: 30 MINUTES
READY IN: 40 MINUTES
SERVINGS: 16

2 (8 ounce) packages cream cheese, softened
3/4 cup pepper sauce, such as Franks Red Hot®
1 cup Ranch-style salad dressing
2 cups diced cooked chicken
1 cup shredded Cheddar cheese

Preheat the oven to 350°F (175°C).

In a medium bowl, stir together the cream cheese and hot pepper sauce until well blended. Mix in the Ranch dressing, chicken and Cheddar cheese. Spread into a 9x13 inch baking dish.

Bake for 30 minutes in the preheated oven. If oil collects on the top, dab it off using a paper towel. Serve with tortilla chips.

Definitely a hit at my party! I made it exactly according to the recipe and my guests really gobbled it up. I did use canned chicken and it was sooo easy.

—AZMOM

AMOUNT PER SERVING: CALORIES: 240   TOTAL FAT: 21.8 g   CHOLESTEROL: 57 mg   SODIUM: 357 mg
TOTAL CARBS: 1.6 g   DIETARY FIBER: 0.1 g   PROTEIN: 9.4 g

AS SHOWN IN THE PICTURE

Annie's Fruit Salsa and Cinnamon Chips

Submitted by: ALISON

PREP TIME: 15 MINUTES
READY IN: 55 MINUTES
SERVINGS: 10

2 kiwis, peeled and diced
2 Golden Delicious apples - peeled, cored and diced
8 ounces raspberries
1 pound strawberries, chopped
2 tablespoons white sugar
1 tablespoon brown sugar
3 tablespoons fruit preserves, any flavor
10 (10 inch) flour tortillas
Butter flavored cooking spray
2 cups cinnamon sugar

In a large bowl, thoroughly mix kiwis, Golden Delicious apples, raspberries, strawberries, white sugar, brown sugar and fruit preserves. Cover and chill in the refrigerator at least 15 minutes.

Preheat oven to 350°F (175°C).

Coat one side of each flour tortilla with butter flavored cooking spray. Cut into wedges and arrange in a single layer on a large baking sheet. Sprinkle wedges with desired amount of cinnamon sugar. Spray again with cooking spray.

Bake in the preheated oven 8 to 10 minutes. Repeat with any remaining tortilla wedges. Allow to cool approximately 15 minutes. Serve with chilled fruit and spice mixture.

I've been making this recipe for years and it's a hit with everyone. You can basically use any kind of fruits you wish and you won't compromise the flavor of this salsa. The cinnamon chips are very tasty with the cinnamon and sugar sprinkled on them and the crunch from baking them in the oven....I love this recipe!

—MOBUN7

I added some fresh mint and lime juice and it was the perfect balance of sweet and tart. Great recipe!

—TRACEY MITCHELL

Has anyone tried adding a bit of chopped cilantro and jalapeno pepper to this mix (for a little kick)? Maybe finely chopped red onion? Diced grilled fresh pineapple might also be nice.

—COOKER20

AMOUNT PER SERVING: CALORIES: 466   TOTAL FAT: 5.5 g   CHOLESTEROL: 0 mg   SODIUM: 349 mg
TOTAL CARBS: 99.3 g   DIETARY FIBER: 6 g   PROTEIN: 7 g

AS SHOWN IN THE PICTURE

Kettle Corn

Submitted by: SUE

PREP TIME: 5 MINUTES
COOK TIME: 15 MINUTES
READY IN: 20 MINUTES
SERVINGS: 5

1/2 cup unpopped popcorn kernels
1/4 cup white sugar
1/4 cup vegetable oil

Place the popcorn and sugar in a large pot with vegetable oil. Over a medium heat, begin to pop the popcorn. Constantly shake the pot to ensure that the popcorn kernels and oil do not burn. Once the popping has slowed, remove the pot from heat.

This popcorn is addictive!! I think I have made a batch each day since trying it last weekend. Perfect if you crave sweet and salty.

—BETHANYPACE

AMOUNT PER SERVING: CALORIES: 209   TOTAL FAT: 11.9 g   CHOLESTEROL: 0 mg   SODIUM: <1 mg
TOTAL CARBS: 24.8 g   DIETARY FIBER: 2.9 g   PROTEIN: 2.4 g

Pecan Snack

Submitted by: BEA

PREP TIME: 10 MINUTES
COOK TIME: 1 HOUR
SERVINGS: 32

1 egg white
1 tablespoon water
1 pound pecans
3/4 cup white sugar
1 teaspoon ground cinnamon
1 teaspoon salt

Preheat oven to 250°F (120°C).

In a large bowl, beat egg white with water until frothy. Stir in pecans and mix to coat. Combine sugar, cinnamon and salt and stir into pecan mixture. Spread on a baking sheet.

Bake in preheated oven 1 hour, stirring every 15 minutes. Store in an airtight container.

YUMMY - I like them a touch sweeter so I reduced the salt to 1/2 teaspoon and added a bit more cinnamon. Also the egg white should be beaten to stiff peaks. The coating tasted lighter and crispier the second day for some reason. Make 3 pounds because you will not be able to stop eating these!

—GINA

AMOUNT PER SERVING: CALORIES: 117   TOTAL FAT: 10.2 g   CHOLESTEROL: 0 mg   SODIUM: 74 mg
TOTAL CARBS: 6.7 g   DIETARY FIBER: 1.4 g   PROTEIN: 1.4 g

AS SHOWN IN THE PICTURE

Grilled Salmon Skewers

Submitted by: DAKOTA KELLY

PREP TIME: 15 MINUTES
COOK TIME: 8 MINUTES
READY IN: 53 MINUTES
SERVINGS: 12

1 pound salmon filet without skin
1/4 cup soy sauce
1/4 cup honey
1 tablespoon rice vinegar
1 teaspoon minced fresh ginger root
1 clove fresh garlic, minced
Pinch of freshly ground black pepper
12 fresh lemon wedges
12 skewers

Slice salmon lengthwise into 12 long strips, and thread each onto a soaked wooden skewer. Place in a shallow dish.

In a bowl, whisk together the soy sauce, honey, vinegar, ginger, garlic, and pepper. Pour over skewers, turning to coat. Let stand at room temperature for 30 minutes. When finished marinating, transfer marinade to a small saucepan, and simmer for several minutes.

Preheat an outdoor grill for medium-high heat.

Lightly oil grill grate. Thread 1 lemon wedge onto the end of each skewer. Cook skewers on the preheated grill for 4 minutes per side, brushing often with marinade, or until fish flakes easily with a fork.

AMOUNT PER SERVING: CALORIES: 89   TOTAL FAT: 3.7 g   CHOLESTEROL: 19 mg   SODIUM: 324 mg   TOTAL CARBS: 7.9 g   DIETARY FIBER: 0.7 g   PROTEIN: 7 g

---

Best Ever Jalapeno Poppers

Submitted by: HEATHER FARGIS

PREP TIME: 45 MINUTES
COOK TIME: 15 MINUTES
READY IN: 1 HOUR
SERVINGS: 32

12 ounces cream cheese, softened
1 (8 ounce) package shredded Cheddar cheese
1 tablespoon bacon bits
12 ounces jalapeno peppers, halved and seeded
1 cup milk
1 cup all-purpose flour
1 cup dry bread crumbs
2 quarts oil for frying

In a medium bowl, mix the cream cheese, Cheddar cheese and bacon bits. Spoon this mixture into the jalapeno pepper halves.

Put the milk and flour into two separate small bowls. Dip the stuffed jalapenos first into the milk then into the flour, making sure they are well coated with each. Allow the coated jalapenos to dry for about 10 minutes.

Dip the jalapenos in milk again and roll them through the breadcrumbs. Allow them to dry, then repeat to ensure the entire surface of the jalapeno is coated.

In a medium skillet, heat the oil to 365°F (180°C). Deep fry the coated jalapenos 2 to 3 minutes each, until golden brown. Remove and let drain on a paper towel.

AMOUNT PER SERVING: CALORIES: 149   TOTAL FAT: 12 g   CHOLESTEROL: 20 mg   SODIUM: 115 mg   TOTAL CARBS: 6.8 g   DIETARY FIBER: 0.5 g   PROTEIN: 3.9 g

Cocktail Meatballs

Submitted by: JENNIE

PREP TIME: 10 MINUTES
COOK TIME: 40 MINUTES
READY IN: 50 MINUTES
SERVINGS: 8

1 pound ground beef
1/2 cup dried bread crumbs
1/3 cup chopped onion
1/4 cup milk
1 egg
1 teaspoon salt
1/2 teaspoon Worcestershire sauce
1/8 teaspoon ground black pepper
1/4 cup shortening
12 fluid ounces tomato-based Chili sauce
1 1/4 cups grape jelly

In a large bowl, combine ground beef, bread crumbs, onion, milk, egg, salt, Worcestershire sauce, and ground black pepper. Mix together, and shape into meatballs.

In a large skillet, heat shortening over medium heat. Add meatballs, and cook until browned, about 5 to 7 minutes. Remove from skillet, and drain on paper towels. Add chili sauce and jelly to skillet; heat, stirring, until jelly is melted. Return meatballs to skillet, and stir until coated. Reduce heat to low. Simmer, uncovered, for 30 minutes.

Another party favorite and so easy to make. I cheat and use frozen meatballs and then throw them in a crockpot for a few hours with the cocktail sauce and grape jelly. They are always the first to go.

—KELLYANN6281

AMOUNT PER SERVING: CALORIES: 458   TOTAL FAT: 22.8 g   CHOLESTEROL: 75 mg   SODIUM: 1,047 mg
TOTAL CARBS: 14 g   DIETARY FIBER: 3.5 g   PROTEIN: 1.8 g

AS SHOWN IN THE PICTURE

Ginger Orange Glazed Chicken Wings

Submitted by: HEATHER

PREP TIME: 20 MINUTES
COOK TIME: 45 MINUTES
READY IN: 9 HOURS 5 MINUTES
SERVINGS: 4

1/2 cup frozen orange juice concentrate, thawed and undiluted
3 tablespoons fresh lemon juice
1/4 cup hoisin sauce
1 tablespoon vegetable oil
1/4 cup sugar
3 tablespoons minced peeled ginger
3 cloves fresh garlic, minced
2 pounds chicken wings
3 medium green onions, thinly sliced

In a large, resealable bag, mix the orange juice concentrate, lemon juice, hoisin sauce, vegetable oil, sugar, ginger, and fresh garlic. Add chicken wings, seal, and shake to coat evenly. Refrigerate overnight.

Preheat oven to 400°F (200°C). Line a large baking sheet with aluminum foil.

Spread wings on foil with marinade, and bake for 45 minutes, until brown and shiny. Transfer to serving platter, and garnish with green onions.

AMOUNT PER SERVING: CALORIES: 347   TOTAL FAT: 15.2 g   CHOLESTEROL: 48 mg   SODIUM: 307 mg
TOTAL CARBS: 36.2 g   DIETARY FIBER: 1.2 g   PROTEIN: 1.7 g

Bacon and Cheddar Stuffed Mushrooms

Submitted by: **KRISTA HUGHES**

PREP TIME: 15 MINUTES
COOK TIME: 15 MINUTES
READY IN: 30 MINUTES
SERVINGS: 8

3 slices bacon
8 crimini mushrooms
1 tablespoon butter
1 tablespoon chopped onion
3/4 cup shredded Cheddar cheese

Place bacon in a large, deep skillet. Cook over medium high heat until evenly browned. Drain, dice and set aside. Preheat oven to 400°F (200°C). Remove mushroom stems. Set aside caps. Chop the stems.

In a large saucepan over medium heat, melt the butter. Slowly cook and stir the chopped stems and onion until the onion is soft. Remove from heat.

In a medium bowl, stir together the mushroom stem mixture, bacon and 1/2 cup Cheddar. Mix well and scoop the mixture into the mushroom caps. Bake in the preheated oven 15 minutes, or until the cheese has melted. Remove the mushrooms from the oven, and sprinkle with the remaining cheese.

AMOUNT PER SERVING: CALORIES: 120 TOTAL FAT: 11 g CHOLESTEROL: 22 mg SODIUM: 164 mg
TOTAL CARBS: 0.8 g DIETARY FIBER: 0.4 g PROTEIN: 4.4 g

AS SHOWN IN THE PICTURE

Chicken Quesadillas

Submitted by: **HEATHER**

PREP TIME: 20 MINUTES
COOK TIME: 25 MINUTES
READY IN: 45 MINUTES
SERVINGS: 20

1 pound skinless, boneless chicken breast halves
1 (1.27 ounce) packet fajita seasoning
1 tablespoon vegetable oil
2 green bell peppers, chopped
2 red bell peppers, chopped
1 onion, chopped
10 (10 inch) flour tortillas
1 (8 ounce) package shredded Cheddar cheese
1 tablespoon bacon bits
1 (8 ounce) package shredded Monterey Jack cheese

Preheat the broiler.

Cut the chicken into small cubes and prepare with the fajita seasoning mix. Broil 5 minutes, or until the chicken is no longer pink on the inside

Preheat oven to 350°F (175°C).

Heat the oil in a large saucepan over medium heat. Mix in the seasoned chicken, green bell peppers, red bell peppers and onion. Slowly cook and stir 10 minutes, or until the vegetables are tender.

Layer 1/2 of each tortilla with Cheddar cheese, chicken mixture and desired amount of bacon bits. Top with Monterey Jack. Fold the tortillas in half.

Bake in the preheated oven 10 minutes, or until the cheese has melted.

AMOUNT PER SERVING: CALORIES: 250 TOTAL FAT: 10.7 g CHOLESTEROL: 35 mg SODIUM: 445 mg
TOTAL CARBS: 23.4 g DIETARY FIBER: 1.7 g PROTEIN: 14.3 g

Crispy Vegetable Pakoras

Submitted by: **KARLA**

PREP TIME: 15 MINUTES
COOK TIME: 10 MINUTES
READY IN: 25 MINUTES
SERVINGS: 6

1 cup chickpea flour
1/2 teaspoon ground coriander
1 teaspoon salt
1/2 teaspoon ground turmeric
1/2 teaspoon chili powder
1/2 teaspoon garam masala
2 cloves garlic, crushed
3/4 cup water
1 quart oil for deep frying
1/2 head cauliflower florets
2 onions, sliced into rings

Sift the chickpea flour into a medium bowl. Mix in the coriander, salt, turmeric, chili powder, garam masala and garlic.

Make a well in the center of the flower. Gradually pour the water into the well and mix to form a thick, smooth batter.

Over medium high heat in a large, heavy saucepan, heat the oil to 375°F (190°C).

Coat the cauliflower and onions in the batter and fry them in small batches until golden brown, about 4 to 5 minutes. Drain on paper towels before serving.

AMOUNT PER SERVING: CALORIES: 212 TOTAL FAT: 15.9 g CHOLESTEROL: 0 mg SODIUM: 407 mg
TOTAL CARBS: 14.9 g DIETARY FIBER: 2.6 g PROTEIN: 4.4 g

Bacon Water Chestnut Rolls

Submitted by: **MARY ANN MUELLER**

PREP TIME: 20 MINUTES
COOK TIME: 30 MINUTES
READY IN: 50 MINUTES
SERVINGS: 24

1 (8 ounce) can water chestnuts, halved
1/2 pound bacon, cut in half
1/4 cup mayonnaise
1/2 cup packed light brown sugar
1/4 cup tomato-based chili sauce

Preheat oven to 350 °F (175°C).

Wrap each chestnut with a bacon strip. Place the rolls seam-side down in a baking dish.

Bake 30 minutes or until bacon is crisp and cooked through. When baked, drain the dish of fat.

In a medium-size mixing bowl, combine mayonnaise, brown sugar and hot sauce. Mix well and pour over baked bacon-chestnut rolls.

Very good. I cooked the bacon until crisp and then poured the sauce on top and baked until it bubbled... that was yummy!

—**LUV2COOK**

AMOUNT PER SERVING: CALORIES: 94 TOTAL FAT: 7.3 g CHOLESTEROL: 8 mg SODIUM: 123 mg TOTAL CARBS: 6.4 g
DIETARY FIBER: 0.3 g PROTEIN: 1 g

Smoked Salmon Sushi Roll

Submitted by: VIVIAN

PREP TIME: 30 MINUTES
READY IN: 5 HOURS
SERVINGS: 6

2 cups Japanese sushi rice
6 tablespoons rice wine vinegar
6 sheets nori (dry seaweed)
1 avocado, peeled, pitted and sliced
1 cucumber, peeled and sliced
8 ounces smoked salmon, cut into long strips
2 tablespoons wasabi paste

Soak rice for 4 hours. Drain rice and cook in a rice cooker with 2 cups of water. Rice must be slightly dry as vinegar will be added later.

Immediately after rice is cooked, mix in 6 tablespoons rice vinegar to the hot rice. Spread rice on a plate until completely cool.

Place 1 sheet of seaweed on bamboo mat, press a thin layer of cool rice on the seaweed. Leave at least 1/2 inch top and bottom edge of the seaweed uncovered. This is for easier sealing later. Dot some wasabi on the rice. Arrange cucumber, avocado and smoked salmon to the rice. Position them about 1 inch away from the bottom edge of the seaweed.

Slightly wet the top edge of the seaweed. Roll from bottom to the top edge with the help of the bamboo mat tightly. Cut roll into 8 equal pieces and serve. Repeat for other rolls.

If I hadn't come across this recipe, I never would have dared to make my own sushi. It took a considerable amount of time to prepare the first time, but now it's a breeze! Very tasty and satisfying. I highly recommend splurging on quality ingredients, as it really does make quite a difference. Thank you for this recipe!

—GOCHISOSAMADESHITA

I never would've dreamed making sushi..it seems so mysterious and sophisticated. But after reading rave reviews, I jumped right in and was very happy with the outcome. Initially, I thought that 6 tsp of rice vinegar was too much, but after the rice cooled it was perfect. Next time I will add sesame seeds to add a little flavor. What makes it even better, is having miso soup and green tea..yummy!

—NEB123

AMOUNT PER SERVING: CALORIES: 291 TOTAL FAT: 7.1 g CHOLESTEROL: 9 mg SODIUM: 407 mg
TOTAL CARBS: 44.8 g DIETARY FIBER: 3.3 g PROTEIN: 11.1 g

AS SHOWN IN THE PICTURE

B.L.T. Salad with Basil Mayo Dressing

Submitted by: KIMBER

PREP TIME: 15 MINUTES
COOK TIME: 10 MINUTES
READY IN: 25 MINUTES
SERVINGS: 4

1/2 pound bacon
1/2 cup mayonnaise
2 tablespoons red wine vinegar
1/4 cup finely chopped fresh basil
4 slices French bread, cut into half inch pieces
1 teaspoon salt
1 teaspoon ground black pepper
1 tablespoon canola oil
1 pound romaine lettuce - rinsed, dried, and torn into bite-size pieces
1 pint cherry tomatoes, quartered

Place bacon in a large, deep skillet. Cook over medium high heat until evenly browned. Drain, crumble and set aside, reserving 2 tablespoons of the drippings.

In a small bowl, whisk together the reserved bacon drippings, mayonnaise, vinegar and basil and let dressing stand, covered, at room temperature.

In a large skillet over medium heat, toss the bread pieces with the salt and pepper. Drizzle with the oil, continue tossing and cook over medium-low heat until golden brown.

In a large bowl mix together the romaine, tomatoes, bacon and croutons. Pour the dressing over the salad and toss well.

AMOUNT PER SERVING: CALORIES: 648 TOTAL FAT: 59.2 g CHOLESTEROL: 54 mg SODIUM: 1,320 mg
TOTAL CARBS: 20.9 g DIETARY FIBER: 3.7 g PROTEIN: 10 g

Fresh Broccoli Salad

Submitted by: NORA

PREP TIME: 15 MINUTES
COOK TIME: 15 MINUTES
READY IN: 30 MINUTES
SERVINGS: 9

1/2 pound bacon
2 heads fresh broccoli
1 red onion
3/4 cup raisins
3/4 cup sliced almonds
1 cup mayonnaise
1/2 cup white sugar
2 tablespoons white wine vinegar

Place bacon in a deep skillet and cook over medium high heat until evenly browned. Cool and crumble.

Cut the broccoli into bite-size pieces and cut the onion into thin bite-size slices. Combine with the bacon, raisins, your favorite nuts and mix well.

To prepare the dressing, mix the mayonnaise, sugar and vinegar together until smooth. Stir into the salad, let chill and serve.

You can save time by using pre-made slaw dressing. Adding dried cranberries instead of raisins give a hint of tartness that tastes great!

—SPIDER

AMOUNT PER SERVING: CALORIES: 465 TOTAL FAT: 38.2 g CHOLESTEROL: 31 mg SODIUM:343 mg
TOTAL CARBS: 27.4 g DIETARY FIBER: 3.5 g PROTEIN: 6.6 g

AS SHOWN IN THE PICTURE

Harvest Salad

Submitted by: TIFFANY

PREP TIME: 15 MINUTES
READY IN: 15 MINUTES
SERVINGS: 6

1/2 cup chopped walnuts

1 bunch spinach, rinsed and torn into bite-size pieces

1/2 cup dried cranberries

1/2 cup crumbled blue cheese

2 tomatoes, chopped

1 avocado, peeled, pitted and diced

1/2 red onion, thinly sliced

2 tablespoons red raspberry jam (with seeds)

2 tablespoons red wine vinegar

1/3 cup walnut oil

Freshly ground black pepper to taste

Salt to taste

Preheat oven to 375°F (190°C). Arrange walnuts in a single layer on a baking sheet. Toast in oven for 5 minutes, or until nuts begin to brown.

In a large bowl, toss together the spinach, walnuts, cranberries, blue cheese, tomatoes, avocado, and red onion.

In a small bowl, whisk together jam, vinegar, walnut oil, pepper, and salt. Pour over the salad just before serving, and toss to coat.

This is great! I used candied walnuts and pecans. I also used avocados and omitted the tomato.

—VALERIE

AMOUNT PER SERVING: CALORIES: 339 TOTAL FAT: 27.4 g CHOLESTEROL: 8 mg SODIUM: 274 mg
TOTAL CARBS: 20.7 g DIETARY FIBER: 5.3 g PROTEIN: 6.7 g

Fennel and Watercress Salad

Submitted by: BARRETT

PREP TIME: 20 MINUTES
READY IN: 20 MINUTES
SERVINGS: 20

1/2 cup chopped dried cranberries

1/4 cup red wine vinegar

1/4 cup balsamic vinegar

1 tablespoon minced garlic

1 1/4 teaspoons salt

1 cup extra virgin olive oil

6 bunches watercress, rinsed, dried and trimmed

3 bulbs fennel, trimmed, cored and thinly sliced

3 small heads radicchio, cored and chopped

1 cup pecan halves, toasted

In a bowl, combine the cranberries, red wine vinegar, balsamic vinegar, garlic and salt. Whisk in the olive oil.

In a large salad bowl, combine the watercress, fennel, radicchio and pecans. Stir the vinaigrette and pour over salad. Toss well and serve at once.

What a great combination of flavors! This salad is unique and delicious.

—E-BISKIT

AMOUNT PER SERVING: CALORIES: 178 TOTAL FAT: 15.4 g CHOLESTEROL: 0 mg SODIUM: 202 mg
TOTAL CARBS: 8.5 g DIETARY FIBER: 3.1 g PROTEIN: 3.1 g

AS SHOWN IN THE PICTURE

Greek Veggie Salad

Submitted by: DEBBIE

PREP TIME: 15 MINUTES
READY IN: 15 MINUTES
SERVINGS: 8

1 head cauliflower, chopped
1 head broccoli, chopped
2 cups cherry tomatoes
1 (6 ounce) can small pitted black olives, drained
1 (6 ounce) package tomato basil feta cheese, crumbled
1 (16 ounce) bottle zesty Italian dressing

In a large bowl, combine the cauliflower, broccoli, cherry tomatoes, olives and cheese. Add enough dressing to coat, toss and refrigerate overnight.

Excellent! I made a few changes, added 1 peeled, seeded and chopped cucumber and a 14 oz. can of artichoke hearts in water. Looks gorgeous as well as tastes good.

—CRIS

AMOUNT PER SERVING: CALORIES: 313 TOTAL FAT: 27.3 g CHOLESTEROL: 19 mg SODIUM: 1,368 mg
TOTAL CARBS: 12.8 g DIETARY FIBER: 4.3 g PROTEIN: 6.2 g

Spinach Salad with Pepper Jelly Dressing

Submitted by: SARAHGURLOO

PREP TIME: 5 MINUTES
COOK TIME: 2 MINUTES
READY IN: 7 MINUTES
SERVINGS: 2

3 tablespoons mild pepper jelly
2 tablespoons olive oil
1/8 teaspoon salt
1/8 teaspoon Dijon mustard
2 cups baby spinach leaves
2 ounces goat cheese, sliced
2 tablespoons chopped walnuts

In a small bowl, whisk together the pepper jelly, olive oil, salt and mustard to make the dressing. Heat in the microwave for 30 seconds. Let cool.

Place the spinach in a large bowl, and toss with the dressing. Divide between two serving bowls. Top each one with slices of goat cheese and sprinkle with walnuts.

I've made this recipe several times and always receive rave reviews. The dressing is easy and wonderful on any spinach salad. I often use with whatever I have on hand, berries and purple onion as well as feta and blue cheese can easily be substituted.

—VICKI-SAVANNAH

AMOUNT PER SERVING: CALORIES: 359 TOTAL FAT: 26.9 g CHOLESTEROL: 22 mg SODIUM: 331 mg
TOTAL CARBS: 22.9 g DIETARY FIBER: 1.6 g PROTEIN: 8.2 g

Easy Arugula Salad

Submitted by: KELLID26

PREP TIME: 15 MINUTES
READY IN: 15 MINUTES
SERVINGS: 4

4 cups young arugula leaves, rinsed and dried
1 cup cherry tomatoes, halved
1/4 cup pine nuts
2 tablespoons grapeseed oil or olive oil
1 tablespoon rice vinegar
Salt to taste
Freshly ground black pepper to taste
1/4 cup grated Parmesan cheese
1 large avocado, peeled, pitted and sliced

In a large plastic bowl with a lid, combine arugula, cherry tomatoes, pine nuts, oil, vinegar, and Parmesan cheese. Season with salt and pepper to taste. Cover, and shake to mix.

Divide salad onto plates, and top with slices of avocado.

I couldn't find arugula so I substituted baby greens, and it was AWESOME. Simple, together in mere minutes, and we ate it all! Delicious! The pine nuts are a wonderful touch. Great salad.

—KCHOSKINS

AMOUNT PER SERVING: CALORIES: 264   TOTAL FAT: 24.1 g   CHOLESTEROL: 5 mg   SODIUM: 423 mg
TOTAL CARBS: 9.2 g   DIETARY FIBER: 4.7 g   PROTEIN: 6.9 g

AS SHOWN IN THE PICTURE

Grilled Chicken Salad with Seasonal Fruit

Submitted by: KARENA

PREP TIME: 15 MINUTES
COOK TIME: 20 MINUTES
READY IN: 35 MINUTES
SERVINGS: 6

1 pound skinless, boneless chicken breast halves
1/2 cup pecans
1/3 cup red wine vinegar
1/2 cup white sugar
1 cup vegetable oil
1/2 onion, minced
1 teaspoon ground mustard
1 teaspoon salt
1/4 teaspoon ground white pepper
2 heads Bibb lettuce, rinsed, dried and torn
1 cup sliced fresh strawberries

Preheat the grill for high heat.

Lightly oil the grill grate. Grill chicken 8 minutes on each side, or until juices run clear. Remove from heat, cool, and slice.

Meanwhile, place pecans in a dry skillet over medium-high heat. Cook pecans until fragrant, stirring frequently, about 8 minutes. Remove from heat, and set aside.
In a blender, combine the red wine vinegar, sugar, vegetable oil, onion, mustard, salt, and pepper. Process until smooth.

Arrange lettuce on serving plates. Top with grilled chicken slices, strawberries, and pecans. Drizzle with the dressing to serve.

AMOUNT PER SERVING: CALORIES: 566   TOTAL FAT: 46 g   CHOLESTEROL: 43 mg   SODIUM: 429 mg   TOTAL CARBS: 23 g
DIETARY FIBER: 2.3 g   PROTEIN: 17.8 g

Chutney Chicken Salad

Submitted by: S A R A H

PREP TIME: 15 MINUTES
READY IN: 15 MINUTES
SERVINGS: 9

1/2 cup mayonnaise
1/2 cup chutney
1 teaspoon curry powder
2 teaspoons lime zest
1/4 cup fresh lime juice
1/2 teaspoon salt
4 cups diced, cooked chicken breast meat

In a large bowl, whisk together the mayonnaise, chutney, curry powder, lime zest, lime juice and salt. Add chicken and toss with the dressing until well coated. Add more mayonnaise to taste, if desired. Cover and refrigerate until serving.

My husband really enjoyed this. Added some sliced seedless red grapes and slivered almonds. Used leftover roast chicken from Sams Club.

—J D V M D

AMOUNT PER SERVING: CALORIES: 228 TOTAL FAT: 14.4 g CHOLESTEROL: 54 mg SODIUM: 240 mg
TOTAL CARBS: 7.1 g DIETARY FIBER: 0.5 g PROTEIN: 17.4 g

Amy's Barbecue Chicken Salad

Submitted by: A M Y E H

PREP TIME: 15 MINUTES
COOK TIME: 12 MINUTES
READY IN: 35 MINUTES
SERVINGS: 8

2 skinless, boneless chicken breast halves
1 head red leaf lettuce, rinsed and torn
1 head green leaf lettuce, rinsed and torn
1 fresh tomato, chopped
1 bunch cilantro, chopped
1 (15.25 ounce) can whole kernel corn, drained
1 (15 ounce) can black beans, drained
1 (2.8 ounce) can French fried onions
1/2 cup Ranch dressing
1/2 cup barbeque sauce

Preheat the grill for high heat.

Lightly oil the grill grate. Place chicken on the grill, and cook 6 minutes per side, or until juices run clear. Remove from heat, cool, and slice.

In a large bowl, mix the red leaf lettuce, green leaf lettuce, tomato, cilantro, corn, and black beans. Top with the grilled chicken slices and French fried onions.

In a small bowl, mix the Ranch dressing and barbeque sauce. Serve on the side as a dipping sauce, or toss with the salad to coat.

AMOUNT PER SERVING: CALORIES: 291 TOTAL FAT: 14.8 g CHOLESTEROL: 21 mg SODIUM: 698 mg
TOTAL CARBS: 29 g DIETARY FIBER: 6.6 g PROTEIN: 12.4 g

Cherry Chicken Salad

Submitted by: MIA BINGENHEIMER

PREP TIME: 15 MINUTES
READY IN: 45 MINUTES
SERVINGS: 4

3 cooked, boneless chicken breast halves, diced
1/3 cup dried cherries
1/3 cup diced celery
1/3 cup toasted, chopped pecans
1/3 cup low fat mayonnaise
1 tablespoon buttermilk
1/2 teaspoon salt
1/2 teaspoon ground black pepper
1/3 cup cubed apples (optional)

In a large bowl, combine the chicken, dried cherries, celery, nuts, mayonnaise, milk, salt and pepper and apple if desired. Toss together well and refrigerate until chilled. Serve on toasted cracked wheat bread or croissants.

Perfect. Used cranberries inside of cherries, used walnuts instead of pecans—because this is what I had on hand. I ate the whole thing (not at one sitting of course)! Can not wait to make this again.

—MONICA

AMOUNT PER SERVING: CALORIES: 334   TOTAL FAT: 20.4 g   CHOLESTEROL: 69 mg   SODIUM: 505 mg

TOTAL CARBS: 13.8 g   DIETARY FIBER: 2.5 g   PROTEIN:24.4 g

Pecan Crusted Chicken Salad

Submitted by: LIANAD

PREP TIME: 15 MINUTES
COOK TIME: 25 MINUTES
READY IN: 40 MINUTES
SERVINGS: 4

1 cup creamy garlic salad dressing
1 cup finely chopped pecans
4 skinless, boneless chicken breast halves
1 head romaine lettuce leaves, torn into half inch wide strips
1 (15 ounce) can mandarin oranges, drained
1 cup dried cranberries
4 ounces blue cheese, crumbled
1/2 cup Ranch dressing

Preheat oven to 400°F (200°C).

Place the creamy garlic dressing and pecans in separate bowls. Dip each chicken breast in the dressing then in the pecans to coat. Arrange chicken on a baking sheet.

Bake chicken 25 minutes in the preheated oven, until juices run clear. Cool slightly, and cut into strips.

On serving plates, arrange equal amounts of the lettuce, mandarin oranges, cranberries, and blue cheese. Top with equal amounts chicken, and serve with Ranch dressing.

This was awesome! Great combination and flavor. I used blue cheese dressing instead of ranch and gorgonzola cheese.

—NANCY VEJVODA

AMOUNT PER SERVING: CALORIES: 953   TOTAL FAT: 70.2 g   CHOLESTEROL: 97 mg   SODIUM: 1,473 mg

TOTAL CARBS: 47.2 g   DIETARY FIBER: 6.6 g   PROTEIN: 35.7 g

AS SHOWN IN THE PICTURE

Chinese Chicken Salad

Submitted by: ANN BLACK

PREP TIME: 20 MINUTES
READY IN: 20 MINUTES
SERVINGS: 6

3 1/2 boneless chicken breast halves, cooked and diced

1 head lettuce, torn into small pieces

4 green onions, sliced

4 stalks celery, sliced thin

1/2 cup walnuts, chopped

2 tablespoons sesame seeds, toasted

6 ounces Chinese noodles, heated briefly to crisp

6 tablespoons seasoned rice vinegar

4 tablespoons white sugar

1 teaspoon salt

1/2 cup peanut oil

In a large salad bowl combine the chicken, lettuce, green onion, celery, nuts, seeds and noodles. Mix all together. Set aside.

To make dressing: put vinegar in a small bowl. Dissolve sugar and salt in vinegar before adding oil. Shake or beat well.

Add dressing to salad and toss to coat. Serve and enjoy!

Wonderful! I served this with Chinese-style pork ribs and house fried rice. It was a perfect light complement to some heavier soy sauce laden foods. Excellent.

—MEGAN ETHER

AMOUNT PER SERVING: CALORIES: 516 TOTAL FAT: 31.6 g CHOLESTEROL: 48 mg SODIUM: 758 mg
TOTAL CARBS: 38.1 g DIETARY FIBER: 6.7 g PROTEIN: 24 g

Santa Fe Chicken Salad

Submitted by: JUDY NEARY

PREP TIME: 30 MINUTES
COOK TIME: 20 MINUTES
READY IN: 50 MINUTES
SERVINGS: 4

1/2 cup mayonnaise

1/2 cup Italian-style salad dressing

4 skinless, boneless chicken breasts

1 head iceberg lettuce

1 head romaine lettuce, rinsed and dried

2 bunches green onions, chopped

1 large tomato, chopped

1 1/2 cups shredded Cheddar and Monterey cheese blend

5 (10 inch) flour tortillas

1/2 cup ranch-style salad dressing

1/2 cup salsa

In a gallon size plastic bag or 9x9 baking dish, mix together the mayonnaise and Italian dressing. Place chicken in mixture and marinate overnight in the refrigerator.

Chop, wash, and dry the iceberg and romaine lettuce. Mix and divide among four dinner-size plates. Divide and place the tomato and green onions among the plates. Sprinkle the top of each salad with shredded cheese.

Remove chicken from marinade and grill or broil until cooked. While chicken is cooking, cut tortillas into three thick strips and cut each strip into 'matchsticks'. Place on a cookie sheet and put under broiler until golden brown. Let cool. Cut the chicken into strips and divide among plates. Top with tortilla 'crispies'.

To prepare the dressing, combine the salsa and ranch dressing in a blender and mix until smooth. Pour over each salad.

AMOUNT PER SERVING: CALORIES: 1,122 TOTAL FAT: 64.4 g CHOLESTEROL: 123 mg SODIUM: 1,693 mg
TOTAL CARBS: 73.8 g DIETARY FIBER: 10.3 g PROTEIN: 50.6 g

AS SHOWN IN THE PICTURE

Caesar Salad Supreme

Submitted by: KAREN WEIR

PREP TIME: 20 MINUTES
COOK TIME: 15 MINUTES
READY IN: 35 MINUTES
SERVINGS: 6

6 cloves garlic, peeled
3/4 cup mayonnaise
5 anchovy fillets, minced
6 tablespoons grated Parmesan cheese, divided
1 teaspoon Worcestershire sauce
1 teaspoon Dijon mustard
1 tablespoon lemon juice
Salt to taste
Ground black pepper to taste
1/4 cup olive oil
4 cups day-old bread, cubed
1 head romaine lettuce, torn into bite-size pieces

Mince 3 cloves of garlic, and combine in a small bowl with mayonnaise, anchovies, 2 tablespoons of the Parmesan cheese, Worcestershire sauce, mustard, and lemon juice. Season to taste with salt and black pepper. Refrigerate until ready to use.

Heat oil in a large skillet over medium heat. Cut the remaining 3 cloves of garlic into quarters, and add to hot oil. Cook and stir until brown, and then remove garlic from pan. Add bread cubes to the hot oil. Cook, turning frequently, until lightly browned. Remove bread cubes from oil, and season with salt and pepper.

Place lettuce in a large bowl. Toss with dressing, remaining Parmesan cheese, and seasoned bread cubes.

AMOUNT PER SERVING: CALORIES: 383 TOTAL FAT: 33.7 g CHOLESTEROL: 23 mg SODIUM: 533 mg

TOTAL CARBS: 15.3 g DIETARY FIBER: 1.6 g PROTEIN: 6.4 g

Mama's Potato Salad

Submitted by: JULIEPUHLMAN

PREP TIME: 20 MINUTES
COOK TIME: 10 MINUTES
READY IN: 1 HOUR
SERVINGS: 20

5 pounds potatoes, peeled and cubed
2 cups mayonnaise
1/2 cup yellow mustard
1 cup chopped onion
2 tablespoons prepared horseradish
Sea salt to taste
8 hard-cooked eggs, chopped
3 dill pickles, chopped (optional)
Freshly ground black pepper to taste

Place the potatoes in a large pot with enough water to cover. Bring to a boil, and cook for about 10 minutes, or until tender. Drain, and place in a serving bowl.

Stir the onion, salt and pepper into the potatoes while they are still hot. This allows the potatoes to absorb the flavor. Allow to cool for about 20 minutes.

Add the mayonnaise, mustard and horseradish to the salad, and mix well. Gently stir in the eggs and dill pickles. Finish off with a generous grinding of black pepper on top. Chill for about 30 minutes before serving.

The perfect potato salad! Delicious and so easy to make! I did add some diced radishes for extra color and flavor! This is definitely a keeper!

—DAWN

AMOUNT PER SERVING: CALORIES: 285 TOTAL FAT: 98 g CHOLESTEROL: 0 mg SODIUM: 370 mg TOTAL CARBS: 23.1 g

DIETARY FIBER: 2.4 g PROTEIN: 4.9 g

AS SHOWN IN THE PICTURE

Asian Chicken Noodle Salad

Submitted by: XING JIN

PREP TIME: 15 MINUTES
COOK TIME: 10 MINUTES
READY IN: 25 MINUTES
SERVINGS: 4

1 (3 ounce) package ramen noodle pasta, crushed
1/2 cup sunflower seeds
1/2 cup pine nuts
2 tablespoons butter, melted
3 cups shredded bok choy
5 green onions, thinly sliced
1 cup diced, cooked chicken breast meat
1 (5 ounce) can water chestnuts, drained
12 pods snow peas
1/2 cup vegetable oil
1/4 cup rice wine vinegar
1 tablespoon soy sauce
1/4 cup white sugar
1 tablespoon lemon juice

Preheat oven to 350°F (175°C). In a large bowl, mix the noodles, sunflower seeds, and pine nuts with melted butter until evenly coated. Spread the mixture in a thin layer on a baking sheet.

Bake 7 to 10 minutes in the preheated oven, stirring occasionally, until evenly toasted. Remove from heat, and cool slightly.

In a large bowl toss together the noodle mixture, bok choy, green onions, chicken, water chestnuts, and snow peas. Prepare the dressing by blending the oil, vinegar, soy sauce, sugar, and lemon juice. Pour over salad, and toss to evenly coat. Serve immediately, or refrigerate until chilled.

I made this recipe for a potluck and everyone enjoyed it. Don't skip baking/roasting the noodles and nuts since that is what made the salad flavorful. I would definitely make this again!

—BLIMSILVERNAIL

Great recipe to play with! I substituted baby spinach for the bok choy, and pumpkin seeds instead of pine nuts. I also added a tablespoon of sesame seeds to the nuts and 1 tsp of sesame seed oil to the dressing which I poured on the hot noodle mixture immediately after taking it from the oven. I have also tried it with jumbo shrimp but like the chicken better. It's a meal in itself and a favorite in our house!

—HEATHER

I love this recipe! I have made it with and without chicken. To make it easier on myself, I used pre-packaged coleslaw mix. I always get rave reviews every time I bring this to a get-together!

—KIM O

AMOUNT PER SERVING: CALORIES: 736   TOTAL FAT: 55.8 g   CHOLESTEROL: 42 mg   SODIUM: 1,076 mg
TOTAL CARBS: 43.9 g   DIETARY FIBER: 5.3 g   PROTEIN: 20.3 g

AS SHOWN IN THE PICTURE

Apple Avocado Salad with Tangerine Dressing

PREP TIME: 20 MINUTES
READY IN: 20 MINUTES
SERVINGS: 10

Submitted by: DONNA SMALLY

1 (10 ounce) package baby greens
1/4 cup chopped red onion
1/2 cup chopped walnuts
1/3 cup crumbled blue cheese
2 teaspoons lemon zest
1 apple, peeled, cored and sliced
1 avocado, peeled, pitted and diced
4 mandarin oranges, juiced
1/2 lemon, juiced
1/2 teaspoon lemon zest
1 clove garlic, minced
2 tablespoons olive oil
Salt to taste

In a large bowl, toss together the baby greens, red onion, walnuts, blue cheese, and lemon zest. Mix in the apple and avocado just before serving.

In a container with a lid, mix the mandarin orange juice, lemon juice, lemon zest, garlic, olive oil, and salt. Drizzle over the salad as desired.

This was an excellent salad. I wasn't able to find fresh mandarin oranges, so I just pureed 1/2 of a small can of drained ones. Worked great and my company loved it!

—JILLZW

AMOUNT PER SERVING: CALORIES: 143   TOTAL FAT: 11.2 g   CHOLESTEROL: 3 mg   SODIUM: 107 mg
TOTAL CARBS: 10.4 g   DIETARY FIBER: 3.5 g   PROTEIN: 3 g

Raw Vegetable Salad

PREP TIME: 15 MINUTES
COOK TIME: 15 MINUTES
READY IN: 30 MINUTES
SERVINGS: 6

Submitted by: PAMELA BROWN

6 slices bacon
3 cups chopped broccoli
3 cups cauliflower, chopped
3 cups chopped celery
1 (10 ounce) package frozen green peas, thawed
1 cup sweetened, dried cranberries
1/4 cup white sugar
1 teaspoon salt
1 tablespoon white wine vinegar
2 tablespoons grated onion
1/4 cup Parmesan cheese
1 1/2 cups mayonnaise
1 cup raw Spanish peanuts

Place bacon in a large, deep skillet. Cook over medium high heat until evenly browned. Drain, crumble and set aside.

In a large bowl, combine the broccoli, cauliflower, celery, peas and cranberries.

Whisk together the sugar, salt, vinegar, grated onion, cheese and mayonnaise. Pour dressing over the salad; add nuts and bacon and toss well.

YUM!! This is so good. I did substitute dried cherries for the cranberries, and almonds for the peanuts, but followed the rest. So good!

—GADABOUT

AMOUNT PER SERVING: CALORIES: 878   TOTAL FAT: 73.6 g   CHOLESTEROL: 55 mg   SODIUM: 1,120 mg
TOTAL CARBS: 44.4 g   DIETARY FIBER: 9.2 g   PROTEIN: 16.4 g

Mediterranean Greek Salad

Submitted by: HEATHER SHEVLIN

PREP TIME: 10 MINUTES
READY IN: 10 MINUTES
SERVINGS: 8

3 cucumbers, seeded and sliced
1 1/2 cups crumbled feta cheese
1 cup black olives, pitted and sliced
3 cups diced roma tomatoes
1/3 cup diced oil packed sun-dried tomatoes, drained, oil reserved
1/2 red onion, sliced

In a large salad bowl, toss together the cucumbers, feta cheese, olives, roma tomatoes, sun-dried tomatoes, 2 tablespoons reserved sun-dried tomato oil, and red onion. Chill until serving.

This salad was amazing!! The sun dried tomatoes and the olives were fantastic! I also added a little red wine vinegar and olive oil. Make sure you use fresh veggies it makes a big difference. This was even delicious the next day!

—AGGIEB

AMOUNT PER SERVING: CALORIES: 131 TOTAL FAT: 8.9 g CHOLESTEROL: 25 mg SODIUM: 489 mg
TOTAL CARBS: 9.1 g DIETARY FIBER: 2.3 g PROTEIN: 5.5 g

Tabbouleh

Submitted by: KATHERINE DENNING

PREP TIME: 45 MINUTES
READY IN: 4 HOURS 45 MINUTES
SERVINGS: 8

1 cup bulgur
3 tomatoes, seeded and chopped
2 cucumbers, peeled and chopped
3 green onions, chopped
3 cloves garlic, minced
1 cup chopped fresh parsley
1/3 cup fresh mint leaves
2 teaspoons salt
1/2 cup lemon juice
2/3 cup olive oil

Place cracked wheat in bowl and cover with 2 cups boiling water. Soak for 30 minutes; drain and squeeze out excess water.

In a mixing bowl, combine the wheat, tomatoes, cucumbers, onions, garlic, parsley, mint, salt, lemon juice, and olive oil. Toss and refrigerate for at least 4 hours before serving. Toss again prior to serving.

I used to make this basic recipe when I was in college and I've been looking for it ever since. I cut back the olive oil to 1/4 or 1/3 cup, otherwise this recipe is just awesome. Use fresh lemons and let this salad set for 24 hours. Be sure to mix before serving.

—TEMKIN

AMOUNT PER SERVING: CALORIES: 248 TOTAL FAT: 18.6 g CHOLESTEROL: 0 mg SODIUM: 595 mg
TOTAL CARBS: 19.8 g DIETARY FIBER: 4.5 g PROTEIN: 3.6 g

Wild Rice Salad

Submitted by: GINA

PREP TIME: 20 MINUTES
COOK TIME: 40 MINUTES
READY IN: 2 HOURS
SERVINGS: 12

1 (6 ounce) package wild rice
3/4 cup light mayonnaise
1 teaspoon white vinegar
1 teaspoon white sugar
Salt and pepper to taste
2 cups cooked, cubed turkey meat
1/4 cup diced green onion
1 cup seedless red grapes
6 ounces blanched slivered almonds

Cook rice according to package directions. Remove from heat and set aside to cool.

In a medium bowl, whisk together the mayonnaise, vinegar, sugar, salt and pepper. Stir in rice, turkey, onion and grapes until evenly coated with dressing. Cover and refrigerate for 1 to 2 hours. Before serving, sprinkle slivered almonds over the top of the salad.

I make this salad all the time! I love it! Make sure you use light or fat free mayo, regular gives it less flavor and a more greasy feel to it. I add a tad more sugar and use cider vinegar. Another great variation is to add mandarin oranges and cranberries.

—BMASOG

AMOUNT PER SERVING: CALORIES: 221 TOTAL FAT: 13.4 g CHOLESTEROL: 23 mg SODIUM: 138 mg
TOTAL CARBS: 14.3 g DIETARY FIBER: 2.1 g PROTEIN: 11.4 g

AS SHOWN IN THE PICTURE

Black Bean and Corn Salad

Submitted by: BONNIE MOORE

PREP TIME: 15 MINUTES
READY IN: 12 HOURS 15 MINUTES
SERVINGS: 6

1/2 cup balsamic vinaigrette salad dressing
1/4 teaspoon seasoned pepper
1/4 teaspoon dried cilantro
1/8 teaspoon ground cayenne pepper
1/4 teaspoon ground cumin
2 (15 ounce) cans black beans, rinsed and drained
2 (15 ounce) cans whole kernel corn, drained
1/2 cup chopped onion
1/2 cup chopped green onions
1/2 cup red bell pepper, chopped

In a small bowl, mix together vinaigrette, seasoned pepper, cilantro, cayenne pepper, and cumin. Set dressing aside.

In a large bowl, stir together beans, corn, onion, green onions, and red bell pepper. Toss with dressing. Cover, and refrigerate overnight. Toss again before serving.

Excellent!!! So full of flavor. Served some of this to a friend of mine and she loved it. I used mixed beans instead of black beans and added parsley instead of cilantro because I didn't have all ingredients. I'll definitely be making this on a regular basis!

—BABYMOMMA

AMOUNT PER SERVING: CALORIES: 304 TOTAL FAT: 8.6 g CHOLESTEROL: 0 mg SODIUM: 966 mg TOTAL CARBS: 49.1 g
DIETARY FIBER: 11.1 g PROTEIN: 11.7 g

AS SHOWN IN THE PICTURE

The Ultimate Pasta Salad

Submitted by: HELENE

PREP TIME: 15 MINUTES
COOK TIME: 10 MINUTES
READY IN: 1 HOUR 25 MINUTES
SERVINGS: 12

1 (16 ounce) package uncooked tri-colored spiral pasta

1 head fresh broccoli, cut into bite size pieces

1 head fresh cauliflower, chopped into bite size pieces

1 red onion, chopped

2 teaspoons minced garlic

8 ounces pepperoni slices, cut into quarters

1 (8 ounce) package mozzarella cheese, cut into cubes

1 (6 ounce) can large pitted black olives, drained and sliced

1/2 cup olive oil, or to taste

1/2 cup red wine vinegar, or to taste

Salt and pepper to taste

Italian seasoning to taste

Bring a large pot of lightly salted water to a boil. Place pasta in the pot, cook for 8 to 10 minutes, until al dente, and drain. Transfer to a bowl, cover, and chill 1 hour in the refrigerator.

Toss chilled pasta with the broccoli, cauliflower, red onion, garlic, pepperoni, mozzarella cheese, olives, olive oil, and red wine vinegar. Season with salt, pepper, and Italian seasoning. Chill in the refrigerator until serving.

This was very good, but we added some zesty italian dressing to it. I also used cheddar, and colby jack cheese instead of mozzarella. I made it the night before so everything could marinate.

—CARLYNSMOMMY

I also have been making a similar recipe for years. I use Caesar-Italian bottled dressing, and instead of mozzarella cheese I sprinkle in some grated Parmesan cheese. My family has loved this pasta salad for years!

—JANEYT

I used zesty Italian dressing. I added shrimp and crab meat. No pepperoni, but ham bits and some cheddar cheese. Yummy!

—KEATTA

AMOUNT PER SERVING: CALORIES: 394 TOTAL FAT: 22.5 g CHOLESTEROL: 26 mg SODIUM: 646 mg
TOTAL CARBS: 33.9 g DIETARY FIBER: 3.8 g PROTEIN: 14.9 g

AS SHOWN IN THE PICTURE

Chicken Tortilla Soup

Submitted by: **STAR POOLEY**

PREP TIME: 20 MINUTES
COOK TIME: 20 MINUTES
READY IN: 40 MINUTES
SERVINGS: 8

1 tablespoon olive oil
1 onion, chopped
3 cloves garlic, minced
2 teaspoons chili powder
1 teaspoon dried oregano
1 (28 ounce) can crushed tomatoes
1 (10.5 ounce) can condensed chicken broth
1 1/4 cups water
1 cup whole corn kernels, cooked
1 cup white hominy
1 (4 ounce) can chopped green chile peppers
1 (15 ounce) can black beans, rinsed and drained
1/4 cup chopped fresh cilantro
2 boneless chicken breast halves, cooked and cut into bite-sized pieces
Crushed tortilla chips
Sliced avocado
Shredded Monterey Jack cheese
Chopped green onions

In a medium stock pot, heat oil over medium heat. Saute onion and garlic in oil until soft. Stir in chili powder, oregano, tomatoes, broth, and water. Bring to a boil, and simmer for 5 to 10 minutes.

Stir in corn, hominy, chiles, beans, cilantro, and chicken. Simmer for 10 minutes.

Ladle soup into individual serving bowls, and top with crushed tortilla chips, avocado slices, cheese, and chopped green onion.

The fresh ingredients filled my kitchen with yummy aromas! I used cumin instead of oregano and added fresh lime juice. A beautiful, simple dinner when served with a plate of do-it-yourself toppings (avocado, cheese, cilantro sprigs, chopped green onions, and lime wedges). I served it with corn bread muffins and watermelon margaritas!

—PINKITCHEN

This was fantastic. The only change I made was to add 1/2 cup of uncooked rice as the soup simmered. This is a very filling soup. The whole family loved it!

—SUSAN G

This soup is amazing! I cooked the chicken in the garlic and onion. I also added cumin. Instead of a can of black beans, in the frozen veggies section there is a bagged 'fiesta mix' of black beans, corn, onion, red and green peppers and poblano chili. I added that in addition to the hominy and a can of corn. The soup was thick but very yummy and filling. Top with cheese, sour cream, and crushed tortilla chips.

—DARLINGNIKKI

AMOUNT PER SERVING: CALORIES: 378   TOTAL FAT:19.5 g   CHOLESTEROL: 46 mg   SODIUM: 951 mg
TOTAL CARBS: 30.3 g   DIETARY FIBER: 8.4 g   PROTEIN: 23 g

Excellent Broccoli Cheese Soup

Submitted by: NATHAN TRUAX

PREP TIME: 15 MINUTES
COOK TIME: 30 MINUTES
READY IN: 45 MINUTES
SERVINGS: 18

3/4 cup butter
3/4 cup all-purpose flour
9 cups chicken stock
9 cups milk
1 teaspoon salt
1 1/2 teaspoons white pepper
5 cups fresh broccoli florets
1 1/2 pounds processed cheese, shredded
3 cups shredded Cheddar cheese

Melt the butter in a large pot over medium heat, and mix in the flour. Reduce heat to low, and cook, stirring constantly, about 2 minutes. Mix in the chicken stock and milk, and season with salt and white pepper. Bring to a boil, reduce heat to low, and simmer about 10 minutes.

Bring a pot of lightly salted water to a boil. Place the broccoli in the boiling water, and cook 2 minutes, or until just tender. Remove from heat, drain, and set aside.

Gradually mix the processed cheese and Cheddar cheese into the large pot until melted. Mix in the broccoli. Continue cooking about 5 minutes.

AMOUNT PER SERVING: CALORIES: 361   TOTAL FAT: 26 g   CHOLESTEROL: 75 mg   SODIUM: 1,185 mg
TOTAL CARBS: 14.8 g   DIETARY FIBER: 1 g   PROTEIN: 17.9 g

African Peanut Soup

Submitted by: PIETOGO

PREP TIME: 15 MINUTES
COOK TIME: 55 MINUTES
READY IN: 1 HOUR 10 MINUTES
SERVINGS: 10

2 tablespoons olive oil
2 medium onions, chopped
2 large red bell peppers, chopped
4 cloves garlic, minced
1 (28 ounce) can crushed tomatoes, with liquid
8 cups vegetable broth or stock
1/4 teaspoon pepper
1/4 teaspoon chili powder (optional)
2/3 cup extra crunchy peanut butter
1/2 cup uncooked brown rice

Heat oil in a large stock pot over medium high heat. Cook onions and bell peppers until lightly browned and tender, stirring in garlic when almost done to prevent burning. Stir in tomatoes, vegetable stock, pepper, and chili powder. Reduce heat to low and simmer, uncovered, for 30 minutes.

Stir in rice, cover, and simmer another fifteen minutes or until rice is tender. Stir in peanut butter until well blended, and serve.

I loved this recipe. I blackened the peppers and skinned them, then pureed them. This adds a slight smoky flavor that goes well with the peanuts. I will make this again.

—MSCLIO

AMOUNT PER SERVING: CALORIES: 220   TOTAL FAT: 12.2 g   CHOLESTEROL: 0 mg   SODIUM: 558 mg
TOTAL CARBS: 23.5 g   DIETARY FIBER: 5 g   PROTEIN: 7.4 g

Creamy Tomato-Basil Soup

Submitted by: ALOK

PREP TIME: 10 MINUTES
COOK TIME: 45 MINUTES
READY IN: 55 MINUTES
SERVINGS: 8

1/4 cup butter
1/4 cup olive oil
1 1/2 cups chopped onions
3 pounds tomatoes, cored, peeled, and quartered
1/2 cup chopped fresh basil leaves
Salt to taste
Ground black pepper to taste
1 quart chicken broth
1 cup heavy cream
8 sprigs fresh basil for garnish

Heat the butter and olive oil in a large pot over medium heat. Stir in onions and cook until tender. Mix in tomatoes and chopped basil. Season with salt and pepper. Pour in the chicken broth, reduce heat to low, and continue cooking 15 minutes.

Transfer soup to a blender (or use an immersible hand blender), and blend until smooth. Return to the pot, and bring to a boil. Reduce heat to low, and gradually mix in the heavy cream. Pour soup through a strainer before serving. Garnish each serving with a sprig of basil.

AMOUNT PER SERVING: CALORIES: 278 TOTAL FAT: 25.2 g CHOLESTEROL: 56 mg SODIUM: 632 mg

TOTAL CARBS: 12.4 g DIETARY FIBER: 2.8 g PROTEIN: 3.7 g

Wild Rice And Chicken Soup

Submitted by: GLENDA BALDWIN

PREP TIME: 15 MINUTES
COOK TIME: 50 MINUTES
READY IN: 1 HOUR 10 MINUTES
SERVINGS: 6

3 (10.5 ounce) cans chicken broth
2 cups water
1/2 cup wild rice
1/2 cup chopped green onions
1/2 cup butter
3/4 cup all-purpose flour
3/4 teaspoon salt
1/2 teaspoon poultry seasoning
1/4 teaspoon ground black pepper
2 cups heavy cream
2 cups cubed, cooked chicken meat
1 (4 ounce) jar sliced pimento peppers, drained

Combine the broth, water, and rice in a large soup pot, and bring to a boil. Reduce heat, and cover. Simmer for 35 to 40 minutes, until rice is tender.

Saute onions in butter or margarine in a medium saucepan, over low heat. Stir in flour, salt, poultry seasoning, and pepper. Cook, stirring constantly, until mixture is bubbly and thick. Stir in cream. Cook for 6 minutes, or until mixture thickens slightly, stirring constantly. Stir into broth.

Add cubed chicken and pimentos. Heat through.

Great soup. The sage really adds to the flavor. I added some extra vegetables to make it a one dish meal.

—LALISONA

AMOUNT PER SERVING: CALORIES: 639 TOTAL FAT: 48.5 g CHOLESTEROL: 187 mg SODIUM: 1,444 mg

TOTAL CARBS: 26.9 g DIETARY FIBER: 1.9 g PROTEIN: 25 g

AS SHOWN IN THE PICTURE

Hot and Sour Chicken Soup

Submitted by: MORPHIUS_RAE

PREP TIME: 10 MINUTES
COOK TIME: 20 MINUTES
READY IN: 30 MINUTES
SERVINGS: 4

3 cups chicken broth

1/2 cup water

2 cups sliced fresh mushrooms

1/2 cup sliced bamboo shoots, drained

3 slices fresh ginger root

2 cloves garlic, crushed

2 teaspoons soy sauce

1/4 teaspoon red pepper flakes

1 pound skinless, boneless chicken breast halves - cut into thin strips

1 tablespoon sesame oil

2 green onions, chopped

1/4 cup chopped fresh cilantro (optional)

3 tablespoons red wine vinegar

2 tablespoons cornstarch

1 egg, beaten

In a saucepan, combine the chicken broth, water, mushrooms, bamboo shoots, ginger, garlic, soy sauce, and hot pepper flakes. Bring to a boil, then reduce the heat to low, cover and simmer while you assemble the rest of the ingredients.

Place the chicken slices into a bowl and toss with the sesame oil to coat. In a separate bowl, stir together the cornstarch and vinegar, and set aside.

Increase the heat under the broth to medium-high, and return to a rolling boil. Add the chicken slices. Return to a boil, and then drizzle in the egg while stirring slowly to create long strands of egg. Stir in the vinegar and cornstarch. Simmer over medium heat, stirring occasionally, until chicken is cooked through and the broth has thickened slightly, about 3 minutes. Serve garnished with green onions and cilantro.

I have made this twice in the past week and love it. The first time I used chicken and the second time shrimp. Both were excellent. I also served it over white rice, which was delicious. I love the fact it is quick to make and flavorful.

—KELSEYDAWG

Very easy, yummy recipe! I used tofu instead of chicken and it was great. I also substituted rice vinegar for the red wine. This will become a favorite for me.

—TANIA

Used dried shiitake slices instead of fresh mushrooms. Also added in some slivered water chestnuts for an extra crunch. Yum!

—CHERRY007

This is a very tasty soup. To make it a bit more authentic tasting I doubled the starch for consistency and added 1/4 tsp of white pepper.

—SEAN

AMOUNT PER SERVING: CALORIES: 228   TOTAL FAT: 8.8 g   CHOLESTEROL: 112 mg   SODIUM: 972 mg
TOTAL CARBS: 9.6 g   DIETARY FIBER: 1.3 g   PROTEIN: 27.3 g

MAIN DISHES $\left(\,69\,\right)$

AS SHOWN IN THE PICTURE

Marinated Chicken Kabobs

Submitted by: D. DETTMANN

PREP TIME: 15 MINUTES
COOK IN: 20 MINUTES
READY IN: 2 HOURS 35 MINUTES
SERVINGS: 8

1 cup vegetable oil
1/2 cup soy sauce
1/2 cup light corn syrup
1/4 cup lemon juice
2 tablespoons sesame seeds
1/2 teaspoon garlic powder
Salt to taste
4 skinless, boneless chicken breast halves, cut into 1 1/2 inch pieces
1 (8 ounce) package fresh mushrooms
2 onions, quartered
1 green bell pepper, cut into large chunks

In a medium bowl, blend vegetable oil, soy sauce, light corn syrup, lemon juice, sesame seeds, garlic powder, and garlic salt. Place chicken in the mixture. Cover, and marinate in the refrigerator at least 2 hours.

Preheat an outdoor grill to medium heat, and lightly oil grate. Thread chicken onto skewers alternately with mushrooms, onions, and green bell pepper. Pour marinade into a saucepan, and bring to a boil. Cook for 5 to 10 minutes.

Place skewers on the prepared grill. Cook 15 to 20 minutes, turning frequently, until chicken is no longer pink and juices run clear. Baste with the boiled marinade frequently during the last 10 minutes.

AMOUNT PER SERVING: CALORIES: 818 TOTAL FAT: 58.6 g CHOLESTEROL: 68 mg SODIUM: 2,043 mg
TOTAL CARBS: 45.7 g DIETARY FIBER: 3.1 g PROTEIN: 32.3 g

Honey Mustard Chicken

Submitted by: CAROL ALTER

PREP TIME: 15 MINUTES
COOK IN: 1 HOUR
READY IN: 9 HOURS 15 MINUTES
SERVINGS: 8

1 (4 pound) whole chicken, cut into 8 pieces
1 teaspoon paprika
1/4 teaspoon ground black pepper
1/2 teaspoon curry powder
3 tablespoons prepared Dijon-style mustard
1/4 cup honey
2 tablespoons apricot jam

Sprinkle chicken with paprika, pepper, and curry powder. Place in a roasting pan.

Combine mustard, honey, and jam in a small bowl. Pour over chicken, and marinate for 1 hour or overnight.

Bake in a preheated 350°F (175°C) oven for 1 hour, basting often.

Both my husband and I LOVE this recipe. I use orange marmalade and chicken legs and thighs instead and I don't marinade it because I usually don't have the time. It comes out superb every time and I have made it several times.

— FEEDING-A-FAMILY-OF-6

AMOUNT PER SERVING: CALORIES: 618 TOTAL FAT: 39.7 g CHOLESTEROL: 195 mg SODIUM: 347 mg
TOTAL CARBS: 14.7 g DIETARY FIBER: 0.3 g PROTEIN: 48.8 g

Lemon Butter Chicken

Submitted by: PAYNES

PREP TIME: 15 MINUTES
COOK IN: 25 MINUTES
READY IN: 40 MINUTES
SERVINGS: 4

1 tablespoon butter
1/3 cup Italian style dressing
1 lemon, zested and juiced
1 tablespoon Worcestershire sauce
8 chicken tenderloins
Lemon pepper to taste
Garlic salt to taste
Onion powder to taste

Preheat oven to 350°F (175°C). Place the butter in a 9x9 inch baking dish, and melt in the oven. Remove from heat, and mix in Italian salad dressing, lemon juice, and Worcestershire sauce.

Arrange the chicken tenderloins in the baking dish, coating with the melted butter mixture. Season both sides of chicken with lemon pepper, garlic salt, and onion powder. Sprinkle with lemon zest.

Bake 25 minutes in the preheated oven, or until chicken juices run clear.

AMOUNT PER SERVING: CALORIES: 248 TOTAL FAT: 15.1 g CHOLESTEROL: 70 mg SODIUM: 421 mg
TOTAL CARBS: 5.9 g DIETARY FIBER: 1.3 g PROTEIN: 23.4 g

Easier Chicken Marsala

Submitted by: D. ALEXANDER

PREP TIME: 10 MINUTES
COOK TIME: 20 MINUTES
READY IN: 30 MINUTES
SERVINGS: 4

1/4 cup all-purpose flour
1/2 teaspoon garlic salt
1/4 teaspoon ground black pepper
1/2 teaspoon dried oregano
4 boneless, skinless chicken breast halves
1 tablespoon olive oil
1 tablespoon butter
1 cup sliced fresh mushrooms
1/2 cup Marsala wine

In a medium bowl, stir together the flour, garlic salt, pepper, and oregano. Dredge chicken in the mixture to lightly coat.

Heat olive oil and butter in a large skillet over medium heat. Fry the chicken in the skillet for 2 minutes, or until lightly browned on one side. Turn chicken over, and add mushrooms. Cook about 2 minutes, until other side of chicken is lightly browned. Stir mushrooms so that they cook evenly.

Pour Marsala wine over the chicken. Cover skillet, and reduce heat to low; simmer for 10 minutes, or until chicken is no longer pink and juices run clear.

AMOUNT PER SERVING: CALORIES: 284 TOTAL FAT: 10.1 g CHOLESTEROL: 80 mg SODIUM: 322 mg
TOTAL CARBS: 11 g DIETARY FIBER: 0.5 g PROTEIN: 27.9 g

Spicy Garlic Lime Chicken

Submitted by: C. PEREZ

PREP TIME: 5 MINUTES
COOK IN: 20 MINUTES
READY IN: 25 MINUTES
SERVINGS: 4

3/4 teaspoon salt
1/4 teaspoon black pepper
1/4 teaspoon cayenne pepper
1/8 teaspoon paprika
1/4 teaspoon garlic powder
1/8 teaspoon onion powder
1/4 teaspoon dried thyme
1/4 teaspoon dried parsley
4 boneless, skinless chicken breast halves
2 tablespoons butter
1 tablespoon olive oil
2 teaspoons garlic powder
3 tablespoons lime juice

In a small bowl, mix together salt, black pepper, cayenne, paprika, garlic powder, onion powder, thyme and parsley. Sprinkle spice mixture generously on both sides of chicken breasts.

Heat butter and olive oil in a large heavy skillet over medium heat. Saute chicken until golden brown, about 6 minutes on each side. Sprinkle with 2 teaspoons garlic powder and lime juice. Cook 5 minutes, stirring frequently to coat evenly with sauce.

Definitely a make again recipe. I used fresh minced onion, garlic and de-seeded chili peppers instead of the powdered versions. Also, I sauteed minced garlic with the oil and butter before adding chicken.

— LOVEMYKIDS

AMOUNT PER SERVING: CALORIES: 220 TOTAL FAT: 10.7 g CHOLESTEROL: 84 mg SODIUM: 572 mg
TOTAL CARBS: 2.5 g DIETARY FIBER: 0.3 g PROTEIN: 27.7 g

Focaccia Chicken Sandwiches

Submitted by: SILVERSOLARA

PREP TIME: 20 MINUTES
COOK TIME: 40 MINUTES
READY IN: 1 HOUR
SERVINGS: 8

2 tablespoons prepared brown mustard
3 skinless, boneless chicken breast halves
2 cups shredded mozzarella cheese
2 cups broccoli florets
1 loaf focaccia bread, cut in half horizontally

Preheat the oven to 350°F (175°C). Spread brown mustard onto the chicken breasts to coat, and place them in a baking dish. Bake for about 30 minutes in the preheated oven, or until cooked through.

Meanwhile, bring 1/2 inch of water to a boil in a small saucepan with a lid. Add the broccoli, and cook for 7 minutes, or until tender but still bright green. Drain, and set aside.

Shred or cube the chicken, and place onto the bottom half of the focaccia bread. Spread the broccoli over the chicken, and top with mozzarella cheese.

Bake this part of the sandwich (without the top) for about 10 minutes, or until the cheese is melted. Place the top of the bread over the filling, and bake for another 5 minutes to heat through. Cut into small squares to serve.

AMOUNT PER SERVING: CALORIES: 284 TOTAL FAT: 7.3 g CHOLESTEROL: 42 mg SODIUM: 547 mg
TOTAL CARBS: 30.6 g DIETARY FIBER: 2.2 g PROTEIN: 23 g

AS SHOWN IN THE PICTURE

Tangy Chicken Fajitas

Submitted by: JANET SCHAUFELE

PREP TIME: 10 MINUTES
COOK IN: 20 MINUTES
READY IN: 3 HOURS 30 MINUTES
SERVINGS: 6

1/2 cup olive oil
1/2 cup distilled white vinegar
1/2 cup fresh lime juice
2 (.7 ounce) packages dry Italian-style salad dressing mix
3 whole boneless, skinless chicken breasts, cubed
1 onion, sliced
1 green bell pepper, sliced

In a large glass bowl combine the oil, vinegar, lime juice, and dry salad dressing mix. Mix together. Add chicken strips, onion and bell pepper. Cover dish and refrigerate. Marinate for 3 to 6 hours.

In a large skillet, heat oil. Remove chicken, onion and bell pepper from marinade and saute in oil until chicken is cooked through (juices run clear) and onion is translucent.

Awesome! A keeper for sure. I did this up on the grill and it was absolutely delicious! I didn't even marinate for more than 2-1/2 or 3 hours.

— ED LIN

AMOUNT PER SERVING: CALORIES: 256 TOTAL FAT: 18.8 g CHOLESTEROL: 34 mg SODIUM: 888 mg
TOTAL CARBS: 7.4 g DIETARY FIBER: 0.8 g PROTEIN: 14.1 g

Garlic Chicken Fried Chicken

Submitted by: TANCAL29

PREP TIME: 20 MINUTES
COOK TIME: 15 MINUTES
READY IN: 35 MINUTES
SERVINGS: 4

2 teaspoons garlic powder, or to taste
1 teaspoon ground black pepper
1 teaspoon salt
1 teaspoon paprika
1/2 cup seasoned bread crumbs
1 cup all-purpose flour
1/2 cup milk
1 egg
4 skinless, boneless chicken breast halves - pounded thin
1 cup oil for frying, or as needed

In a shallow dish, mix together the garlic powder, pepper, salt, paprika, bread crumbs and flour. In a separate dish, whisk together the milk and egg.

Heat the oil in an electric skillet set to 350°F (175°C). Dip the chicken into the egg and milk, then dredge in the dry ingredients until evenly coated.

Fry chicken in the hot oil for about 5 minutes per side, or until the chicken is cooked through and juices run clear. Remove from the oil with a slotted spatula, and serve.

Excellent recipe. I finally found a chicken recipe that my husband likes, and I have tried out quite a few in the past 3 years. I have had problems with chicken coming out dry and tough, but with this recipe the chicken was very moist and tender. definitely a keeper.

— WEEPING HEAD

AMOUNT PER SERVING: CALORIES: 389 TOTAL FAT: 11 g CHOLESTEROL: 123 mg SODIUM: 1,070 mg
TOTAL CARBS: 37.7 g DIETARY FIBER: 1.9 g PROTEIN: 32.8 g

Hawaiian Chicken

Submitted by: BARBARA CHILDERS

PREP TIME: 5 MINUTES
COOK IN: 25 MINUTES
READY IN: 8 HOURS 30 MINUTES
SERVINGS: 6

6 skinless, boneless chicken breast halves
2 cups teriyaki sauce, divided
6 pineapple rings
1/2 cup butter, melted
3/4 cup packed brown sugar
3/4 cup soy sauce
3/4 cup unsweetened pineapple juice
6 tablespoons Worcestershire sauce

Place the chicken breast halves in a dish with the 1 1/2 cups of teriyaki sauce. Cover and refrigerate 8 hours or overnight.

Preheat a grill for high heat. Lightly oil the grill grate. Place chicken breasts on grill, and discard marinade. Cook for 8 minutes per side, or until juices run clear. Brush with the remaining teriyaki sauce during the last 5 minutes. When almost done, place one pineapple ring on top of each breast, and brush with melted butter.

In a small saucepan over medium heat, mix the brown sugar, soy sauce, pineapple juice, and Worcestershire sauce. Cook, stirring occasionally, until sugar is dissolved. Serve with chicken for dipping!

AMOUNT PER SERVING: CALORIES: 541 TOTAL FAT: 18.2 g CHOLESTEROL: 109 mg SODIUM: 5,906 mg
TOTAL CARBS: 63.4 g DIETARY FIBER: 0.9 g PROTEIN: 32.1 g

AS SHOWN IN THE PICTURE

Spinach Stuffed Chicken Breast

Submitted by: JERSEYGIRL_CHELL

PREP TIME: 15 MINUTES
COOK TIME: 45 MINUTES
READY IN: 1 HOUR
SERVINGS: 4

1 (10 ounce) package fresh spinach leaves
1/2 cup sour cream
1/2 cup shredded pepperjack cheese
4 cloves garlic, minced
4 skinless, boneless chicken breast halves, pounded to half inch thickness
1 pinch ground black pepper
8 slices bacon

Preheat the oven to 375°F (190°C).

Place spinach in a large glass bowl, and heat in the microwave for 3 minutes, stirring every minute or so, or until wilted. Stir in sour cream, pepperjack cheese, and garlic.

Lay the chicken breasts out on a clean surface, and spoon some of the spinach mixture onto each one. Roll up chicken to enclose the spinach, then wrap each chicken breast with two slices of bacon. Secure with toothpicks, and arrange in a shallow baking dish.

Bake uncovered for 35 minutes in the preheated oven, then increase heat to 500°F (260°C), or use the oven's broiler to cook for an additional 5 to 10 minutes to brown the bacon.

AMOUNT PER SERVING: CALORIES: 360 TOTAL FAT: 21.5 g CHOLESTEROL: 110 mg SODIUM: 472 mg
TOTAL CARBS: 5.5 g DIETARY FIBER: 2 g PROTEIN: 36.1 g

AS SHOWN IN THE PICTURE

Aussie Chicken

Submitted by: REBECCA

PREP TIME: 25 MINUTES
COOK IN: 25 MINUTES
READY IN: 1 HOUR 20 MINUTES
SERVINGS: 4

4 skinless, boneless chicken breast halves, pounded to half inch thickness

2 teaspoons seasoning salt

6 slices bacon, cut in half

1/2 cup prepared mustard

1/2 cup honey

1/4 cup light corn syrup

1/4 cup mayonnaise

1 tablespoon dried onion flakes

1 tablespoon vegetable oil

1 cup sliced fresh mushrooms

2 cups shredded Colby-Monterey Jack cheese

2 tablespoons chopped fresh parsley

Really very good! Pounding the chicken flat is important. I marinated the breasts in Italian dressing and Worcestershire sauce, and sautéed the mushrooms in the bacon fat. Delish!
— KATIE SEBASTIAN

Rub the chicken breasts with the seasoning salt, cover and refrigerate for 30 minutes.

Preheat oven to 350°F (175°C). Place bacon in a large, deep skillet. Cook over medium high heat until crisp. Set aside.

In a medium bowl, combine the mustard, honey, corn syrup, mayonnaise and dried onion flakes. Remove half of sauce, cover and refrigerate to serve later.

Heat oil in a large skillet over medium heat. Place the breasts in the skillet and saute for 3 to 5 minutes per side, or until browned. Remove from skillet and place the breasts into a 9x13 inch baking dish. Apply the honey mustard sauce to each breast, then layer each breast with mushrooms and bacon. Sprinkle top with shredded cheese.

Bake in preheated oven for 15 minutes, or until cheese is melted and chicken juices run clear. Garnish with parsley and serve with the reserved honey mustard sauce.

One of the best recipes in my cookbook! I use the bacon drippings instead of vegetable oil and sometimes I use provolone and sharp cheddar cheese when I want an extra kick. YUM!
— CHROMO

Whenever a version of this dish is offered at a restaurant, my husband orders it. Now we don't have to eat out, because I can make it at home! It turned out great!!
— AMANDA J

AMOUNT PER SERVING: CALORIES: 976   TOTAL FAT: 64.1 g   CHOLESTEROL: 140 mg   SODIUM: 1,714 mg
TOTAL CARBS: 57.9 g   DIETARY FIBER: 1.5 g   PROTEIN: 47.2 g

Oven Fried Parmesan Chicken

Submitted by: JUDY WILSON

PREP TIME: 15 MINUTES
COOK IN: 1 HOUR 15 MINUTES
READY IN: 1 HOUR 30 MINUTES
SERVINGS: 6

1 clove crushed garlic
1/4 pound butter, melted
1 cup dried bread crumbs
1/3 cup grated Parmesan cheese
2 tablespoons chopped fresh parsley
1 teaspoon salt
1/8 teaspoon ground black pepper
1 (4 pound) chicken, cut into pieces

Preheat oven to 350°F (175°C).

In a shallow glass dish or bowl, combine the crushed garlic with the melted butter or margarine. In another small bowl mix together the bread crumbs, cheese, parsley, salt and pepper. Dip chicken pieces into garlic butter, then into crumb mixture to coat.

Place coated chicken pieces into a lightly greased 9x13 inch baking dish. Drizzle with remaining garlic butter and bake uncovered in the preheated oven for 1 to 1 1/4 hours, or until chicken is cooked through and juices run clear.

AMOUNT PER SERVING: CALORIES: 884 TOTAL FAT: 63.6 g CHOLESTEROL: 273 mg SODIUM: 1,015 mg
TOTAL CARBS: 13.5 g DIETARY FIBER: 0.5 g PROTEIN: 61.1 g

AS SHOWN IN THE PICTURE

Chicken with Garlic, Basil, and Parsley

Submitted by: KITTY731

PREP TIME: 10 MINUTES
COOK IN: 40 MINUTES
READY IN: 50 MINUTES
SERVINGS: 4

1 tablespoon dried parsley, divided
1 tablespoon dried basil, divided
4 skinless, boneless chicken breast halves
4 cloves garlic, thinly sliced
1/2 teaspoon salt
1/2 teaspoon crushed red pepper flakes
2 tomatoes, sliced

Preheat oven to 350°F (175°C). Coat a 9x13 inch baking dish with cooking spray.

Sprinkle 1 teaspoon parsley and 1 teaspoon basil evenly over the bottom of the baking dish. Arrange chicken breast halves in the dish, and sprinkle evenly with garlic slices. In a small bowl, mix the remaining 2 teaspoons parsley, remaining 2 teaspoons basil, salt, and red pepper; sprinkle over the chicken. Top with tomato slices.

Bake covered in the preheated oven 25 minutes. Remove cover, and continue baking 15 minutes, or until chicken juices run clear.

AMOUNT PER SERVING: CALORIES: 152 TOTAL FAT: 3.1 g CHOLESTEROL: 67 mg SODIUM: 357 mg
TOTAL CARBS: 4.6 g DIETARY FIBER: 1.2 g PROTEIN: 25.5 g

Easy Grilled Chicken Teriyaki

Submitted by: T'S MOM

PREP TIME: 15 MINUTES
COOK IN: 15 MINUTES
READY IN: 1 HOUR 30 MINUTES
SERVINGS: 4

4 skinless, boneless chicken breast halves
1 cup teriyaki sauce
1/4 cup lemon juice
2 teaspoons minced fresh garlic
2 teaspoons sesame oil

Place chicken, teriyaki sauce, lemon juice, garlic, and sesame oil in a large resealable plastic bag. Seal bag, and shake to coat. Place in refrigerator for 24 hours, turning every so often.

Preheat grill for high heat.

Lightly oil the grill grate. Remove chicken from bag, discarding any remaining marinade. Grill for 6 to 8 minutes each side, or until juices run clear when chicken is pierced with a fork.

Even marinated for one hour, this recipe was excellent. I added some sweet thai chili sauce for a little spicy kick.

— SIBLINO

AMOUNT PER SERVING: CALORIES: 240 TOTAL FAT: 7.5 g CHOLESTEROL: 67 mg SODIUM: 691 mg TOTAL CARBS: 16.6 g DIETARY FIBER: 0.1 g PROTEIN: 25.3 g

---

Tomato Curry Chicken

Submitted by: FRANNY

PREP TIME: 15 MINUTES
COOK TIME: 1 HOUR
READY IN: 1 HOUR 15 MINUTES
SERVINGS: 4

4 skinless, boneless chicken breast halves
2 tablespoons butter
1 onion, chopped
2/3 cup beer
1 (10.75 ounce) can condensed tomato soup
1 teaspoon curry powder
1/2 teaspoon dried basil
1/2 teaspoon ground black pepper
1/4 cup grated Parmesan cheese

Preheat oven to 350°F (175°C).

Place chicken in a 9x13 inch baking dish. Melt butter in a medium skillet over medium heat. Saute onion, then stir in beer, soup, curry powder, basil and pepper. Reduce heat to low and simmer for about 10 minutes, then pour over chicken.

Bake for 1 hour; sprinkle with cheese for last 10 minutes of baking.

This was really good. I like spices so I added a variety over what the recipe calls for (2 tsp curry, 3/4 tsp garam masala, and 1/4 tsp cumin, cardamom, chili powder and cinnamon). The best part about this is that it doesn't require a special trip to the grocery store!

— HORSEFLESH

AMOUNT PER SERVING: CALORIES: 291 TOTAL FAT: 10.4 g CHOLESTEROL: 89 mg SODIUM: 678 mg TOTAL CARBS: 14.8 g DIETARY FIBER: 1.2 g PROTEIN: 31.7 g

Pesto Chicken Florentine

Submitted by: JAMIE

PREP TIME: 10 MINUTES
COOK IN: 35 MINUTES
READY IN: 45 MINUTES
SERVINGS: 4

2 tablespoons olive oil

2 cloves garlic, finely chopped

4 skinless, boneless chicken breast halves, cut into strips

2 cups fresh spinach leaves

1 (4.5 ounce) package dry Alfredo sauce mix

2 tablespoons pesto

1 (8 ounce) package dry penne pasta

1 tablespoon grated Romano cheese

Heat oil in a large skillet over medium high heat. Add garlic, saute for 1 minute; then add chicken and cook for 7 to 8 minutes on each side. When chicken is close to being cooked through (no longer pink inside), add spinach and saute all together for 3 to 4 minutes.

Meanwhile, prepare Alfredo sauce according to package directions. When finished, stir in 2 tablespoons pesto; set aside.

In a large pot of salted boiling water, cook pasta for 8 to 10 minutes or until al dente. Rinse under cold water and drain.

Add chicken/spinach mixture to pasta, then stir in pesto/Alfredo sauce. Mix well, top with cheese and serve.

AMOUNT PER SERVING: CALORIES: 571 TOTAL FAT: 19.3 g CHOLESTEROL: 84 mg SODIUM: 1,707 mg
TOTAL CARBS: 57.3 g DIETARY FIBER: 2.6 g PROTEIN: 41.9 g

Irish Chicken and Dumplings

Submitted by: CLAIRE MCLAUGHLIN

PREP TIME: 20 MINUTES
COOK TIME: 2 HOURS 30 MINUTES
READY IN: 2 HOURS 50 MINUTES
SERVINGS: 4

2 (10.75 ounce) cans condensed cream of chicken soup

4 skinless, boneless chicken breast halves

3 cups water

1 cup chopped celery

2 onions, quartered

1 teaspoon salt

1/2 teaspoon poultry seasoning

1/2 teaspoon ground black pepper

4 potatoes, quartered

5 carrots, sliced

1 (10 ounce) package frozen green peas

3 cups baking mix

1 1/3 cups milk

In large, heavy pot, combine soup, water, chicken, celery, onion, salt, poultry seasoning, and pepper. Cover and cook over low heat about 1 1/2 hours.

Add potatoes and carrots; cover and cook another 30 minutes.

Remove chicken from pot, shred it, and return to pot. Add peas and cook only 5 minutes longer.

Add dumplings. To make dumplings: Mix baking mix and milk until a soft dough forms. Drop by tablespoonfuls onto boiling stew. Simmer covered for 10 minutes, then uncover and simmer an additional 10 minutes.

AMOUNT PER SERVING: CALORIES: 722 TOTAL FAT: 11 g CHOLESTEROL: 70 mg SODIUM: 3,031 mg
TOTAL CARBS: 114.8 g DIETARY FIBER: 10.4 g PROTEIN: 41.2 g

AS SHOWN IN THE PICTURE

Bourbon Pecan Chicken

Submitted by: PGRAFF

PREP TIME: 20 MINUTES
COOK IN: 10 MINUTES
READY IN: 30 MINUTES
SERVINGS: 8

1/2 cup finely chopped pecans

1/2 cup dry bread crumbs

1/4 cup clarified butter, melted

8 skinless, boneless chicken breast halves

1/4 cup Dijon mustard

1/4 cup dark brown sugar

2 2/3 tablespoons bourbon whiskey

2 tablespoons soy sauce

1 teaspoon Worcestershire sauce

3/4 cup unsalted butter, chilled and cut into small cubes

1/2 cup sliced green onions

Stir together the pecans, bread crumbs, and 2 tablespoons of clarified butter. Spread the mixture out on a plate. Press the chicken breasts into the mixture to coat on both sides. Heat the remaining 2 tablespoons of clarified butter in a large skillet over medium heat. Place the coated chicken breasts in the pan, and fry on both sides until nicely browned and chicken meat is cooked through, about 10 minutes per side.

In a small saucepan, whisk together the Dijon mustard, brown sugar, bourbon, soy sauce, and Worcestershire sauce until smooth. Bring to a simmer over medium-low heat, then remove from the burner, and whisk in the 3/4 cup of unsalted butter one piece at a time. Do not return to the heat.

Arrange the chicken breasts on a large serving plate. Pour the sauce over the chicken, and sprinkle with green onion.

The sauce is tangy and rich; I drizzled it lightly over the platter of breaded fried chicken breasts and put leftover sauce in a gravy boat on the table for guests to season to their desire. The pecan taste and smell really comes out when you fry these. This one is a keeper; will make again.
— COLLEEN

We made this for dinner last night and it was an excellent dish. We paired it with rice and asparagus and everyone loved it.
— J MARCY

AWESOME!! This was so good. I have never been so impressed with a chicken dish! Since I was making it the first time for a special occasion, I didn't attempt the clarified butter coating. I just combined the pecans and breadcrumbs and coated in the traditional method (flour, then egg wash, then crumbs). It worked perfectly - nice thick coating.
— HUGSMOMMY

GREAT ALTERNATIVE TO PLAIN OLD BREADED CHICKEN!! I tried this recipe out on my family (with two picky teens), my in-laws, my dad and sister. Everybody thought it was great and said the sauce was excellent. Word of advice, fry at a little lower heat than you would normally fry chicken since pecans can burn easily. It takes a bit longer to cook but burned pecan taste horrible and can ruin a dish. I served it with squash casserole, fresh green beans and corn bread.
— TIFFANY H

AMOUNT PER SERVING: CALORIES: 487   TOTAL FAT: 33.8 g   CHOLESTEROL: 135 mg   SODIUM: 522 mg
TOTAL CARBS: 14.8 g   DIETARY FIBER: 1.2 g   PROTEIN: 29 g

AS SHOWN IN THE PICTURE

Summer Chicken Burgers

Submitted by: ELLIE ADAM

PREP TIME: 30 MINUTES
COOK IN: 30 MINUTES
READY IN: 1 HOUR 30 MINUTES
SERVINGS: 4

1 ripe avocado, sliced
1 tablespoon lemon juice
1 tablespoon butter
1 large Vidalia onions, sliced into rings
4 boneless, skinless chicken breast halves
Salt and pepper to taste
4 hamburger buns
4 tablespoons mayonnaise
4 slices provolone cheese

In a small bowl, combine sliced avocado and lemon juice. Add water to cover; set aside. Preheat an outdoor grill for high heat and lightly oil grate.

Heat butter in a large heavy skillet over medium-high heat. Saute the onions until browned and caramelized; set aside.

Season the chicken with salt and pepper. Place on grill, and cook until no longer pink and juices run clear, about 5 minutes on each side. Place buns on grill just long enough to toast them.

Spread buns with mayonnaise to taste, then layer with chicken, caramelized onion, provolone and avocado.

AMOUNT PER SERVING: CALORIES: 589 TOTAL FAT: 32.9 g CHOLESTEROL: 104 mg SODIUM: 681 mg
TOTAL CARBS: 33.6 g DIETARY FIBER: 5.1 g PROTEIN: 40.3 g

Marinated Turkey Breast

Submitted by: DANIELLE

PREP TIME: 20 MINUTES
COOK TIME: 30 MINUTES
READY IN: 5 HOURS
SERVINGS: 12

2 cloves garlic, peeled and minced
1 tablespoon finely chopped fresh basil
1/2 teaspoon ground black pepper
2 (3 pound) boneless turkey breast halves
6 whole cloves
1/4 cup vegetable oil
1/4 cup soy sauce
2 tablespoons lemon juice
1 tablespoon brown sugar

In a small bowl, mix together the garlic, basil, and pepper. Rub over the turkey breasts. Insert one clove into each end of the turkey breasts, and one in the center.

In a large shallow dish, blend vegetable oil, soy sauce, lemon juice, and brown sugar. Place the breasts in the dish, and turn to coat. Cover, and marinate in the refrigerator at least 4 hours.

Preheat grill for high heat. Lightly oil the grill grate. Discard marinade, place turkey breasts on the grill. Close the lid, and grill turkey breasts about 15 minutes on each side, or to an internal temperature of 170°F (68°C).

AMOUNT PER SERVING: CALORIES: 317 TOTAL FAT: 6 g CHOLESTEROL: 164 mg SODIUM: 610 mg TOTAL CARBS: 2.3 g
DIETARY FIBER: 0.3 g PROTEIN: 59.8 g

Cajun Chicken Pasta

Submitted by: TAMMY SCHILL

PREP TIME: 15 MINUTES
COOK IN: 15 MINUTES
READY IN: 30 MINUTES
SERVINGS: 2

4 ounces linguine pasta
2 boneless, skinless chicken breast halves, sliced into thin strips
2 teaspoons Cajun seasoning
2 tablespoons butter
1 green bell pepper, chopped
1/2 red bell pepper, chopped
4 fresh mushrooms, sliced
1 green onion, minced
1 1/2 cups heavy cream
1/4 teaspoon dried basil
1/4 teaspoon lemon pepper
1/4 teaspoon salt
1/8 teaspoon garlic powder
1/8 teaspoon ground black pepper
2 tablespoons grated Parmesan cheese

Bring a large pot of lightly salted water to a boil. Add linguini pasta, and cook for 8 to 10 minutes, or until al dente; drain.

Meanwhile, place chicken and Cajun seasoning in a bowl, and toss to coat.

In a large skillet over medium heat, saute chicken in butter until no longer pink and juices run clear, about 5 to 7 minutes. Add green and red bell peppers, sliced mushrooms and green onions; cook for 2 to 3 minutes. Reduce heat, and stir in heavy cream. Season the sauce with basil, lemon pepper, salt, garlic powder and ground black pepper, and heat through.

In a large bowl, toss linguini with sauce. Sprinkle with grated Parmesan cheese.

We loved it. I really didn't measure any of the ingredients...just threw it all together...a spice here and there... used shrimp instead of chicken. added some canned diced tomatoes... It was very tasty, will make again.

— CHEFNAN

I made this last night and thought it was very good. I added lemon zest and some lemon juice and a little more cheese.

— SDONOVAN1

Love this recipe! I added some crispy, crumbled bacon which complemented the dish nicely!

— FOODLOVER25

We love this recipe. I use a chicken already cooked from the store and 1/2 and 1/2 instead of the heavy cream.

— KORIEKISS

AMOUNT PER SERVING: CALORIES: 1,114   TOTAL FAT: 82.3 g   CHOLESTEROL: 348 mg   SODIUM: 1,184 mg
TOTAL CARBS: 55.2 g   DIETARY FIBER: 4.6 g   PROTEIN: 42.8 g

Mushroom and Swiss Chicken

Submitted by: NATALIE ROWE

PREP TIME: 25 MINUTES
COOK TIME: 45 MINUTES
READY IN: 1 HOUR 10 MINUTES
SERVINGS: 4

3 tablespoons olive oil
2 cloves crushed garlic
4 skinless, boneless chicken breasts
3 tablespoons red wine vinegar
1 tablespoon Cajun-style seasoning
1 cup chopped green onion
1 (8 ounce) package sliced fresh mushrooms
4 slices Swiss cheese

Preheat oven to 350°F (175°C).

Combine oil and garlic in a 9x13 inch baking dish. Add chicken breasts and coat well with the oil and garlic. Sprinkle with the vinegar and Cajun seasoning.

Bake for 30 minutes. Remove chicken from oven and cover with green onion and mushrooms; then add a few more sprinkles of oil and vinegar and return dish to oven for 15 to 20 minutes more. Remove from oven and immediately place 1 slice of cheese on top of each chicken breast; cheese will melt. Serve immediately.

AMOUNT PER SERVING: CALORIES: 360   TOTAL FAT: 19.7 g   CHOLESTEROL: 95 mg   SODIUM: 513 mg
TOTAL CARBS: 7.4 g   DIETARY FIBER: 1.9 g   PROTEIN: 37.2 g

Pasta, Chicken and Artichokes

Submitted by: KAY

PREP TIME: 25 MINUTES
COOK IN: 15 MINUTES
READY IN: 40 MINUTES
SERVINGS: 4

4 ounces uncooked pasta
1 teaspoon olive oil
1 teaspoon minced garlic
3 skinless, boneless chicken breast halves, cut into strips
1/4 cup chicken broth
1/4 cup fresh chopped broccoli
1/4 cup chopped tomatoes
1/4 (14 ounce) can artichoke hearts, drained and sliced
1/4 cup fresh sliced mushrooms
1 tablespoon red bell pepper, julienned
4 ounces pasta, cooked and drained
Salt and pepper to taste
1 tablespoon grated Parmesan cheese
1 teaspoon chopped fresh parsley

Bring a large pot of water to a boil. Cook pasta in boiling water until done. Drain, and set aside.

In a large saute pan, heat olive oil over medium high heat; brown the chicken and garlic in oil (about 5 minutes). Remove from the pan, and set aside.

Pour the chicken broth into the pan; then add the broccoli and tomato, and cook for about 5 minutes. Stir in the artichoke hearts, mushrooms, red bell pepper, cooked chicken, and pasta; cook for 3 to 5 more minutes, or until hot. Season to taste with salt and pepper.

Transfer to a serving bowl, and top with Parmesan cheese and parsley. Serve.

AMOUNT PER SERVING: CALORIES: 270   TOTAL FAT: 7.8 g   CHOLESTEROL: 48 mg   SODIUM: 347 mg
TOTAL CARBS: 25.7 g   DIETARY FIBER: 21 g   PROTEIN: 23.4 g

Cranberry Chicken

Submitted by: HEATHER

PREP TIME: 15 MINUTES
COOK IN: 1 HOUR 15 MINUTES
READY IN: 9 HOURS 30 MINUTES
SERVINGS: 6

6 skinless, boneless chicken breasts
1 1/2 (1 ounce) packages dry onion soup mix
1 (16 ounce) can jellied cranberry sauce
1 cup French dressing

Place chicken breasts in a glass or other non-reactive casserole dish.

In a mixing bowl, combine the soup mix, cranberry sauce, and dressing. Pour over the chicken breasts. Cover with plastic wrap, and refrigerate for at least 8 hours.

Cover loosely with foil. Bake at 350°F (175°C) and bake for 1 hour and 15 minutes, or until done.

Really great flavors...even for those who would never have imagined combining cranberries with chicken. It has a lovely sweet flavor and a tangy zip that is perfect paired with Stove Top Stuffing! Almost a little reminiscent of turkey and dressing, but way better!

— INSPIRINGOTHERS

AMOUNT PER SERVING: CALORIES: 481 TOTAL FAT: 22.3 g CHOLESTEROL: 68 mg SODIUM: 1,087 mg
TOTAL CARBS: 40.3 g DIETARY FIBER: 1.2 g PROTEIN: 27.9 g

Baked Apricot Chicken

Submitted by: JEANNE JONES

PREP TIME: 15 MINUTES
COOK TIME: 1 HOUR
READY IN: 1 HOUR 15 MINUTES
SERVINGS: 4

1 cup apricot preserves
1 cup French dressing
1 (1 ounce) package dry onion soup mix
12 chicken thighs

Preheat oven to 350°F (175°C).

In a medium bowl combine the jam, dressing and soup mix. Mix together.

Place chicken pieces in a 9x13 inch baking dish. Pour apricot mixture over chicken and bake uncovered in the preheated oven for 50 to 60 minutes.

I used chicken leg quarters with this, and increase the temperature about 10 degrees, and cooking time to a little over an hour. This was yum-yum-yum. Chicken was very moist. Thanks for a great recipe I will use again!

— MICHELLE M

AMOUNT PER SERVING: CALORIES: 1,027 TOTAL FAT: 60.3 g CHOLESTEROL: 176 mg SODIUM: 1,333 mg
TOTAL CARBS: 69.9 g DIETARY FIBER: 0.4 g PROTEIN: 47.8 g

AS SHOWN IN THE PICTURE

Enchiladas Suisas

Submitted by: LISA C.

PREP TIME: 45 MINUTES
COOK IN: 20 MINUTES
READY IN: 1 HOUR 5 MINUTES
SERVINGS: 6

2 tablespoons butter
2/3 cup chopped Spanish onion
2 tablespoons all-purpose flour
1 1/2 cups chicken broth
1 cup chopped green chile peppers
1 clove garlic, minced
3/4 teaspoon salt
1 dash ground cumin
12 (8 inch) corn tortillas
Canola oil for frying
1 cup shredded Monterey Jack cheese
1 cup shredded mild Cheddar cheese
2 cups shredded, cooked chicken breast meat
1 cup heavy cream
1/4 cup chopped green onion
1/2 cup sliced green olives
1 pint cherry tomatoes

Loved this! My husband and I could definitely taste a difference between those tortillas that we fried slightly in oil before stuffing and those that we did not. The "toasted" ones were much tastier.
— COOKINGDIVA

Prepare salsa verde: Melt butter in saucepan over medium heat. Saute the onion until soft. Stir in the flour. Add the broth, then add the chiles, garlic, salt, and cumin. Simmer about 15 minutes to blend flavors, then set aside. Preheat oven to 350°F (175°C.)

In a heavy skillet, lightly fry tortillas in shallow oil, being careful not to make them too crisp to roll. Combine the cheeses and keep 1/2 cup aside for topping. Dip each tortilla in salsa verde (both sides.) Place 2 heaping tablespoons chicken and about 2 tablespoons cheese down the center of each; roll and place seam side down in a shallow dish.

After all the rolled tortillas are in the dish, spoon additional salsa verde over them and then cover evenly with heavy cream. Sprinkle with remaining 1/2 cup cheese mixture, and with the green onions.

Bake uncovered in preheated oven for 20 minutes. Serve immediately, garnished with the olives, cherry tomatoes, and with additional salsa on the side.

Great recipe! I usually substitute a lower fat dairy product for the cream and it has always tasted great!
— JAMIE

These enchiladas were wonderful! Frying the corn tortillas gives them an authentic Mexican taste. I will try using just a small amount of oil next time. I made half the amount of enchiladas (6) and used all of the sauce. It still made a whole pan full. I also put some chopped cilantro inside the enchiladas because I love cilantro. I was worried about the cream, but not to worry, it turns out delicious! Very good!
— MOMOF3

AMOUNT PER SERVING: CALORIES: 744   TOTAL FAT: 52.6 g   CHOLESTEROL: 136 mg   SODIUM: 1,239 mg
TOTAL CARBS: 42.4 g   DIETARY FIBER: 5.1 g   PROTEIN: 29 g

AS SHOWN IN THE PICTURE

Gram's Chicken Pot Pie

Submitted by: JILL

PREP TIME: 45 MINUTES
COOK TIME: 35 MINUTES
READY IN: 1 HOUR 20 MINUTES
SERVINGS: 6

1 (2 to 3 pound) whole chicken

1 (10.75 ounce) can condensed cream of mushroom soup

1 (10 ounce) package frozen green peas, thawed

2 cups water, or as needed

1 teaspoon chicken bouillon granules

2 (9 inch) deep dish frozen pie crusts, thawed

In a large heavy pot, place chicken and water to cover. Bring to a boil and let simmer uncovered for 30 minutes, adding water as needed. When chicken is boiled and tender, pick all the meat off of the bones.

Preheat oven to 400°F (200°C).

Open 1 can of cream of mushroom soup and pour into a small saucepan. Add frozen peas and carrots, water and chicken bouillon to taste. Simmer all together until the soup is smooth. Add chicken meat and mix all together.

Pour chicken and soup mixture into one pie crust and cover with the other crust. Seal the edges and cut a small steam hole in the top crust. Bake in the preheated oven 30 to 35 minutes or until crust is brown.

AMOUNT PER SERVING: CALORIES: 807 TOTAL FAT: 52.4 g CHOLESTEROL: 142 mg SODIUM: 937 mg

TOTAL CARBS: 40.3 g DIETARY FIBER: 3 g PROTEIN: 41.1 g

Old-Fashioned Chicken and Noodles

Submitted by: ROGE

PREP TIME: 20 MINUTES
COOK TIME: 1 HOUR 30 MINUTES
READY IN: 1 HOUR 50 MINUTES
SERVINGS: 8

1 (2 to 3 pound) whole chicken, cut into pieces

4 stalks celery, diced

1 carrot, shredded

1 onion, halved

Ground black pepper to taste

3 (32 ounce) containers chicken broth

2 eggs, beaten

1 cup warm water

2 tablespoons vegetable oil

1 teaspoon salt

3 cups all-purpose flour

In a large pot over medium heat, combine chicken, celery and their tops, carrot, onion and its peel, and pepper. Pour broth over and bring to a boil. Cover, reduce heat and simmer until chicken is tender and falls from the bone, about 45 minutes.

While chicken is cooking, make noodles. In a large bowl, combine eggs, water, oil, salt and enough of the flour to make a stiff dough.

Strain chicken stock, reserving meat, celery and carrots. Pull meat from bones and return strained stock and meat, celery and carrots to pot. Bring to a boil. Make noodles by cutting dough from a broth-dipped spoon or using scissors or your fingers to make small, chickpea sized, noodles and dropping them in the boiling water. When the noodles rise to the surface they are done.

AMOUNT PER SERVING: CALORIES: 449 TOTAL FAT: 18 g CHOLESTEROL: 115 mg SODIUM: 1,793 mg

TOTAL CARBS: 40.2 g DIETARY FIBER: 2 g PROTEIN: 29.3 g

AS SHOWN IN THE PICTURE

Mexican Turkey Burgers

Submitted by: DANIEL DEN HOED

PREP TIME: 20 MINUTES
COOK IN: 25 MINUTES
READY IN: 45 MINUTES
SERVINGS: 6

1 tablespoon olive oil
1 medium onion, finely chopped
1 medium green bell pepper, finely chopped
2 cloves garlic, minced
1 cup salsa
1 (15.25 ounce) can whole kernel corn, drained
1 pound ground turkey
1 (1.25 ounce) package taco seasoning mix
1/3 cup dry bread crumbs
6 (10 inch) flour tortillas
6 tablespoons sour cream
2 cups shredded lettuce

YUM, YUM, YUM!! Made this last night without the tortillas (just set the burger on a bed of romaine) and hubby snarfed up two of them. Full of flavor, although next time I might use a little less taco seasoning (3/4 instead of a whole packet). Definitely saving this one for the future.

— C.MILLER

Preheat oven to 450°F (230°C). Coat a medium baking dish with cooking spray.

Heat the olive oil in a skillet over medium heat, and saute the onion, green pepper, and garlic 5 minutes. Remove from heat, and cool slightly.

In a small bowl, mix the salsa and 1/2 the corn. In a large bowl, mix the onion mixture with the turkey, taco seasoning, and 2 tablespoons of the salsa mixture. Divide into 6 patties, and press into the breadcrumbs to lightly coat on all sides. Arrange coated patties in the prepared baking dish.

Bake the patties 10 minutes in the preheated oven. Drain any liquid from the dish, turn patties, and spread with the remaining salsa mixture. Continue baking 10 minutes, to an internal temperature of 165°F (75°C).

Warm the tortillas in the microwave, about 30 seconds on High. Wrap the cooked turkey patties in the warmed tortillas with sour cream and lettuce. Sprinkle with remaining corn to serve.

Fabulous! Definitely not another boring old burger! I followed the recipe exactly except I made the burgers oblong and smaller because I had smaller tortillas. Also, we didn't have sour cream and they were delicious anyway but I can see how the coolness of the sour cream would be great!

— MICHELLE A

This is a delicious recipe. I added 1 cup of black beans to the recipe for protein and fiber. I topped with fat free shredded cheddar and 99% fat free ground turkey breast. I topped with avocado slices, sour cream, and homemade salsa.

— BTSYLYNN

AMOUNT PER SERVING: CALORIES: 543   TOTAL FAT: 18.8 g   CHOLESTEROL: 62 mg   SODIUM: 1,229 mg
TOTAL CARBS: 68.4 g   DIETARY FIBER: 5.6 g   PROTEIN: 25.5 g

Grilled Halibut with Cilantro Garlic Butter

Submitted by: SERENADELORENZO

PREP TIME: 25 MINUTES
COOK TIME: 8 MINUTES
READY IN: 33 MINUTES
SERVINGS: 4

4 (6 ounce) fillets halibut
1 lime, cut into wedges
Salt and pepper to taste
1 tablespoon olive oil
3 cloves garlic, coarsely chopped
1/2 cup chopped fresh cilantro
1 tablespoon fresh lime juice
2 tablespoons butter

Preheat a grill to high heat. Squeeze the juice from the lime wedges over fish fillets, then season them with salt and pepper.

Grill fish fillets for about 5 minutes on each side, until browned and fish can be flaked with a fork. Remove to a warm serving plate.

Heat the oil in a skillet over medium heat. Add the garlic; cook and stir just until fragrant, about 2 minutes. Stir in the butter, remaining lime juice and cilantro. Serve fish with the cilantro butter sauce.

AMOUNT PER SERVING: CALORIES: 276 TOTAL FAT: 13.1 g CHOLESTEROL: 69 mg SODIUM: 250 mg
TOTAL CARBS: 3.1 g DIETARY FIBER: 0.7 g PROTEIN: 35.4 g

Blackened Tuna

Submitted by: DENYS

PREP TIME: 10 MINUTES
COOK TIME: 10 MINUTES
READY IN: 20 MINUTES
SERVINGS: 6

1 1/2 pounds fresh tuna steaks, one inch thick
2 tablespoons Cajun seasoning
2 tablespoons olive oil
2 tablespoons butter

Generously coat tuna with Cajun seasoning.

Heat oil and butter in a large skillet over high heat. When oil is nearly smoking, place steaks in pan. Cook on one side for 3 to 4 minutes, or until blackened. Turn steaks, and cook for 3 to 4 minutes, or to desired doneness.

This is simple, quick, and very tasty - I couldn't ask for anything more on a busy weeknight. I have made this twice with tuna, once with salmon, and tonight with swordfish. Yum, yum yum.

—ALOSHA7777

AMOUNT PER SERVING: CALORIES: 243 TOTAL FAT: 14 g CHOLESTEROL: 54 mg SODIUM: 557 mg TOTAL CARBS: 1.1 g
DIETARY FIBER: 0.2 g PROTEIN: 26.8 g

Seafood Fettuccine

Submitted by: LESLIE ANN

PREP TIME: 15 MINUTES
COOK TIME: 20 MINUTES
READY IN: 35 MINUTES
SERVINGS: 8

1 (16 ounce) package dry fettuccine noodles
1 1/2 tablespoons butter or margarine
1 cup chopped green onions
4 garlic cloves, peeled and minced
1 pound medium shrimp, peeled and deveined
1 pound sea scallops
2 cups half-and-half cream
Salt and pepper to taste
2 tablespoons cornstarch (optional)
1 cup freshly grated Parmesan cheese

Bring a large pot of lightly salted water to a boil. Add pasta and cook for 8 to 10 minutes or until al dente; drain.

Melt butter in a large, non-stick skillet over medium-high heat. Stir in onions and garlic, and cook for 1 minute. Add shrimp and scallops, stirring to combine, and cook 3 minutes more. Reduce heat to medium-low.

Pour half-and-half, salt, and pepper into the pan and bring to a simmer, stirring constantly. Do not boil. Gradually sprinkle 1/2 cup Parmesan cheese over seafood mixture and continue stirring another minute. Remove from heat.

Toss cooked pasta into the pan, coating thoroughly. Sprinkle with remaining Parmesan cheese, and serve.

AMOUNT PER SERVING: CALORIES: 476 TOTAL FAT: 14.9 g CHOLESTEROL: 154 mg SODIUM: 811 mg
TOTAL CARBS: 47.6 g DIETARY FIBER: 2.8 g PROTEIN: 35 g

Spicy Shrimp Creole

Submitted by: PAMELA SHAW

PREP TIME: 15 MINUTES
COOK IN: 45 MINUTES
READY IN: 1 HOUR
SERVINGS: 8

3 tablespoons vegetable oil
2 cups julienne celery
2 onions, chopped
4 cloves crushed garlic
1 teaspoon white sugar
2 tablespoons all-purpose flour
1 teaspoon salt
1 teaspoon ground black pepper
1/2 teaspoon cayenne pepper
2 (14.5 ounce) cans crushed tomatoes
1 (15 ounce) can tomato sauce
1 bay leaf, crushed
1 tablespoon hot pepper sauce
2 pounds medium shrimp, peeled and deveined

Heat oil in a Dutch oven on medium heat. Saute celery, onions, and garlic in the Dutch oven until the onions are pearly white and the celery has begun to soften.

Mix sugar, flour, salt, pepper and cayenne pepper into the Dutch oven. Add crushed tomatoes and tomato sauce, both pieces of bay leaf, and hot sauce. Bring the mixture to a boil, then turn the heat to low.

Let the mixture simmer for 30 minutes, stirring occasionally. Approximately 15 minutes before serving, add shrimp to the pot and stir well. If necessary, raise the temperature to medium-low to ensure the Creole is bubbling but not burning. Scoop out the bay leaf halves before serving. Serve when the shrimp is pink and thoroughly cooked.

AMOUNT PER SERVING: CALORIES: 242 TOTAL FAT: 7.6 g CHOLESTEROL: 173 mg SODIUM: 985 mg
TOTAL CARBS: 18.5 g DIETARY FIBER: 3.9 g PROTEIN: 26.3 g

AS SHOWN IN THE PICTURE

Oven Baked Jambalaya

Submitted by: JOSLYN H.

PREP TIME: 45 MINUTES
COOK IN: 2 HOUR
READY IN: 2 HOURS 45 MINUTES
SERVINGS: 16

1/2 cup butter
1 large onion, diced
1 large green bell pepper, chopped
4 stalks celery, chopped
4 cloves garlic, minced
1 (6 ounce) can tomato paste
3 tablespoons Creole Seasoning Blend
4 teaspoons Worcestershire sauce
2 (28 ounce) cans whole peeled tomatoes
7 cups chicken stock
3 cups chopped cooked ham
3 cups cooked andouille sausage, sliced
3 cups cooked chicken, cut into bite-sized pieces
3 cups frozen cooked shrimp
4 cups uncooked long-grain white rice

Preheat oven to 350°F (175°C).

Melt butter in large stock pot. Saute onion, green pepper, celery and garlic until tender, being careful not to burn the garlic. Add tomato paste and cook to brown slightly, stirring constantly. Stir in Creole seasoning blend and Worcestershire sauce. Pour into a large roasting pan. Squeeze tomatoes to break up into pieces, and add to mixture in pan. Stir in juice from tomatoes, chicken stock, ham, sausage, chicken, shrimp and rice. Mix well. Cover tightly with aluminum foil.

Bake in preheated oven for 1 1/2 hours, stirring once halfway through baking time.

This is so delicious. Very authentic. I make 4 smaller casseroles (9"x9") and bake one that night and freeze the remaining three. Very good meal to have on hand.
—KIRBYSHELTIE

I made this jambalaya for a party and it was awesome. Everyone raved about how tasty it was and I raved at how easy it was to prepare. The only thing I did differently was that I added some bay leaves to give it that extra something and it was great. Wonderful recipe!
—MAY06BRIDE

This recipe is the best! It cooks up just as promised and leaves room for experimentation. I used red and green pepper and extra celery (to up the veggie content). I have made it with both cooked and raw shrimp and it turned out equally well. Instead of andouille sausage (difficult to find in these parts), I used hot Italian sausage. All in all a great recipe!
—VALKINGS

AMOUNT PER SERVING: CALORIES: 555   TOTAL FAT: 26.6 g   CHOLESTEROL: 136 mg   SODIUM: 1,430 mg
TOTAL CARBS: 47.4 g   DIETARY FIBER: 2.6 g   PROTEIN: 30.6 g

AS SHOWN IN THE PICTURE

Grilled Marinated Shrimp

Submitted by: ROBBIE RICE

PREP TIME: 30 MINUTES
COOK IN: 10 MINUTES
READY IN: 2 HOURS 40 MINUTES
SERVINGS: 6

1 cup olive oil
1/4 cup chopped fresh parsley
1 lemon, juiced
2 tablespoons hot pepper sauce
3 cloves garlic, minced
1 tablespoon tomato paste
2 teaspoons dried oregano
1 teaspoon salt
1 teaspoon ground black pepper
2 pounds large shrimp, peeled and deveined with tails attached
Skewers

In a mixing bowl, mix together olive oil, parsley, lemon juice, hot sauce, garlic, tomato paste, oregano, salt, and black pepper. Reserve a small amount for basting later. Pour remaining marinade into a large resealable plastic bag with shrimp. Seal, and marinate in the refrigerator for 2 hours.

Preheat grill for medium-low heat. Thread shrimp onto skewers, piercing once near the tail and once near the head. Discard marinade.

Lightly oil grill grate. Cook shrimp for 5 minutes per side, or until opaque, basting frequently with reserved marinade.

AMOUNT PER SERVING: CALORIES: 447 TOTAL FAT: 37.5 g CHOLESTEROL: 230 mg SODIUM: 799 mg
TOTAL CARBS: 3.7 g DIETARY FIBER: 1.4 g PROTEIN: 25.3 g

Thai Spiced Barbecue Shrimp

Submitted by: NEDB

PREP TIME: 1 HOUR
COOK TIME: 6 MINUTES
READY IN: 1 HOUR 6 MINUTES
SERVINGS: 8

3 tablespoons fresh lemon juice
1 tablespoon soy sauce
1 tablespoon Dijon mustard
2 cloves garlic, minced
1 tablespoon brown sugar
2 teaspoons curry paste
1 pound medium shrimp, peeled and deveined

In a shallow dish or resealable bag, mix together the lemon juice, soy sauce, mustard, garlic, brown sugar and curry paste. Add shrimp, and seal or cover. Marinate in the refrigerator for 1 hour.

Preheat a grill for high heat. When the grill is hot, lightly oil the grate. Thread the shrimp onto skewers, or place in a grill basket for easy handling. Transfer the marinade to a saucepan, and boil for a few minutes.

Grill shrimp for 3 minutes per side, or until opaque. Baste occasionally with the marinade.

5 stars for this versatile recipe. I have used this recipe to marinade chicken/shrimp/fish steaks before grilling. Serving over couscous is a great addition!

—AEWSCOTT1

AMOUNT PER SERVING: CALORIES: 73 TOTAL FAT: 1.2 g CHOLESTEROL: 86 mg SODIUM: 270 mg TOTAL CARBS: 3.5 g
DIETARY FIBER: 0.1 g PROTEIN: 11.8 g

Creamy Pesto Shrimp

Submitted by: LORETTA BUFFA

PREP TIME: 15 MINUTES
COOK IN: 15 MINUTES
READY IN: 30 MINUTES
SERVINGS: 8

1 pound linguine pasta
1/2 cup butter
2 cups heavy cream
1/2 teaspoon ground black pepper
1 cup grated Parmesan cheese
1/3 cup pesto
1 pound large shrimp, peeled and deveined

Bring a large pot of lightly salted water to a boil. Add linguine pasta, and cook for 8 to 10 minutes, or until al dente; drain.

In a large skillet, melt the butter over medium heat. Stir in cream, and season with pepper. Cook 6 to 8 minutes, stirring constantly.

Stir Parmesan cheese into cream sauce, stirring until thoroughly mixed. Blend in the pesto, and cook for 3 to 5 minutes, until thickened.

Stir in the shrimp, and cook until they turn pink, about 5 minutes. Serve over the hot linguine.

AMOUNT PER SERVING: CALORIES: 660   TOTAL FAT: 43.4 g   CHOLESTEROL: 212 mg   SODIUM: 552 mg
TOTAL CARBS: 43.1 g   DIETARY FIBER: 2.7 g   PROTEIN: 24.5 g

AS SHOWN IN THE PICTURE

Crab Cakes

Submitted by: ABBY

PREP TIME: 15 MINUTES
COOK TIME: 30 MINUTES
READY IN: 45 MINUTES
SERVINGS: 16

4 pounds crabmeat
1 egg
1 tablespoon lemon zest
1/4 teaspoon Old Bay Seasoning™
2 tablespoons fresh basil, chopped
1 cup saltine crackers, crushed
1 cup mayonnaise
4 tablespoons vegetable oil
3 egg yolks
3 ounces fresh lime juice
2 tablespoons chopped fresh cilantro
Salt and pepper to taste
1 3/4 cups vegetable oil

In a large mixing bowl, combine crabmeat, 1 egg, lemon zest, 1/8 teaspoon Old Bay Seasoning, chopped basil, crushed crackers and mayonnaise. Mix thoroughly.

Form 5 ounce patties out of the crab mixture (should make about 16 patties), and chill until cold before cooking.

In a skillet, heat 4 tablespoons of oil over medium heat. Saute the crab cakes for 4 minutes on each side or until golden brown.

In a blender place the egg yolks, remaining Old Bay Seasoning, lime juice, cilantro, salt and pepper. Blend for 10 seconds. Keeping the blender running, slowly drizzle the oil into the blender. Blend until sauce is creamy.

AMOUNT PER SERVING: CALORIES: 501   TOTAL FAT: 41.4 g   CHOLESTEROL: 148 mg   SODIUM: 586 mg
TOTAL CARBS: 5.3 g   DIETARY FIBER: 0.2 g   PROTEIN: 26.8 g

AS SHOWN IN THE PICTURE

Cioppino

Submitted by: STAR POOLEY

PREP TIME: 10 MINUTES
COOK IN: 45 MINUTES
READY IN: 55 MINUTES
SERVINGS: 13

3/4 cup butter
2 onions, chopped
2 cloves garlic, minced
1 bunch fresh parsley, chopped
2 (14.5 ounce) cans stewed tomatoes
2 (14.5 ounce) cans chicken broth
2 bay leaves
1 tablespoon dried basil
1/2 teaspoon dried thyme
1/2 teaspoon dried oregano
1 cup water
1 1/2 cups white wine
1 1/2 pounds large shrimp, peeled and deveined
1 1/2 pounds bay scallops
18 small clams
18 mussels, cleaned and debearded
1 1/2 cups crabmeat
1 1/2 pounds cod fillets, cubed

This recipe must be the best Cioppino of its kind. I do add more seafood than requested in the recipe which doesn't alter the flavor of the soup. 5 stars!
—JANET VONG

Over medium-low heat melt butter in a large stockpot, add onions, garlic and parsley. Cook slowly, stirring occasionally until onions are soft.

Add tomatoes to the pot (break them into chunks as you add them). Add chicken broth, bay leaves, basil, thyme, oregano, water and wine. Mix well. Cover and simmer 30 minutes.

Stir in the shrimp, scallops, clams, mussels and crabmeat. Stir in fish, if desired. Bring to boil. Lower heat, cover and simmer 5 to 7 minutes until clams open. Ladle soup into bowls and serve with warm, crusty bread!

Wow, this was amazing! It definitely tasted like a restaurant-quality dish. I had a dinner party for 4 people started with a simple lettuce salad with pine nuts and a lemon-basil dressing. Then we had crab cakes. The cioppino was the main course. (Followed by a crème brulee.) The beauty of this recipe is its flexibility! I like my cioppino very tomato-based, so even though I halved the recipe, I put in a 28-oz can of tomatoes, as well as a 14-oz can of tomato sauce. Also, I used a merlot (red wine) instead of white, because I tend to associate tomato-based dished with a red wine accent. I used a combination of fresh and frozen seafood. I used fresh basil and a seafood seasoning. Served it with freshly grated parmesan cheese on top, fresh ground pepper and a big loaf of fresh, crusty bread.
—POST-IT POET

Fabulous! Substituted clam juice for the water. Also, added shallots to the garlic & used fresh bay leaves and fresh basil (doubled all herbs) & some Emeril's Essence for seasoning. I used red snapper for a firm fish & crab legs instead of meat...I dished up the broth with a few pieces of seafood & then served the shellfish etc. in a bowl. Nice presentation!
—TRISH WILTSHIRE

AMOUNT PER SERVING: CALORIES: 315   TOTAL FAT: 13.2 g   CHOLESTEROL: 162 mg   SODIUM: 773 mg
TOTAL CARBS: 8.9 g   DIETARY FIBER: 1.3 g   PROTEIN: 34.7 g

AS SHOWN IN THE PICTURE

Grilled Rock Lobster Tails

Submitted by: JOE NEKRASZ

PREP TIME: 15 MINUTES
COOK IN: 12 MINUTES
READY IN: 27 MINUTES
SERVINGS: 2

1 tablespoon lemon juice
1/2 cup olive oil
1 teaspoon salt
1 teaspoon paprika
1/8 teaspoon white pepper
1/8 teaspoon garlic powder
2 (10 ounce) rock lobster tails

Preheat grill for high heat.

Squeeze lemon juice into a small bowl, and slowly whisk in olive oil. Whisk in salt, paprika, white pepper, and garlic powder. Split lobster tails lengthwise with a large knife, and brush flesh side of tail with marinade.

Lightly oil grill grate. Place tails, flesh side down, on preheated grill. Cook for 10 to 12 minutes, turning once, and basting frequently with marinade. Discard any remaining marinade. Lobster is done when opaque and firm to the touch.

AMOUNT PER SERVING: CALORIES: 743 TOTAL FAT: 60.9 g CHOLESTEROL: 170 mg SODIUM: 2,036 mg
TOTAL CARBS: 4.3 g DIETARY FIBER: 0.3 g PROTEIN: 44.4 g

Maple Salmon

Submitted by: STARFLOWER

PREP TIME: 10 MINUTES
COOK TIME: 20 MINUTES
READY IN: 1 HOUR
SERVINGS: 4

1/4 cup maple syrup
2 tablespoons soy sauce
1 clove garlic, minced
1/4 teaspoon garlic salt
1/8 teaspoon ground black pepper
1 pound salmon

In a small bowl, mix the maple syrup, soy sauce, garlic, garlic salt, and pepper.

Place salmon in a shallow baking dish, and coat with the maple syrup mixture. Cover the dish, and marinate salmon in the refrigerator 30 minutes, turning once.

Preheat oven to 400°F (200°C).

Place the baking dish in the preheated oven, and bake salmon 20 minutes, or until easily flaked with a fork.

Yummy - this was really good. It gets 5 stars because not only was it delicious, it was such a quick and easy meal to put together. I did add about a half teaspoon of ground ginger, but apart from that I followed the recipe exactly; this one is a keeper for sure.

—KELCAMPBELL

AMOUNT PER SERVING: CALORIES: 265 TOTAL FAT: 12.4 g CHOLESTEROL: 67 mg SODIUM: 639 mg
TOTAL CARBS: 14.2 g DIETARY FIBER: 0.1 g PROTEIN: 23.1 g

Trout Amandine

Submitted by: LOLA

PREP TIME: 15 MINUTES
COOK IN: 20 MINUTES
READY IN: 35 MINUTES
SERVINGS: 2

2 whole (10 ounce) trout, pan-dressed
Salt and pepper to taste
1/4 cup all-purpose flour
4 tablespoons butter
1/2 cup blanched slivered almonds
2 tablespoons lemon juice
1 tablespoon chopped fresh parsley, for garnish
8 slices lemon, for garnish

Rinse and pat dry trout. Season inside and out with salt and pepper to taste. Dredge trout in flour.

Heat 2 tablespoons butter in large skillet over high heat until melted. Add trout and brown both sides. Lower heat to medium and cook for about 5 minutes on each side or until cooked through. Remove trout to a serving plate and keep warm.

Wipe out pan and add 2 tablespoons butter. Cook butter over medium heat until it just begins to brown. Add the almonds and brown.

Pour sauce and almonds over fish and sprinkle with lemon juice and parsley. Garnish with fresh lemon slices.

AMOUNT PER SERVING: CALORIES: 895   TOTAL FAT: 59.1 g   CHOLESTEROL: 225 mg   SODIUM: 387 mg
TOTAL CARBS: 25.7 g   DIETARY FIBER: 6.2 g   PROTEIN: 67.8 g

Baked Dijon Salmon

Submitted by: ARNIE WILLIAMS

PREP TIME: 20 MINUTES
COOK TIME: 15 MINUTES
READY IN: 35 MINUTES
SERVINGS: 4

1/4 cup butter, melted
3 tablespoons Dijon mustard
1 1/2 tablespoons honey
1/4 cup dry bread crumbs
1/4 cup finely chopped pecans
4 teaspoons chopped fresh parsley
4 (4 ounce) fillets salmon
Salt and pepper to taste
1 lemon, for garnish

Preheat oven to 400°F (200°C).

In a small bowl, stir together butter, mustard, and honey. Set aside. In another bowl, mix together bread crumbs, pecans, and parsley.

Brush each salmon fillet lightly with honey mustard mixture, and sprinkle the tops of the fillets with the bread crumb mixture.

Bake salmon 12 to 15 minutes in the preheated oven, or until it flakes easily with a fork. Season with salt and pepper, and garnish with a wedge of lemon.

AMOUNT PER SERVING: CALORIES: 429   TOTAL FAT: 30.5 g   CHOLESTEROL: 97 mg   SODIUM: 527 mg
TOTAL CARBS: 16.7 g   DIETARY FIBER: 2.3 g   PROTEIN: 25.1 g

Lemongrass and Citrus Poached Salmon

Submitted by: CHEF DAVE

PREP TIME: 15 MINUTES
COOK IN: 10 MINUTES
READY IN: 25 MINUTES
SERVINGS: 10

2 1/2 pounds salmon fillet
1 quart chicken stock
1 quart orange juice
2 cups white wine
1 small yellow onion, chopped
2 tablespoons minced garlic
2 cups chopped lemon grass
1 teaspoon salt
1 teaspoon white pepper

Remove skin from salmon, then cut into desired portions.

In a large pot, combine chicken stock, orange juice, white wine, onion, garlic and lemon grass. Season with salt and white pepper. Bring to a boil for 5 minutes. Reduce heat to a low boil. Place the salmon in the poaching liquid until flaky and tender, about 5 minutes.

Incredibly easy to make, and ready in minutes. I added a tablespoon of molasses to the broth. It gave it a nice color and a smoky/sweet taste. Serve with rice and sautéed mushrooms and snap peas with some garlic.

—KIERNAN46

AMOUNT PER SERVING: CALORIES: 318   TOTAL FAT: 13.4 g   CHOLESTEROL: 67 mg   SODIUM: 702 mg
TOTAL CARBS: 15.9 g   DIETARY FIBER: 0.4 g   PROTEIN: 24.6 g

AS SHOWN IN THE PICTURE

Grilled Salmon

Submitted by: TINA

PREP TIME: 15 MINUTES
COOK TIME: 16 MINUTES
READY IN: 2 HOURS 31 MINUTES
SERVINGS: 6

1 1/2 pounds salmon fillets
Lemon pepper to taste
Garlic powder to taste
Salt to taste
1/3 cup soy sauce
1/3 cup brown sugar
1/3 cup water
1/4 cup vegetable oil

Season salmon fillets with lemon pepper, garlic powder, and salt.

In a small bowl, stir together soy sauce, brown sugar, water, and vegetable oil until sugar is dissolved. Place fish in a large resealable plastic bag with the soy sauce mixture, seal, and turn to coat. Refrigerate for at least 2 hours.

Preheat grill for medium heat.

Lightly oil grill grate. Place salmon on the preheated grill, and discard marinade. Cook salmon for 6 to 8 minutes per side, or until the fish flakes easily with a fork.

AMOUNT PER SERVING: CALORIES: 318   TOTAL FAT: 20.1 g   CHOLESTEROL: 56 mg   SODIUM: 1,104 mg
TOTAL CARBS: 13.2 g   DIETARY FIBER: 0.1 g   PROTEIN: 20.3 g

Cheesy Salmon Pasta

Submitted by: VIRGOLUV

PREP TIME: 15 MINUTES
COOK IN: 15 MINUTES
READY IN: 30 MINUTES
SERVINGS: 4

1 (8 ounce) package uncooked spaghetti
1 1/2 tablespoons olive oil
1 cup chopped sweet onions
3 green onions, finely chopped
2 tablespoons prepared basil pesto
2 (6 ounce) cans salmon, drained and flaked
1/2 cup Parmesan cheese

Bring a large pot of lightly salted water to a boil. Add pasta and cook for 8 to 10 minutes or until al dente; drain.

Heat olive oil in a skillet over medium heat. Stir in the onions, green onions, and pesto. Cook until tender. Mix in salmon, and cook until heated through. Stir in 1/2 the Parmesan cheese, and continue cooking 5 minutes. Toss with the cooked pasta, and sprinkle with remaining Parmesan cheese to serve.

This recipe is FABULOUS. I used medium shells instead of spaghetti, simply because it's easier to eat. And I was about to reheat some leftovers of it but after one quick cold bite realized IT'S GREAT REFRIGERATED TOO! This is the perfect dish!

—MANDYHARMON

AMOUNT PER SERVING: CALORIES: 487   TOTAL FAT: 19.6 g   CHOLESTEROL: 50 mg   SODIUM: 754 mg
TOTAL CARBS: 45.1 g   DIETARY FIBER: 3.6 g   PROTEIN: 31.4 g

Lemon Pasta Sauce

Submitted by: HOLLY

PREP TIME: 10 MINUTES
COOK TIME: 20 MINUTES
READY IN: 30 MINUTES
SERVINGS: 5

4 tablespoons butter
1 cup heavy whipping cream
2 tablespoons fresh lemon juice
1 teaspoon lemon zest
1 teaspoon grated lime zest
1 cup beef broth
10 ounces uncooked pasta

In a sauce pan or skillet large enough to hold the pasta when it is done, combine the butter, cream, and beef broth or bouillon and simmer over medium heat until reduced by about half. Add the lemon juice, lemon and lime zest and set aside.

Bring a large pot of lightly salted water to a boil. Add pasta and cook for 8 to 10 minutes or until al dente; drain. Toss pasta with sauce; serve.

Very good, but I made some changes. First, I sauteed 1 small minced yellow onion with about 1/4 cup of white wine, and a few tblsp butter. I added the remaining ingredients. Finally, I put 2 chicken breasts in a casserole dish, and poured the sauce over the top. I topped it with some grated Monterey Jack cheese, and baked it at 350 for about 25-30 mins.

—CHELSEY E

AMOUNT PER SERVING: CALORIES: 412   TOTAL FAT: 28.2 g   CHOLESTEROL: 131 mg   SODIUM: 284 mg
TOTAL CARBS: 32.7 g   DIETARY FIBER: 2.3 g   PROTEIN: 8 g

Potato Curry

Submitted by: JSCHAFFE

PREP TIME: 15 MINUTES
COOK IN: 45 MINUTES
READY IN: 1 HOUR
SERVINGS: 4

3 tablespoons ghee
1 teaspoon cumin seeds
1 teaspoon turmeric
1 teaspoon ground coriander
1 teaspoon salt
1/2 teaspoon mustard seed
1/2 teaspoon ground cayenne pepper
6 medium potatoes, peeled and diced
2 cups water
1 cup yogurt
2/3 cup frozen green peas

Heat the ghee in a skillet over medium heat, and mix in the cumin, turmeric, coriander, salt, mustard seed, and cayenne pepper. Place potatoes in the skillet, and stir to evenly coat with the ghee. Cook 10 minutes, stirring often. Pour water into the skillet. Reduce heat to low, and simmer 30 minutes, until potatoes are tender.

Mix the yogurt and peas into the saucepan. Continue cooking until heated through.

Very delicious. I added cut up chicken at the same time that I added the potatoes. The chicken was very tender, and the dish was very filling.

—ALHAAN

AMOUNT PER SERVING: CALORIES: 403   TOTAL FAT: 11 g   CHOLESTEROL: 28 mg   SODIUM: 680 mg
TOTAL CARBS: 66.3 g   DIETARY FIBER: 9.3 g   PROTEIN: 11.3 g

Quinoa and Black Beans

Submitted by: HILARY LYONS

PREP TIME: 15 MINUTES
COOK TIME: 35 MINUTES
READY IN: 50 MINUTES
SERVINGS: 10

1 teaspoon vegetable oil
1 onion, chopped
3 cloves garlic, peeled and chopped
3/4 cup uncooked quinoa
1 1/2 cups vegetable broth
1 teaspoon ground cumin
1/4 teaspoon cayenne pepper
Salt and pepper to taste
1 cup frozen corn kernels
2 (15 ounce) cans black beans, rinsed and drained
1/2 cup chopped fresh cilantro

Heat the oil in a medium saucepan over medium heat. Stir in the onion and garlic, and saute until lightly browned.

Mix quinoa into the saucepan and cover with vegetable broth. Season with cumin, cayenne pepper, salt, and pepper. Bring the mixture to a boil. Cover, reduce heat, and simmer 20 minutes.

Stir frozen corn into the saucepan, and continue to simmer about 5 minutes until heated through. Mix in the black beans and cilantro.

This is a great recipe. I have made it a few times already and I love it more and more each time. (I usually only use 1 can of beans.) Also, a general tip for quinoa: it cooks better if you soak it in water for an hour or so before rinsing it out and using it.

—JHARMONY

AMOUNT PER SERVING: CALORIES: 154   TOTAL FAT: 1.7 g   CHOLESTEROL: 0 mg   SODIUM: 513 mg   TOTAL CARBS: 28.3 g
DIETARY FIBER: 7.4 g   PROTEIN: 7.7 g

AS SHOWN IN THE PICTURE

Vegetable Stuffed Cannelloni

Submitted by: JILL

PREP TIME: 45 MINUTES
COOK IN: 1 HOUR 5 MINUTES
READY IN: 1 HOUR 50 MINUTES
SERVINGS: 8

8 cannelloni noodles
5 cloves garlic, minced
5 shallots, chopped
2 tablespoons olive oil
1 cup dry sherry
2 cups heavy whipping cream
Salt and pepper to taste
1 onion, chopped
1 cup fresh sliced mushrooms
1 zucchini, chopped
1 small eggplant, diced
2 roasted red bell peppers, diced
1 teaspoon dried basil
1 teaspoon dried oregano
3/4 cup ricotta cheese
1 cup grated Parmesan cheese

In a large pot of salted water, parboil cannelloni. (Parboiling is partially cooking the noodles in boiling water; they will finish cooking when baked.)

Meanwhile, cook 2 cloves garlic and 2 shallots in 1 tablespoon olive oil in a medium saucepan over medium heat for 30 seconds. Pour in sherry, raise heat to high, and reduce liquid by half. Stir in cream, and reduce until there is about 1 1/2 cups liquid. Remove from heat, and season with salt and pepper to taste. Set cream sauce aside.

In a large skillet, heat one tablespoon olive oil over medium heat. Cook onion, 3 shallots, 3 cloves garlic, mushrooms, zucchini, and eggplant in olive oil until all vegetables are tender. Transfer to a large bowl. Stir in red peppers, basil, oregano, ricotta, and Parmesan cheese. Season to taste with salt and pepper. Set filling aside.

Preheat oven to 350°F (175°C). Lightly grease one 9x13 inch baking dish. Stuff vegetable/cheese filling into cannelloni. Place in prepared baking dish, and cover with cream sauce.

Bake in preheated oven for 25 minutes.

This recipe is fantastic. I couldn't find cannelloni noodles, but found that manicotti noodles work just as well. Don't over boil the noodles! They only need a few minutes in water, so save that part for last. This is my new favorite dish.

—PENNYL1

Very good, easy to make. I substituted red wine for the dry sherry and it worked very well. I also used oven ready cannelloni noodles and it saved my preparation time.

—LISASMALL

AMOUNT PER SERVING: CALORIES: 470   TOTAL FAT: 31.7 g   CHOLESTEROL: 99 mg   SODIUM: 446 mg
TOTAL CARBS: 30.2 g   DIETARY FIBER: 3.4 g   PROTEIN: 13.9 g

Penne and Vodka Sauce

Submitted by: RICK NAYLOR

PREP TIME: 10 MINUTES
COOK IN: 15 MINUTES
READY IN: 25 MINUTES
SERVINGS: 4

1 (16 ounce) package penne pasta
2 tablespoons butter
1/4 pound thinly sliced pancetta bacon, chopped
1/3 cup vodka
1/2 cup heavy whipping cream
1 1/2 cups tomato sauce
1/2 cup grated Parmesan cheese

Bring a large pot of lightly salted water to a boil. Add pasta and cook for 8 to 10 minutes or until al dente; drain.

Meanwhile, melt butter or margarine in a large skillet over medium heat. Add pancetta, and saute until lightly browned. Add vodka and stir until it is reduced by half, about 4 to 5 minutes. Stir in tomato sauce and cream. Simmer uncovered for 10 to 12 minutes. Stir every few minutes. Stir in pasta, and heat through. Serve with Parmesan cheese.

AMOUNT PER SERVING: CALORIES: 842 TOTAL FAT: 39.6 g CHOLESTEROL: 85 mg SODIUM: 1,072 mg
TOTAL CARBS: 89.5 g DIETARY FIBER: 5.1 g PROTEIN: 24.4 g

AS SHOWN IN THE PICTURE

Pasta Pomodoro

Submitted by: DINAH

PREP TIME: 15 MINUTES
COOK TIME: 15 MINUTES
READY IN: 30 MINUTES
SERVINGS: 4

2 (8 ounce) packages angel hair pasta
1/4 cup olive oil
1/2 onion, chopped
4 cloves garlic, minced
2 cups roma (plum) tomatoes, diced
2 tablespoons balsamic vinegar
1 (10.75 ounce) can low-sodium chicken broth
Crushed red pepper to taste
Freshly ground black pepper to taste
2 tablespoons chopped fresh basil
1/4 cup grated Parmesan cheese

Bring a large pot of lightly salted water to a boil. Add pasta and cook for 8 minutes or until al dente; drain.

Pour olive oil in a large deep skillet over high-heat. Saute onions and garlic until lightly browned. Reduce heat to medium-high and add tomatoes, vinegar and chicken broth; simmer for about 8 minutes.

Stir in red pepper, black pepper, basil and cooked pasta, tossing thoroughly with sauce. Simmer for about 5 more minutes and serve topped with grated cheese.

AMOUNT PER SERVING: CALORIES: 515 TOTAL FAT: 19.4 g CHOLESTEROL: 6 mg SODIUM: 401 mg
TOTAL CARBS: 70.7 g DIETARY FIBER: 5.3 g PROTEIN: 17 g

AS SHOWN IN THE PICTURE

Artichoke Spinach Lasagna

Submitted by: DAVID

PREP TIME: 20 MINUTES
COOK IN: 1 HOUR
READY IN: 1 HOUR 20 MINUTES
SERVINGS: 8

Cooking spray
9 uncooked lasagna noodles
1 onion, chopped
4 cloves garlic, chopped
1 (14.5 ounce) can vegetable broth
1 tablespoon chopped fresh rosemary
1 (14 ounce) can marinated artichoke hearts, drained and chopped
1 (10 ounce) package frozen chopped spinach, thawed, drained and squeezed dry
1 (28 ounce) jar tomato pasta sauce
3 cups shredded mozzarella cheese, divided
1 (4 ounce) package herb and garlic feta, crumbled

Preheat oven to 350°F (175°C). Spray a 9x13 inch baking dish with cooking spray.

Bring a large pot of lightly salted water to a boil. Add noodles and cook for 8 to 10 minutes or until al dente; drain.

Spray a large skillet with cooking spray and heat on medium-high. Saute onion and garlic for 3 minutes, or until onion is tender-crisp. Stir in broth and rosemary; bring to a boil. Stir in artichoke hearts and spinach; reduce heat, cover and simmer 5 minutes. Stir in pasta sauce.

Spread 1/4 of the artichoke mixture in the bottom of the prepared baking dish; top with 3 cooked noodles. Sprinkle 3/4 cup mozzarella cheese over noodles. Repeat layers 2 more times, ending with artichoke mixture and mozzarella cheese. Sprinkle crumbled feta on top.

Bake, covered, for 40 minutes. Uncover, and bake 15 minutes more, or until hot and bubbly. Let stand

This recipe is delicious! I used dried rosemary instead of fresh, and added a bit more feta. It tastes even better the day after as the flavors intensify a bit. A great and different veggie lasagna recipe—and I'm not a vegetarian!

—STOVERIDER

This dish is quite exceptional. I added chicken to mine, and chose to use chicken broth in place of the vegetable. This one will be made again!

—THEQUALITYCOOKDOTCOM

Delicious and easy to assemble! I sautéed sliced crimini mushrooms along with the onions to give the dish some heft. My normally meat-loving husband gave this dish a big thumbs up!

—SANDYLONGSTON

AMOUNT PER SERVING: CALORIES: 427   TOTAL FAT: 20.3 g   CHOLESTEROL: 58 mg   SODIUM: 1,338 mg
TOTAL CARBS: 40 g   DIETARY FIBER: 5.8 g   PROTEIN: 23.9 g

Vegetarian Four Cheese Lasagna

Submitted by: ROSEMARY

PREP TIME: 15 MINUTES
COOK IN: 1 HOUR
READY IN: 1 HOUR 15 MINUTES
SERVINGS: 8

2 cups peeled and diced pumpkin
1 eggplant, sliced into 1/2 inch rounds
5 tomatoes
1 pint ricotta cheese
9 ounces crumbled feta cheese
2/3 cup pesto
2 eggs, beaten
Salt and pepper to taste
1 (15 ounce) can tomato sauce
Fresh pasta sheets
1 1/3 cups shredded Mozzarella cheese
1 cup grated Parmesan cheese

Excellent! I would give it six stars if I could. Here are the changes I made, zucchini instead of eggplant and cottage cheese, garlic and basil instead of pesto.
—AHOFFORT

I used sun dried tomato pesto and a jar of Portobello mushroom pasta sauce (in place of tomato sauce). It was delicious!
—JALAY

Preheat oven to 350°F (175°C).

Place pumpkin on a baking sheet and roast in oven until browned and tender, about 30 minutes. Meanwhile, grill eggplant on a charcoal grill or fry in a skillet, turning once, until charred and tender, 10 to 15 minutes. Halve tomatoes and place on baking sheet in oven for last 15 minutes of pumpkin time; cook until tender and wrinkly.

In a medium bowl, stir together ricotta, feta, pesto, eggs, salt and pepper until well mixed. Fold roasted pumpkin into ricotta mixture.

Spoon half of the tomato sauce into a 9x13 baking dish. Lay two pasta sheets over the sauce. Arrange a single layer of eggplant slices over pasta and top with half the ricotta mixture. Cover with two more pasta sheets. Arrange the roasted tomatoes evenly over the sheets and spoon the remaining half the ricotta mixture over the tomatoes. Sprinkle with half the mozzarella. Top with remaining two sheets of pasta. Pour remaining tomato sauce over all and sprinkle with remaining mozzarella and Parmesan.

Bake in preheated oven 30 to 40 minutes, until golden and bubbly.

Just delicious! I used yams instead of pumpkin. A great way to get more veggies into the diet. To "lighten" it I used cottage cheese in place of ricotta.
—NDOMMEL

AMOUNT PER SERVING: CALORIES: 470   TOTAL FAT: 30.4 g   CHOLESTEROL: 131 mg   SODIUM: 1,268 mg
TOTAL CARBS: 21.7 g   DIETARY FIBER: 4.2 g   PROTEIN: 30.2 g

Pasta with Fresh Tomatoes and Corn

Submitted by: SIMMI G.

PREP TIME: 20 MINUTES
COOK TIME: 10 MINUTES
READY IN: 30 MINUTES
SERVINGS: 3

8 ounces pasta
4 tablespoons olive oil
2 tablespoons red wine vinegar
1/2 cup whole corn kernels, cooked
4 tomatoes, chopped
1/2 cup chopped green onions
1 teaspoon dried basil
Salt to taste
Ground black pepper to taste
1 tablespoon grated Parmesan cheese
2 teaspoons chopped fresh basil (optional)

In a large pot with boiling salted water cook pasta until al dente. Drain.

Meanwhile, in a large bowl whisk together the olive oil, red wine vinegar, and dried basil. Add salt and pepper to taste. Stir in the tomatoes, corn kernels, and scallions. Let sit for 5 to 10 minutes.

Toss pasta with tomato mixture. Sprinkle with grated parmesan cheese. Garnish with fresh basil, if desired.

LOVED IT! I made as the recipe stated except I used fresh basil and one clove of garlic. What I really loved about it was how easy it was. Again...LOVED IT!

—RENEE

AMOUNT PER SERVING: CALORIES: 445   TOTAL FAT: 21.1 g   CHOLESTEROL: 56 mg   SODIUM: 73 mg

TOTAL CARBS: 55 g   DIETARY FIBER: 6.1 g   PROTEIN: 11.8 g

Pasta with Scallops, Zucchini, and Tomatoes

Submitted by: LISA STINGER

PREP TIME: 15 MINUTES
COOK TIME: 15 MINUTES
READY IN: 30 MINUTES
SERVINGS: 4

1 pound dry fettuccine pasta
1/4 cup olive oil
3 cloves garlic, minced
2 zucchinis, diced
1/2 teaspoon salt
1/2 teaspoon crushed red pepper flakes
1 cup chopped fresh basil
4 roma (plum) tomatoes, chopped
1 pound bay scallops
2 tablespoons grated Parmesan cheese

In a large pot with boiling salted water cook pasta until al dente. Drain.

Meanwhile, in a large skillet heat oil, add garlic and cook until tender. Add the zucchini, salt, red pepper flakes, basil and saute for 10 minutes.
Add chopped tomatoes, bay scallops, and fresh basil (if using) and simmer for 5 minutes, or until scallops are opaque.

Pour sauce over cooked pasta and serve with grated Parmesan cheese.

AMOUNT PER SERVING: CALORIES: 671   TOTAL FAT: 18.2 g   CHOLESTEROL: 39 mg   SODIUM: 535 mg

TOTAL CARBS: 92.4 g   DIETARY FIBER: 6.2 g   PROTEIN: 37.3 g

Twelve Minute Pasta Toss

Submitted by: CINDY

PREP TIME: 20 MINUTES
COOK IN: 12 MINUTES
READY IN: 32 MINUTES
SERVINGS: 8

16 ounces rotini pasta
4 skinless, boneless chicken breast halves, cut into bite size pieces
4 tablespoons olive oil
3 cloves garlic, minced
1 1/4 teaspoons salt
1 1/4 teaspoons garlic powder
1 1/4 teaspoons dried basil
1 1/4 teaspoons dried oregano
1 cup chopped sun-dried tomatoes
1/4 cup grated Parmesan cheese

Cook and drain pasta as directed.

While pasta is cooking, in a 5-quart pot, heat olive oil and saute chicken, garlic, salt, garlic powder, basil, and oregano until chicken is cooked. Add sun-dried tomatoes and cook for two minutes.

Remove from heat and toss with pasta. Serve with grated Parmesan cheese if desired.

This ROCKS! I added about 1/2 cup chopped artichoke hearts with the sun dried tomatoes, MMM! This will be made again & again & again!

—HARDROCKGIRL777

AMOUNT PER SERVING: CALORIES: 365 TOTAL FAT: 9.9 g CHOLESTEROL: 37 mg SODIUM: 470 mg
TOTAL CARBS: 45.8 g DIETARY FIBER: 3 g PROTEIN: 23.6 g

Garlic Pasta with Prawns

Submitted by: BREE

PREP TIME: 5 MINUTES
COOK TIME: 15 MINUTES
READY IN: 20 MINUTES
SERVINGS: 2

8 ounces fusili (spiral) pasta
6 tablespoons olive oil
2 cloves garlic, sliced
8 tiger prawns, peeled and deveined
1/2 cup grated Parmesan cheese, divided
1 teaspoon chopped fresh parsley

Bring a large pot of lightly salted water to a boil. Add pasta and cook for 8 to 10 minutes or until al dente. Drain, then return to pot.

Heat oil in a large heavy skillet over medium heat. Saute garlic for 5 minutes. Toss in prawns, and cook for 5 minutes on each side. Remove prawns, and set aside. Remove garlic slices, and discard.

Pour oil over pasta in pot, and toss to evenly coat. Sprinkle 3/4 of the Parmesan cheese onto pasta, and stir until evenly distributed. Transfer to serving dish. Arrange prawns on top, then sprinkle with remaining Parmesan and parsley.

AMOUNT PER SERVING: CALORIES: 924 TOTAL FAT: 51 g CHOLESTEROL: 20 mg SODIUM: 472 mg TOTAL CARBS: 84 g
DIETARY FIBER: 3.9 g PROTEIN: 34.9 g

Penne Pasta with Spinach and Bacon

Submitted by: **SUPERMAN'S MOM**

PREP TIME: 10 MINUTES
COOK IN: 15 MINUTES
READY IN: 25 MINUTES
SERVINGS: 4

1 (12 ounce) package penne pasta
2 tablespoons olive oil, divided
6 slices bacon, chopped
2 tablespoons minced garlic
1 (14.5 ounce) can diced tomatoes
1 bunch fresh spinach, rinsed and torn into bite-size pieces

Bring a large pot of lightly salted water to a boil. Add the penne pasta, and cook until tender, 8 to 10 minutes.

Meanwhile, heat 1 tablespoon of olive oil in a skillet over medium heat. Place bacon in the skillet and cook until browned and crisp. Add garlic, and cook for about 1 minute. Stir in the tomatoes, and cook until heated through.

Place the spinach into a colander, and drain the hot pasta over it so it is wilted. Transfer to a large serving bowl, and toss with the remaining olive oil, and the bacon and tomato mixture.

AMOUNT PER SERVING: CALORIES: 486 TOTAL FAT: 15.3 g CHOLESTEROL: 12 mg SODIUM: 451 mg
TOTAL CARBS: 68.2 g DIETARY FIBER: 6 g PROTEIN: 17.9 g

Asparagus Lasagna

Submitted by: **WENDY HANSEN**

PREP TIME: 20 MINUTES
COOK TIME: 10 MINUTES
READY IN: 30 MINUTES
SERVINGS: 4

5 wide lasagna noodles
2 tablespoons margarine
2 cloves garlic, chopped
2 tablespoons all-purpose flour
1 1/2 cups milk
1/2 teaspoon dried thyme
1 (15 ounce) can asparagus, drained
1 cup julienned fully cooked ham
1 cup shredded mozzarella cheese

Bring a large pot of lightly salted water to a boil. Cook lasagna noodles in boiling water for 8 to 10 minutes, or until al dente. Drain, and cut noodles in half.

Melt margarine in a skillet over medium heat. Saute garlic just until fragrant. Stir in the flour until no lumps remain. Gradually mix in milk, and season with thyme. Simmer sauce gently until thick. Remove from heat.

Grease a 9x9 inch glass baking dish. Layer noodles, sauce, asparagus, ham, and mozzarella cheese in three layers, each starting with noodles, and ending with shredded cheese on the top.

Cover the dish, and cook in the microwave on HIGH for 9 to 10 minutes, or until cheese is melted and bubbly. Time may vary depending on the oven used. Let stand for 5 to 10 minutes before serving.

AMOUNT PER SERVING: CALORIES: 397 TOTAL FAT: 18.4 g CHOLESTEROL: 55 mg SODIUM: 560 mg
TOTAL CARBS: 33.3 g DIETARY FIBER: 2.3 g PROTEIN: 25.4 g

Spinach Enchiladas

Submitted by: SADONIA2

PREP TIME: 20 MINUTES
COOK IN: 20 MINUTES
READY IN: 40 MINUTES
SERVINGS: 5

1 tablespoon butter
1/2 cup sliced green onions
2 cloves garlic, minced
1 (10 ounce) package frozen chopped spinach, thawed, drained and squeezed dry
1 cup ricotta cheese
1/2 cup sour cream
2 cups shredded Monterey Jack cheese
10 (6 inch) corn tortillas
1 (19 ounce) can enchilada sauce

Preheat the oven to 375°F (190°C).

Melt butter in a saucepan over medium heat. Add garlic and onion; cook for a few minutes until fragrant, but not brown. Stir in spinach, and cook for about 5 more minutes. Remove from the heat, and mix in ricotta cheese, sour cream, and 1 cup of Monterey Jack cheese.

In a skillet over medium heat, warm tortillas one at a time until flexible, about 15 seconds. Spoon about 1/4 cup of the spinach mixture onto the center of each tortilla. Roll up, and place seam side down in a 9x13 inch baking dish. Pour enchilada sauce over the top, and sprinkle with the remaining cup of Monterey Jack.

Bake for 15 to 20 minutes in the preheated oven, until sauce is bubbling and cheese is lightly browned at the edges.

AMOUNT PER SERVING: CALORIES: 577   TOTAL FAT: 39.5 g   CHOLESTEROL: 111 mg   SODIUM: 483 mg
TOTAL CARBS: 35.7 g   DIETARY FIBER: 5.5 g   PROTEIN: 23.4 g

AS SHOWN IN THE PICTURE

Potato and Bean Enchiladas

Submitted by: SYD

PREP TIME: 1 HOUR
COOK TIME: 45 MINUTES
READY IN: 1 HOUR 45 MINUTES
SERVINGS: 12

1 pound potatoes, peeled and diced
1 teaspoon cumin
1 teaspoon chili powder
1 teaspoon salt
1 tablespoon ketchup
1 pound fresh tomatillos, husks removed
1 large onion, chopped
1 bunch fresh cilantro, coarsely chopped, divided
2 (12 ounce) packages corn tortilla
1 (15.5 ounce) can pinto beans, drained
1 (12 ounce) package queso fresco
Oil for frying

Preheat oven to 400°F (205°C). In a bowl, toss diced potatoes together with cumin, chili powder, salt, and ketchup, and place in an oiled baking dish. Bake in the preheated oven for 20 to 25 minutes, or until tender.

Meanwhile, boil tomatillos and chopped onion in water to cover for 10 minutes. Set aside to cool. Once cooled, puree with half of the cilantro until smooth.

Fry tortillas individually in a small amount of hot oil until soft. Mix potatoes together with pinto beans, 1/2 cheese, and 1/2 cilantro. Fill tortillas with potato mixture, and roll up. Place seam side down in an oiled 9x13 inch baking dish. Spoon tomatillo sauce over enchiladas, and spread remaining cheese over sauce. Bake for 20 minutes, or until hot and bubbly.

AMOUNT PER SERVING: CALORIES: 249   TOTAL FAT: 5.5 g   CHOLESTEROL: 9 mg   SODIUM: 450 mg   TOTAL CARBS: 42.5 g
DIETARY FIBER: 6.2 g   PROTEIN: 9.5 g

AS SHOWN IN THE PICTURE

Grilled Mediterranean Vegetable Sandwich

Submitted by: CHRIS M.

PREP TIME: 20 MINUTES
COOK IN: 40 MINUTES
READY IN: 3 HOURS
SERVINGS: 6

1 eggplant, sliced into strips
2 red bell peppers
2 tablespoons olive oil, divided
2 portobello mushrooms, sliced
3 cloves garlic, crushed
4 tablespoons mayonnaise
1 (1 pound) loaf focaccia bread

Preheat oven to 400°F (200°C).

Brush eggplant and red bell peppers with 1 tablespoon olive oil; use more if necessary, depending on sizes of vegetables. Place on a baking sheet and roast in preheated oven. Roast eggplant until tender, about 25 minutes; roast peppers until blackened. Remove from oven and set aside to cool.

Meanwhile, heat 1 tablespoon olive oil and saute mushrooms until tender. Stir crushed garlic into mayonnaise. Slice focaccia in half lengthwise. Spread mayonnaise mixture on one or both halves.

Peel cooled peppers, core and slice. Arrange eggplant, peppers and mushrooms on focaccia. Wrap sandwich in plastic wrap; place a cutting board on top of it and weight it down with some canned foods. Allow sandwich to sit for 2 hours before slicing and serving.

My hubby wants me to find a way to put 6 stars on this. It's GOOD!!! We added fresh mozzarella too.

—ANNSU

Very good. I used two small eggplants and one green pepper (did not have red on hand). Total bake time for both was 25 - 30 minutes. I sautéed the mushrooms garlic/basil oil, and added lemon zest/juice and basil to the mayonnaise mixture. I did not wait the 2 hrs to press the sandwich down. This was great.

—JENN 77

AMOUNT PER SERVING: CALORIES: 356   TOTAL FAT: 14.8 g   CHOLESTEROL: 5 mg   SODIUM: 500 mg
TOTAL CARBS: 48.3 g   DIETARY FIBER: 5.5 g   PROTEIN: 9 g

AS SHOWN IN THE PICTURE

Mom's Big Burgers

Submitted by: GENOWA

PREP TIME: 10 MINUTES
COOK IN: 30 MINUTES
READY IN: 40 MINUTES
SERVINGS: 4

2 pounds lean ground beef
1 (1 ounce) envelope dry onion soup mix
1/2 cup water
2 cloves garlic, chopped
1 tablespoon hot pepper sauce
1 pinch chili powder
1/4 teaspoon ketchup
1/4 teaspoon prepared yellow mustard
1 pinch ground black pepper
4 cracked wheat hamburger buns
4 slices pepperjack cheese
1 avocado, peeled, pitted and sliced
1 bunch green onions

Preheat the oven's broiler.

In a large bowl, mix together the ground beef, onion soup mix, water, garlic, hot pepper sauce, chili powder, ketchup, mustard and pepper using your hands. Pat into 4 large thick patties. Place them on a broiler pan.

Broil the burgers for about 15 minutes per side, or until well done. Place buns on the broiler pan and toast briefly. Place whole green onions on the broiler pan at the same time, and just toast until limp.

Place burger patties onto the bottom halves of the buns and top each one with a slice of cheese and some avocado slices. Top with the top buns. Serve with green onions.

AMOUNT PER SERVING: CALORIES: 784   TOTAL FAT: 47.2 g   CHOLESTEROL: 188 mg   SODIUM: 1,263 mg
TOTAL CARBS: 33.4 g   DIETARY FIBER: 6.3 g   PROTEIN: 58 g

Open-Faced Broiled Roast Beef Sandwich

Submitted by: HELLSWITCH

PREP TIME: 15 MINUTES
COOK IN: 5 MINUTES
READY IN: 20 MINUTES
SERVINGS: 4

2 hoagie buns, split
2 tablespoons mayonnaise
2 teaspoons prepared coarse-ground mustard
1 pound deli sliced roast beef
2 tomatoes, thinly sliced
1/2 red onion, thinly sliced
4 slices provolone cheese
Salt and pepper to taste

Preheat oven on broiler setting.

Cut rolls in half, and toast in a bread toaster. Place on a baking sheet. Spread each half with mayonnaise and mustard. Layer with roast beef, tomato, red onion, Provolone, salt and pepper.

Broil 3 to 6 inches from heat source for 2 to 4 minutes (keep a constant eye on it) until cheese is bubbly and is beginning to brown.

I love this! It is so simple, you can use any combination of meat and cheese. It only takes minutes to make.
—MARISSA

AMOUNT PER SERVING: CALORIES: 398   TOTAL FAT: 19 g   CHOLESTEROL: 78 mg   SODIUM: 1,641 mg
TOTAL CARBS: 22.9 g   DIETARY FIBER: 1.9 g   PROTEIN: 34.4 g

AS SHOWN IN THE PICTURE

Glazed Meatloaf

Submitted by: DELIA

PREP TIME: 10 MINUTES
COOK IN: 1 HOUR 10 MINUTES
READY IN: 1 HOUR 20 MINUTES
SERVINGS: 8

1/2 cup ketchup
1/3 cup brown sugar
1 tablespoon lemon juice
1 teaspoon dry mustard
2 pounds lean ground beef
3 slices bread, shredded
1/4 cup diced onion
1 egg, beaten
1 cube beef bouillon, crumbled
3 tablespoons lemon juice

Preheat oven to 350°F (175°C).

In a small bowl, combine ketchup, brown sugar, 1 tablespoon lemon juice and dry mustard until smooth.

In a large bowl, combine ground beef, shredded bread, onion, egg, bouillon, 3 tablespoons lemon juice, and 1/3 cup of the ketchup mixture until well mixed. Form into a loaf and place in a 9x5 inch loaf pan.

Bake 1 hour. Pour off fat. Pour reserved ketchup mixture over loaf. Bake 10 minutes more.

AMOUNT PER SERVING: CALORIES: 319   TOTAL FAT: 16.8 g   CHOLESTEROL: 93 mg   SODIUM: 396 mg
TOTAL CARBS: 19 g   DIETARY FIBER: 0.5 g   PROTEIN: 22.4 g

Marie's Easy Slow Cooker Pot Roast

Submitted by: MARIE THOMAS

PREP TIME: 20 MINUTES
COOK TIME: 9 HOURS
READY IN: 9 HOURS 20 MINUTES
SERVINGS: 8

4 pounds chuck roast
Salt and pepper to taste
1 packet dry onion soup mix
1 cup water
3 carrots, chopped
1 onion, chopped
3 potatoes, peeled and cubed
1 stalk celery, chopped

Take the chuck roast and season with salt and pepper to taste. Brown on all sides in a large skillet over high heat.

Place in the slow cooker and add the soup mix, water, carrots, onion, potatoes and celery.

Cover and cook on low setting for 8 to 10 hours.

Very good. I did it in the oven at 325 degrees for 3 hours. I added some garlic in with the veggies. The aroma was wonderful and the gravy (after I thickened it with cornstarch) was very flavorful.

—4BOYSMOM

AMOUNT PER SERVING: CALORIES: 542   TOTAL FAT: 30.5 g   CHOLESTEROL: 147 mg   SODIUM: 273 mg
TOTAL CARBS: 18.5 g   DIETARY FIBER: 3 g   PROTEIN: 45.8 g

AS SHOWN IN THE PICTURE

Laurie's Stuffed Peppers

Submitted by: LASELF

PREP TIME: 15 MINUTES
COOK IN: 1 HOUR 15 MINUTES
READY IN: 1 HOUR 30 MINUTES
SERVINGS: 12

1 pound pork sausage

2 pounds ground beef

1 small onion, chopped

1 dash garlic salt

4 (14.5 ounce) cans diced tomatoes, drained

1 (10 ounce) can diced tomatoes with green chile peppers, drained

1 (14 ounce) package uncooked instant rice

6 large green bell peppers

1 cup grated Asiago cheese

Very good dish warm or cold. The sausage is a key ingredient and needs to be of good quality. The asiago cheese compliments it perfectly. I have shared this recipe with friends and family!
—FLOWERGIRL

In a skillet over medium heat, cook the sausage, beef, and onion until sausage and beef are evenly brown and onion is tender. Season with garlic salt. Drain grease. Mix in 2 cans diced tomatoes and 1 can diced tomatoes with green chiles. Reduce heat to low, and simmer 15 minutes.

Prepare the rice according to package directions. Preheat oven to 375°F (190°C).

Cut the peppers in half lengthwise, retaining stems, and remove seeds. Arrange pepper halves in a baking dish, and fill each with about 1/3 cup rice. Top with equal amounts of the meat mixture. Pour remaining meat mixture and remaining 2 cans diced tomatoes around the peppers in the dish.

Bake 45 minutes in the preheated oven, or until bubbly. Top evenly with cheese, and continue baking 10 minutes, or until cheese is melted.

Such a great treat! I used hot sausage and more seasonings (garlic, celery, worcestershire sauce, red pepper flake, Cajun spices). Also, I used regular long grain rice and mixed in with meat mixture. Let simmer for 20 min. Filled 6 peppers and still had enough filling to use in burritos for lunch!! Cheese on top is nice finish (I used pepper jack).
—TRIPLEJ28

The filling is superb - I wouldn't change a thing. I really like the actual chunks of tomato in here, as opposed to the sauce in many other recipes. Because everything is cooked in advance and I like super-soft peppers, I think I'll pre-bake just the pepper shells for half an hour, and then add the meat and cheese until melted and toasty. Oh, I also used andouille instead of regular pork sausage - perfect spice for us.
—M HOWLAND

AMOUNT PER SERVING: CALORIES: 433   TOTAL FAT: 19.8 g   CHOLESTEROL: 76 mg   SODIUM: 830 mg
TOTAL CARBS: 37.4 g   DIETARY FIBER: 3.6 g   PROTEIN: 24.3 g

AS SHOWN IN THE PICTURE

Tomato Bacon Grilled Cheese

Submitted by: MISSY189

PREP TIME: 5 MINUTES
COOK TIME: 20 MINUTES
READY IN: 25 MINUTES
SERVINGS: 4

8 slices bacon
1/4 cup butter, softened
8 slices white bread
8 slices American cheese
8 slices tomato

Place bacon in a large, deep skillet. Cook over medium high heat until evenly brown. Drain, and set aside.

Heat a large skillet over medium heat. Spread butter onto one side of each slice of bread. Lay 4 slices of bread, butter side down, in the skillet. Top with a slice of cheese, 2 slices tomato, bacon, and another slice of cheese. Cover with a slice of bread, butter side out. Fry sandwiches until golden on both sides.

I made these tonight with some soup and they were delish. I did add some mayonnaise to it and it was super. Will make again!

—CHRISSYF

AMOUNT PER SERVING: CALORIES: 566   TOTAL FAT: 40.3 g   CHOLESTEROL: 101 mg   SODIUM: 1,497 mg
TOTAL CARBS: 28.3 g   DIETARY FIBER: 1.7 g   PROTEIN: 22.9 g

BBQ Pork for Sandwiches

Submitted by: K K

PREP TIME: 15 MINUTES
COOK TIME: 4 HOURS 30 MINUTES
READY IN: 4 HOURS 45 MINUTES
SERVINGS: 12

1 (14 ounce) can beef broth
3 pounds boneless pork ribs
1 (18 ounce) bottle barbeque sauce

Pour can of beef broth into slow cooker, and add boneless pork ribs. Cook on High heat for 4 hours, or until meat shreds easily. Remove meat, and shred with two forks. It will seem that it's not working right away, but it will.

Preheat oven to 350°F (175°C). Transfer the shredded pork to a Dutch oven or iron skillet, and stir in barbeque sauce.

Bake in the preheated oven for 30 minutes, or until heated through.

This was great! One of the most easy and delicious recipes I've seen for Pulled Pork.

—ANGYWA

AMOUNT PER SERVING: CALORIES: 323   TOTAL FAT: 18.8 g   CHOLESTEROL: 83 mg   SODIUM: 496 mg
TOTAL CARBS: 5.4 g   DIETARY FIBER: 0.5 g   PROTEIN: 31 g

AS SHOWN IN THE PICTURE

Pork Chops with Fresh Tomato, Onion, Garlic, and Feta

PREP TIME: 15 MINUTES
COOK IN: 20 MINUTES
READY IN: 35 MINUTES
SERVINGS: 4

Submitted by: LOVECOOKING

2 tablespoons olive oil, divided
1 large onion, halved and thinly sliced
4 pork loin chops, one inch thick
Salt to taste
Black pepper to taste
Garlic powder to taste
1/2 pint red grape tomatoes, halved
1/2 pint yellow grape tomatoes, halved
3 cloves garlic, diced
1 tablespoon dried basil
2 1/2 teaspoons balsamic vinegar
4 ounces feta cheese, crumbled

Heat 1 tablespoon oil in a skillet over medium heat. Stir in the onion and cook until golden brown. Set aside.

Heat 1/2 tablespoon oil in the skillet. Season pork chops with salt, pepper, and garlic powder, and place in the skillet. Cook to desired doneness. Set aside and keep warm.

Heat remaining oil in the skillet. Return onions to skillet, and stir in tomatoes, garlic, and basil. Cook and stir about 3 minutes, until tomatoes are tender. Mix in balsamic vinegar, and season with salt and pepper. Top chops with the onion and tomato mixture, and sprinkle with feta cheese to serve.

AMOUNT PER SERVING: CALORIES: 470 TOTAL FAT: 20.4 g CHOLESTEROL: 98 mg SODIUM: 685 mg
TOTAL CARBS: 33.8 g DIETARY FIBER: 5.2 g PROTEIN: 39.9 g

Pleasant Pork Chops

PREP TIME: 15 MINUTES
COOK TIME: 1 HOUR 15 MINUTES
READY IN: 1 HOUR 30 MINUTES
SERVINGS: 6

Submitted by: CLYDE PATTERSON

1 onion, chopped
1 clove garlic, minced
3 tablespoons butter
6 pork chops
Salt and pepper to taste
1 bay leaf
3/4 cup chicken broth
1 cup sour cream
2 teaspoons paprika

Saute onion and garlic in hot butter. Remove from skillet. Trim excess fat from chops and sprinkle with salt and pepper. Brown chops in skillet; pour off fat.

Lower heat, add bay leaf and chicken broth. Cook covered over low heat for 1 hour. Transfer chops to a serving plate, but keep them hot.

Heat juices in skillet and reduce to half. Add the sour cream, onion-garlic mixture and paprika, blending thoroughly. Heat through, but don't boil. Pour over pork chops and serve.

I didn't have a bay leaf so I used 1 teaspoon of italian seasoning instead. It turned out great. We served it with noodles and glazed carrots.

—GOOSEBUMPS101

AMOUNT PER SERVING: CALORIES: 263 TOTAL FAT: 20.5 g CHOLESTEROL: 69 mg SODIUM: 226 mg
TOTAL CARBS: 4.2 g DIETARY FIBER: 0.4 g PROTEIN: 15.7 g

Honeyed Pork Chops

Submitted by: **BOOKCHICKADEE**

PREP TIME: 15 MINUTES
COOK IN: 1 HOUR 10 MINUTES
READY IN: 1 HOUR 25 MINUTES
SERVINGS: 6

2 tablespoons vegetable oil
6 boneless pork chops
3 tablespoons honey
1/2 cup water
1/4 cup soy sauce
1 small onion, chopped
1/4 teaspoon ground ginger
1/8 teaspoon ground black pepper

Preheat oven to 325°F (165°C).

Heat the oil in a skillet over medium heat, and brown the pork chops about 5 minutes on each side. Transfer to a baking dish.

In a bowl, mix the honey, water, soy sauce, onion, ginger, and pepper. Pour over the pork chops in the baking dish.

Bake pork chops 1 hour in the preheated oven, to an internal temperature of 160°F (70°C).

I made this last night and it was fantastic. I added a little garlic powder and marinated over night. I also used low sodium soy sauce (trying to lower my sodium intake). I can't wait to make them again!

—RANDI

AMOUNT PER SERVING: CALORIES: 183   TOTAL FAT: 8.4 g   CHOLESTEROL: 40 mg   SODIUM: 643 mg
TOTAL CARBS: 10.6 g   DIETARY FIBER: 0.3 g   PROTEIN: 16.1 g

Roast Pork with Maple and Mustard Glaze

Submitted by: **CHRISTINE L.**

PREP TIME: 10 MINUTES
COOK IN: 1 HOUR
READY IN: 1 HOUR 10 MINUTES
SERVINGS: 8

2 1/2 pounds boneless pork loin roast
1 cup real maple syrup
4 tablespoons prepared Dijon-style mustard
2 1/2 tablespoons cider vinegar
2 1/2 tablespoons soy sauce
Salt to taste
Ground black pepper to taste

Stir together the maple syrup, mustard, vinegar, soy sauce, salt, and pepper in a small bowl. Set glaze aside.

Place pork roast in a shallow roasting pan. Spread glaze evenly over pork roast.

Roast pork in a 350°F (175°) oven. Cook until internal temperature measured with a meat thermometer reaches 160°, about 45 minutes to 1 1/2 hours. Remove from oven, and let rest about 10 minutes before slicing to serve.

AMOUNT PER SERVING: CALORIES: 292   TOTAL FAT: 8.9 g   CHOLESTEROL: 68 mg   SODIUM: 527 mg
TOTAL CARBS: 28 g   DIETARY FIBER: 0.1 g   PROTEIN: 24.8 g

Honey Glazed Ham

Submitted by: **COLLEEN**

PREP TIME: 20 MINUTES
COOK IN: 1 HOUR 15 MINUTES
READY IN: 1 HOUR 35 MINUTES
SERVINGS: 12

5 pounds ready-to-eat ham
1/4 cup whole cloves
1/4 cup dark corn syrup
2 cups honey
2/3 cup butter

Preheat oven to 325°F (165°C).

Score ham, and stud with the whole cloves. Place ham in foil lined pan.

In the top half of a double boiler, heat the corn syrup, honey and butter. Keep glaze warm while baking ham.

Brush glaze over ham, and bake for 1 hour and 15 minutes in the preheated oven. Baste ham every 10 to 15 minutes with the honey glaze. During the last 4 to 5 minutes of baking, turn on broiler to caramelize the glaze. Remove from oven, and let sit a few minutes before serving.

AMOUNT PER SERVING: CALORIES: 455   TOTAL FAT: 13.6 g   CHOLESTEROL: 115 mg   SODIUM: 2,465 mg
TOTAL CARBS: 55.5 g   DIETARY FIBER: 0.7 g   PROTEIN: 32.4 g

Honey Ribs

Submitted by: **HMICHAUD**

PREP TIME: 10 MINUTES
COOK TIME: 5 HOURS
READY IN: 5 HOURS 10 MINUTES
SERVINGS: 6

1 (10.5 ounce) can beef broth
3 tablespoons honey mustard
1/4 cup honey
1/2 cup water
1/4 cup honey barbeque sauce
1/4 cup soy sauce
1/4 cup maple syrup
3 pounds baby back pork ribs

In the crock of a slow cooker, mix together the beef broth, honey mustard, honey, water, barbeque sauce, soy sauce, and maple syrup. Slice ribs apart, leaving an even amount of meat on each side of the bone. Place them into the slow cooker so that they are covered by the sauce. If there is not enough sauce, you may add a little water or beef broth to compensate.

Cover, and cook on High for 5 hours, or until the meat falls easily from the bones.

Delicious! I made extra sauce, then coated the ribs and broiled them in the oven for an extra 20 minutes...Mmmmm!

—**TASHA D**

AMOUNT PER SERVING: CALORIES: 759   TOTAL FAT: 54.2 g   CHOLESTEROL: 184 mg   SODIUM: 1,122 mg
TOTAL CARBS: 29.1 g   DIETARY FIBER: 0.3 g   PROTEIN: 38 g

AS SHOWN IN THE PICTURE

Sweet and Sour Pork

Submitted by: **PAM**

PREP TIME: 30 MINUTES
COOK IN: 30 MINUTES
READY IN: 2 HOURS
SERVINGS: 4

1 pound pork butt, cut into one inch cubes
1 teaspoon salt
1/4 teaspoon white sugar
1 teaspoon soy sauce
1 egg white
2 green onions, chopped
1 quart vegetable oil for frying
1/2 cup cornstarch
1 tablespoon vegetable oil
3 stalks celery, cut into half inch pieces
1 medium green bell pepper, cut into one inch pieces
1 medium onion, cut into wedges
White sugar to taste
Salt to taste
1 cup water
1/4 teaspoon salt
3/4 cup white sugar
1/3 cup apple cider vinegar
1/4 cup ketchup
1/2 teaspoon soy sauce
1 (8 ounce) can pineapple chunks, undrained
2 tablespoons cornstarch
1/4 cup water

Place cubed pork in a medium bowl, and season with 1 teaspoon salt, 1/4 teaspoon sugar, and 1 teaspoon soy sauce. Mix in the egg white and green onions. Cover, and place in the refrigerator at least 1 hour.

Heat 1 quart oil to 365°F (185°C) in a large, heavy saucepan or deep fryer.

Coat the pork with 1/2 cup cornstarch, and fry in the heated oil about 10 minutes, until evenly browned. Drain on paper towels.

Heat 1 tablespoon oil in a wok over medium heat. Stir in the celery, green bell pepper, and onion, and cook until tender. Season with salt and sugar. Remove from heat, and set aside.

In a large saucepan, mix 1 cup water, 1/4 teaspoon salt, 3/4 cup sugar, apple cider vinegar, ketchup, and 1/2 teaspoon soy sauce. Bring to a boil, and stir in the cooked pork, celery mixture, and the pineapple chunks with juice. Return to boil, and mix in 2 tablespoons cornstarch and 1/4 cup water to thicken. Cook until well blended.

Fantastic and "better than take-out" (so says my NYC take-out-raised husband). The only change in my version was to use a yellow bell pepper as my daughters don't care for green, and to add more pineapple. But overall, this is a PERFECT recipe. Don't wimp out, deep fry the pork; everyone will be thrilled that you did!
—FLANAGANSHAN

I have shied away from attempting Asian food at home because it never tastes like the restaurant quality, but this was different. This was so delicious and hard to believe it came from my kitchen and wasn't from a Chinese restaurant. The best sweet and sour pork I have ever eaten. It was so simple to prepare. My whole family loved this. Everyone had seconds. I used pork tenderloin instead. I served it with steamed Jasmine rice and stir fried green bean/wax bean/baby carrot blend. Yum!
—ILOVE2CK

AMOUNT PER SERVING: CALORIES: 665 TOTAL FAT: 35 g CHOLESTEROL: 43 mg SODIUM: 1,196 mg
TOTAL CARBS: 76.6 g DIETARY FIBER: 2.6 g PROTEIN: 13.9 g

SIDE DISHES 147

AS SHOWN IN THE PICTURE

Broccoli with Garlic Butter and Cashews

Submitted by: **SALSIEPIE**

PREP TIME: 10 MINUTES
COOK IN: 10 MINUTES
READY IN: 20 MINUTES
SERVINGS: 6

1 1/2 pounds fresh broccoli, cut into bite size pieces
1/3 cup butter
1 tablespoon brown sugar
3 tablespoons soy sauce
2 teaspoons white vinegar
1/4 teaspoon ground black pepper
2 cloves garlic, minced
1/3 cup chopped salted cashews

Place the broccoli into a large pot with about 1 inch of water in the bottom. Bring to a boil, and cook for 7 minutes, or until tender but still crisp. Drain, and arrange broccoli on a serving platter.

While the broccoli is cooking, melt the butter in a small skillet over medium heat. Mix in the brown sugar, soy sauce, vinegar, pepper and garlic. Bring to a boil, then remove from the heat. Mix in the cashews, and pour the sauce over the broccoli. Serve immediately.

AMOUNT PER SERVING: CALORIES: 180   TOTAL FAT: 14.2 g   CHOLESTEROL: 28 mg   SODIUM: 642 mg
TOTAL CARBS: 11.7 g   DIETARY FIBER: 3.7 g   PROTEIN: 5.1 g

Green Beans with Cherry Tomatoes

Submitted by: **STARNETSA**

PREP TIME: 5 MINUTES
COOK TIME: 15 MINUTES
READY IN: 20 MINUTES
SERVINGS: 6

1 1/2 pounds green beans, trimmed and cut into two inch pieces
1 1/2 cups water
1/4 cup butter
1 tablespoon sugar
3/4 teaspoon garlic salt
1/4 teaspoon pepper
1 1/2 teaspoons chopped fresh basil
2 cups cherry tomato halves

Place beans and water in a large saucepan. Cover, and bring to a boil. Set heat to low, and simmer until tender, about 10 minutes. Drain off water, and set aside.

Melt butter in a skillet over medium heat. Stir in sugar, garlic salt, pepper and basil. Add tomatoes, and cook stirring gently just until soft. Pour the tomato mixture over the green beans, and toss gently to blend.

Wow. I could seriously eat these beans every night. Both the beans and the tomatoes came from our garden and as the tomatoes were naturally sweet I just used half a teaspoon of sugar. Great side dish!

—**KEZ**

AMOUNT PER SERVING: CALORIES: 122   TOTAL FAT: 8 g   CHOLESTEROL: 21 mg   SODIUM: 318 mg   TOTAL CARBS: 12.6 g
DIETARY FIBER: 4.4 g   PROTEIN: 2.6 g

AS SHOWN IN THE PICTURE

Stuffed Acorn Squash Supreme

Submitted by: **PATRICE GERARD**

PREP TIME: 10 MINUTES
COOK IN: 20 MINUTES
READY IN: 30 MINUTES
SERVINGS: 4

1 (6 ounce) package broccoli and cheese flavored rice mix

1 pound turkey breakfast sausage

1 medium acorn squash, halved and seeded

1/2 cup chopped apple

2 teaspoons crushed coriander seed

1/2 cup shredded Monterey Jack cheese

Prepare rice mix according to package directions; cover, and set aside.

Place squash halves cut side down onto a plate. Cook the squash in a microwave oven for 5 minutes on High, until tender but firm. In a medium skillet over medium heat, cook sausage until evenly browned; drain, and set aside.

In a large bowl, mix together the prepared rice, sausage, apple, and coriander. Stuff each squash half with the mixture. Cover stuffed squash halves with plastic wrap, and heat in the microwave until squash is cooked through and soft, about 5 minutes. Remove plastic, and top stuffed squash with cheese. Continue to cook until cheese is melted, about 1 minute.

AMOUNT PER SERVING: CALORIES: 537 TOTAL FAT: 27.3 g CHOLESTEROL: 108 mg SODIUM: 1,424 mg TOTAL CARBS: 42.8 g DIETARY FIBER: 4.9 g PROTEIN: 34.3 g

---

MeMa Rie's Zippy Zucchini

Submitted by: **NADINE529**

PREP TIME: 10 MINUTES
COOK TIME: 15 MINUTES
READY IN: 25 MINUTES
SERVINGS: 4

1/4 cup extra-virgin olive oil, divided

1 sweet onion, sliced

2 cloves garlic, crushed

5 small zucchini, sliced

Cayenne pepper to taste

2 teaspoons apple cider vinegar

Heat 2 tablespoons olive oil in a skillet over medium heat, and saute onion and garlic until tender and lightly browned. Mix in the zucchini. Continue to cook and stir until zucchini is tender. Season with cayenne pepper. Sprinkle with vinegar. Reduce heat to low, cover skillet, and continue cooking 2 to 3 minutes. Remove cover, and taste. If not at desired 'vinegar' flavor, add another splash, cover, and simmer for another minute.

This recipe was awesome! Both my husband and I really enjoyed it. I did end up adding another teaspoon of the vinegar and seasoning with salt at the end. YUM!!!!!

—**JESSEH**

AMOUNT PER SERVING: CALORIES: 160 TOTAL FAT: 14.3 g CHOLESTEROL: 0 mg SODIUM: 6 mg TOTAL CARBS: 7.3 g DIETARY FIBER: 2.3 g PROTEIN: 2.1 g

Pan-Fried Asparagus

Submitted by: **KIM**

PREP TIME: 5 MINUTES
COOK IN: 15 MINUTES
READY IN: 25 MINUTES
SERVINGS: 4

1/4 cup butter
2 tablespoons olive oil
1 teaspoon coarse salt
1/4 teaspoon ground black pepper
3 cloves garlic, minced
1/2 pound fresh asparagus spears, trimmed

Melt butter in a skillet over medium-high heat. Stir in the olive oil, salt, and pepper. Cook garlic in butter for a minute, but do not brown. Add asparagus, and cook for 10 minutes, turning asparagus to ensure even cooking.

This is delicious. It's the only way I ever end up fixing asparagus because it's so good I never want to try any other recipes.

—WAHNSDLR

AMOUNT PER SERVING: CALORIES: 178 TOTAL FAT: 18.4 g CHOLESTEROL: 31 mg SODIUM: 694 mg
TOTAL CARBS: 3.4 g DIETARY FIBER: 1.3 g PROTEIN: 1.6 g

Shredded Brussels Sprouts

Submitted by: **MOMZRIGHT**

PREP TIME: 20 MINUTES
COOK TIME: 25 MINUTES
READY IN: 45 MINUTES
SERVINGS: 8

1/2 pound sliced bacon
1/4 cup butter
2/3 cup pine nuts
2 pounds Brussels sprouts, cored and shredded
3 green onions, minced
1/2 teaspoon seasoning salt
Pepper to taste

Place bacon in a large, deep skillet. Cook over medium high heat until crisp. Drain, reserving 2 tablespoons grease, crumble and set aside.

In the same skillet, melt butter in with reserved bacon grease over medium heat. Add pine nuts and cook, stirring until browned. Add Brussels sprouts and green onions to the pan, and season with seasoning salt and pepper. Cook over medium heat until sprouts are wilted and tender, 10 to 15 minutes. Stir in crumbled bacon just before serving.

Loved this unique and delicious recipe. Shred these in your food processor to save time, as I did them by hand and it took some time, Deelish!

—JAY

AMOUNT PER SERVING: CALORIES: 220 TOTAL FAT: 16.5 g CHOLESTEROL: 23 mg SODIUM: 295 mg
TOTAL CARBS: 12.3 g DIETARY FIBER: 5 g PROTEIN: 9.6 g

Baked Asparagus with Balsamic Butter Sauce

Submitted by: **CAE**

PREP TIME: 10 MINUTES
COOK IN: 12 MINUTES
READY IN: 25 MINUTES
SERVINGS: 4

1 bunch fresh asparagus, trimmed
Cooking spray
Salt and pepper to taste
2 tablespoons butter
1 tablespoon soy sauce
1 teaspoon balsamic vinegar

Preheat oven to 400°F (200°C).

Arrange the asparagus on a baking sheet. Coat with cooking spray, and season with salt and pepper.

Bake asparagus 12 minutes in the preheated oven, or until tender.

Melt the butter in a saucepan over medium heat. Remove from heat, and stir in soy sauce and balsamic vinegar. Pour over the baked asparagus to serve.

AMOUNT PER SERVING: CALORIES: 80 TOTAL FAT: 6 g CHOLESTEROL: 16 mg SODIUM: 387 mg TOTAL CARBS: 5.7 g DIETARY FIBER: 2.4 g PROTEIN: 2.9 g

Kickin' Collard Greens

Submitted by: **KEN ADAMS**

PREP TIME: 10 MINUTES
COOK TIME: 1 HOUR
READY IN: 1 HOUR 10 MINUTES
SERVINGS: 6

1 tablespoon olive oil
3 slices bacon
1 large onion, chopped
2 cloves garlic, minced
1 teaspoon salt
1 teaspoon pepper
3 cups chicken broth
1 pinch red pepper flakes
1 pound fresh collard greens, cut into two-inch pieces

Heat oil in a large pot over medium-high heat. Add bacon, and cook until crisp. Remove bacon from pan, crumble and return to the pan. Add onion, and cook until tender, about 5 minutes. Add garlic, and cook until just fragrant. Add collard greens, and fry until they start to wilt.

Pour in chicken broth, and season with salt, pepper, and red pepper flakes. Reduce heat to low, cover, and simmer for 45 minutes, or until greens are tender.

As a Southerner, I have been looking for a good "greens" recipe. This is easy and good. I am going to try it with turnip greens next..

—KNEELY56

AMOUNT PER SERVING: CALORIES: 148 TOTAL FAT: 11.7 g CHOLESTEROL: 9 mg SODIUM: 1,006 mg TOTAL CARBS: 7.6 g DIETARY FIBER: 3.3 g PROTEIN: 4.5 g

AS SHOWN IN THE PICTURE

Spinach with a Twist

Submitted by: EJ119

PREP TIME: 15 MINUTES
COOK IN: 15 MINUTES
READY IN: 30 MINUTES
SERVINGS: 4

1 tablespoon olive oil
1 small yellow onion, sliced
1 (14.5 ounce) can diced tomatoes, drained
1 (10 ounce) package frozen chopped spinach, thawed and drained
Salt and pepper to taste
3 ounces Roquefort cheese

Heat the olive oil in a skillet over medium high heat, and saute the onion until tender. Stir in the tomatoes and spinach, and continue cooking until the spinach is wilted. Season with salt and pepper. Stir in the Roquefort cheese, and allow to melt slightly before serving.

This was really, really good. I sautéed garlic in olive oil, used fresh cooked spinach, removing the water before adding it to the garlic and tomatoes, and bleu cheese. Absolutely delicious!!

—DENA IN TEXAS

AMOUNT PER SERVING: CALORIES: 153   TOTAL FAT: 10.1 g   CHOLESTEROL: 19 mg   SODIUM: 694 mg

TOTAL CARBS: 8.1 g   DIETARY FIBER: 3.3 g   PROTEIN: 7.7 g

Spinach Bars

Submitted by: KIM S

PREP TIME: 15 MINUTES
COOK TIME: 30 MINUTES
READY IN: 45 MINUTES
SERVINGS: 12

3 tablespoons butter
3 eggs
1 cup milk
1 cup all-purpose flour
1 teaspoon salt
1/2 teaspoon ground black pepper
1 teaspoon baking powder
1 1/2 teaspoons minced garlic
1/2 cup chopped fresh mushrooms
1 small onion, chopped
4 cups shredded Cheddar cheese
1 (10 ounce) package frozen chopped spinach, thawed and drained

Preheat the oven to 350°F (175°C). Melt butter in a 9x13 inch baking dish while the oven preheats.

In a large bowl, whisk together the eggs, milk, flour, salt, pepper, baking powder and garlic until well blended. Add the mushrooms, spinach and cheese, and stir to blend evenly. Tip the baking dish to coat with melted butter, then pour the spinach mixture into the pan.

Bake for 30 minutes in the preheated oven, until firm and golden. Cut into bars, and serve warm.

Great recipe thanks! I've tried it with all sorts of different cheeses to vary the taste and everyone I've made this for raves and it's so simple which I love!

—KATETATE

AMOUNT PER SERVING: CALORIES: 254   TOTAL FAT: 17.2 g   CHOLESTEROL: 102 mg   SODIUM: 522 mg

TOTAL CARBS: 11.4 g   DIETARY FIBER: 1.2 g   PROTEIN: 13.6 g

Spinach and Rice (Spanakorizo)

Submitted by: **KATHY**

PREP TIME: 5 MINUTES
COOK IN: 45 MINUTES
READY IN: 50 MINUTES
SERVINGS: 4

1/3 cup olive oil
2 onions, chopped
2 pounds fresh spinach, rinsed and stemmed
1 (8 ounce) can tomato sauce
2 cups water
1 teaspoon dried dill weed
1 teaspoon dried parsley
Salt and pepper to taste
1/2 cup uncooked white rice

Heat olive oil in a large skillet over medium-high heat. Saute onions in the oil until soft and translucent. Add spinach, and cook stirring for a few minutes, then pour in the tomato sauce and water. Bring to a boil, and season with parsley, dill, salt and pepper. Stir in rice, reduce heat to low, and simmer uncovered for 20 to 25 minutes, or until rice is tender. Add more water if necessary.

My husband and I loved this recipe! I used a can of vegetable broth for some of the water for extra flavor. I also sprinkled some chopped scallions on the top, along with the feta and fresh lemon juice. Delicious!

—BETH

AMOUNT PER SERVING: CALORIES: 338   TOTAL FAT: 19.2 g   CHOLESTEROL: 0 mg   SODIUM: 598 mg
TOTAL CARBS: 36.5 g   DIETARY FIBER: 8.2 g   PROTEIN: 9.8 g

Apple Cole Slaw

Submitted by: **AUNT MAMIE**

PREP TIME: 15 MINUTES
READY IN: 15 MINUTES
SERVINGS: 6

3 cups chopped cabbage
1 unpeeled red apple, cored and chopped
1 unpeeled Granny Smith apple, cored and chopped
1 carrot, grated
1/2 cup finely chopped red bell pepper
2 green onions, finely chopped
1/3 cup mayonnaise
1/3 cup brown sugar
1 tablespoon lemon juice, or to taste

In a large bowl, combine cabbage, red apple, green apple, carrot, red bell pepper, and green onions. In a small bowl, mix together mayonnaise, brown sugar, and lemon juice. Pour dressing over salad.

Great cole slaw recipe! Different from traditional cole slaw. At first I wasn't sure about the dressing, but it was delicious! No leftovers in our house. I will definitely make this again and maybe add some dried cranberries just to be different. Thank you!

—MUSTANGSUSAN

AMOUNT PER SERVING: CALORIES: 138   TOTAL FAT: 4.6 g   CHOLESTEROL: 3 mg   SODIUM: 105 mg   TOTAL CARBS: 25.2 g
DIETARY FIBER: 2.5 g   PROTEIN: 0.9 g

Fried Cabbage

Submitted by: JEN

PREP TIME: 20 MINUTES
COOK IN: 25 MINUTES
READY IN: 45 MINUTES
SERVINGS: 6

3 slices bacon, chopped
1/4 cup chopped onion
6 cups cabbage, cut into thin wedges
2 tablespoons water
1 pinch white sugar
Salt and pepper to taste
1 tablespoon cider vinegar

Place bacon in a large, deep skillet. Cook over medium-high heat until evenly brown. Remove bacon, and set aside.

Cook onion in the hot bacon grease until tender. Add cabbage, and stir in water, sugar, salt, and pepper. Cook until cabbage wilts, about 15 minutes. Stir in bacon. Splash with vinegar before serving.

Fantastic dish! Mild flavor and easy to make. We like boiled ham and cabbage, but don't often have the time to fix it. I made this cabbage and heated up a fully cooked ham, served with a side of parsley potatoes, and we had ham and cabbage in a fraction of the time. This one's definitely a keeper.

—LAURAK308

AMOUNT PER SERVING: CALORIES: 48   TOTAL FAT: 2.6 g   CHOLESTEROL: 4 mg   SODIUM: 81 mg   TOTAL CARBS: 4.5 g   DIETARY FIBER: 2 g   PROTEIN:2.3 g

Okra and Tomatoes

Submitted by: GWYNN

PREP TIME: 10 MINUTES
COOK TIME: 20 MINUTES
READY IN: 30 MINUTES
SERVINGS: 7

2 slices bacon
1 pound frozen okra, thawed and sliced
1 small onion, chopped
1/2 green bell pepper, chopped
2 celery, chopped
1 (14.5 ounce) can stewed tomatoes
Salt and pepper to taste

Place bacon in a large, deep skillet. Cook over medium high heat until evenly brown. Drain, crumble and set aside.

Remove bacon from pan and saute okra, onion, pepper and celery until tender. Add tomatoes, salt and pepper and cook until well blended.

Garnish with crumbled bacon, if desired.

Super!!! A+++ If I could give it more stars, I would. I didn't realize okra could taste this good w/out being deep fried. I added green chilies because we like food a little more spicy. AWESOME!!

—KCOMFORT

AMOUNT PER SERVING: CALORIES: 90   TOTAL FAT: 5 g   CHOLESTEROL: 5 mg   SODIUM: 206 mg   TOTAL CARBS: 10.2 g   DIETARY FIBER: 3.2 g   PROTEIN: 3.1 g

AS SHOWN IN THE PICTURE

Mediterranean Summer Tomatoes

Submitted by: **SCARLETT**

PREP TIME: 10 MINUTES
READY IN: 15 MINUTES
SERVINGS: 6

5 fresh tomatoes
5 shallots, coarsely chopped
1/2 cup olive oil
1/4 cup balsamic vinegar
1 loaf French bread, for dipping (optional)

Core and slice the tomatoes, and arrange them in a serving dish. Sprinkle the shallots over the tomatoes. Whisk the olive oil and balsamic vinegar together with a fork, then pour over the tomatoes. Let stand for 5 minutes before serving, or refrigerate, covered, for up to 3 days. Eat with French bread, and dip the bread in the marinade when finished with the tomatoes.

Perfect side dish instead of a salad. I also prepared warm baguettes that we enjoyed dipping in the dressing. Yum! I also added fresh garden cucumber slices around the serving tray and it just added to the presentation and tastiness.

—LARABABE

AMOUNT PER SERVING: CALORIES: 424 TOTAL FAT: 20.7 g CHOLESTEROL: 0 mg SODIUM: 478 mg
TOTAL CARBS: 52.6 g DIETARY FIBER: 3.7 g PROTEIN: 8.6 g

Fried Green Tomatoes

Submitted by: **BETH ZUKE**

PREP TIME: 10 MINUTES
COOK TIME: 10 MINUTES
READY IN: 20 MINUTES
SERVINGS: 6

1 cup all-purpose flour
1 teaspoon salt
1 teaspoon pepper
5 green tomatoes, sliced half inch thick
1 cup crushed saltine crackers
2 eggs, beaten
1/2 cup butter

In a small bowl, stir together the flour, salt and pepper. Place the crushed saltine crackers in another bowl, and the beaten eggs in a third bowl.

Melt the butter in a large skillet over medium heat. Dip each tomato slice in the egg to coat, then in the flour mixture. Dip the floured tomato slice back into the egg, and then into the cracker crumbs. Place the coated tomato slices in the hot skillet, and fry until golden brown on each side, about 3 to 5 minutes per side. Add more butter to the pan, if necessary. Serve hot!

We loved these! I used Ritz crackers, the taste was awesome. I have tried several recipes over the years, and they were either soggy, greasy, no flavor, or the outside coating would fall off. These held up perfectly. Will make again!

—SHAWN MARIE

AMOUNT PER SERVING: CALORIES: 312 TOTAL FAT: 18.8 g CHOLESTEROL: 112 mg SODIUM: 731 mg
TOTAL CARBS: 29.9 g DIETARY FIBER: 2.1 g PROTEIN: 6.7 g

Festive Onions

Submitted by: **CHRISTINE JOHNSON**

PREP TIME: 10 MINUTES
COOK IN: 30 MINUTES
READY IN: 40 MINUTES
SERVINGS: 8

4 cups sliced onion
5 tablespoons butter
1 cup heavy whipping cream
Salt to taste
Ground black pepper to taste
2/3 cup Parmesan cheese
2 eggs

Saute onions in butter or margarine until transparent. Place in 2-quart baking dish.

In a small bowl, beat eggs well. Stir in cream, and season with salt and pepper. Pour mixture over onions, and sprinkle cheese.

Bake, uncovered, at 425°F (220°C) for 15 to 20 minutes.

I thought this was a wonderful dish. It needs to be served hot - right out of the oven in order to fully appreciate the creamy sauce.
—DEBBIE MCCARTHY

AMOUNT PER SERVING: CALORIES: 245   TOTAL FAT: 22.1 g   CHOLESTEROL: 120 mg   SODIUM: 257 mg
TOTAL CARBS: 6.3 g   DIETARY FIBER: 1 g   PROTEIN: 6.4 g

Baked Fennel with Parmesan

Submitted by: **RUPERTLSSMITH**

PREP TIME: 10 MINUTES
COOK TIME: 35 MINUTES
READY IN: 45 MINUTES
SERVINGS: 4

2 fennel bulbs
1 tablespoon butter
3/4 cup half-and-half cream
3/4 cup creme fraiche
1/4 cup grated Parmesan cheese

Preheat the oven to 400 degrees. Cut the base off of the fennel bulbs, and cut a cone shape into the base to remove the core. You can see the core because it is whiter than the surrounding green. This is optional, but helps the fennel cook faster. Slice the fennel vertically (upright) into 1/4 inch thick slices.

Melt the butter in a large skillet over medium heat. Add the fennel, and fry for about 5 minutes. Stir in the half-and-half and creme fraiche until well blended. Transfer to a shallow baking dish. Sprinkle Parmesan cheese over the top.

Bake for 30 minutes in the preheated oven, or until the top is golden brown and the fennel is tender enough to pierce with a fork.

AMOUNT PER SERVING: CALORIES: 302   TOTAL FAT: 27 g   CHOLESTEROL: 91 mg   SODIUM: 240 mg
TOTAL CARBS: 12.2 g   DIETARY FIBER: 3.6 g   PROTEIN: 6.9 g

Roasted Vegetables

Submitted by: **SAUNDRA**

PREP TIME: 15 MINUTES
COOK TIME: 40 MINUTES
READY IN: 55 MINUTES
SERVINGS: 12

1 small butternut squash, cubed
2 red bell peppers, seeded and diced
1 sweet potato, peeled and cubed
3 Yukon Gold potatoes, cubed
1 red onion, quartered
1 tablespoon chopped fresh thyme
2 tablespoons chopped fresh rosemary
1/4 cup olive oil
2 tablespoons balsamic vinegar
Salt and freshly ground black pepper

Preheat oven to 475°F (245°C).

In a large bowl, combine the squash, red bell peppers, sweet potato, and Yukon Gold potatoes. Separate the red onion quarters into pieces, and add them to the mixture.

In a small bowl, stir together thyme, rosemary, olive oil, vinegar, salt, and pepper. Toss with vegetables until they are coated. Spread evenly on a large roasting pan.

Roast for 35 to 40 minutes in the preheated oven, stirring every 10 minutes, or until vegetables are cooked through and browned.

AMOUNT PER SERVING: CALORIES: 124 TOTAL FAT: 4.7 g CHOLESTEROL: 0 mg SODIUM: 40 mg TOTAL CARBS: 20.4 g DIETARY FIBER: 4.3 g PROTEIN: 2 g

Roasted Beets and Sauteed Beet Greens

Submitted by: **BN61079**

PREP TIME: 10 MINUTES
COOK TIME: 1 HOUR
READY IN: 1 HOUR 10 MINUTES
SERVINGS: 4

1 bunch beets with greens
1/4 cup olive oil, divided
2 cloves garlic, minced
2 tablespoons chopped onion (optional)
Salt and pepper to taste
1 tablespoon red wine vinegar (optional)

Preheat the oven to 350°F (175°C). Wash the beets thoroughly, leaving the skins on, and remove the greens. Rinse greens, removing any large stems, and set aside. Place the beets in a small baking dish or roasting pan, and toss with 2 tablespoons of olive oil. If you wish to peel the beets, it is easier to do so once they have been roasted.

Cover, and bake for 45 to 60 minutes, or until a knife can slide easily through the largest beet.

When the roasted beets are almost done, heat the remaining 2 tablespoons olive oil in a skillet over medium low heat. Add the garlic and onion, and cook for a minute. Tear the beet greens into 2 to 3 inch pieces, and add them to the skillet. Cook and stir until greens are wilted and tender. Season with salt and pepper.

AMOUNT PER SERVING: CALORIES: 199 TOTAL FAT: 13.8 g CHOLESTEROL: 0 mg SODIUM: 402 mg TOTAL CARBS: 17.4 g DIETARY FIBER: 8.9 g PROTEIN: 4.7 g

AS SHOWN IN THE PICTURE

Herbed Mushrooms with White Wine

Submitted by: **LAURA**

PREP TIME: 10 MINUTES
COOK IN: 15 MINUTES
READY IN: 25 MINUTES
SERVINGS: 6

1 tablespoon olive oil
1 1/2 pounds fresh mushrooms
1 teaspoon Italian seasoning
1/4 cup dry white wine
2 cloves garlic, minced
Salt and pepper to taste
2 tablespoons chopped fresh chives

Heat the oil in a skillet over medium heat. Place mushrooms in the skillet, season with Italian seasoning, and cook 10 minutes, stirring frequently.

Mix the wine and garlic into the skillet, and continue cooking until most of the wine has evaporated. Season with salt and pepper, and sprinkle with chives. Continue cooking 1 minute.

I made this with Portabella mushrooms. Was quick to make and tasty. I think this would be great with fresh basil, in the summer, when it is available from the garden!

—GRACIE

AMOUNT PER SERVING: CALORIES: 55 TOTAL FAT: 2.7 g CHOLESTEROL: 0 mg SODIUM: 69 mg TOTAL CARBS: 5.4 g
DIETARY FIBER: 1.4 g PROTEIN: 2.3 g

Zucchini Patties

Submitted by: **SHERLIE A. MAGARET**

PREP TIME: 10 MINUTES
COOK IN: 20 MINUTES
READY IN: 30 MINUTES
SERVINGS: 4

2 cups grated zucchini
2 eggs, beaten
1/4 cup chopped onion
1/2 cup all-purpose flour
1/2 cup grated Parmesan cheese
1/2 cup shredded mozzarella cheese
Salt to taste
2 tablespoons vegetable oil

In a medium bowl, combine the zucchini, eggs, onion, flour, Parmesan cheese, mozzarella cheese, and salt. Stir well enough to distribute ingredients evenly.

Heat a small amount of oil in a skillet over medium-high heat. Drop zucchini mixture by heaping tablespoonfuls, and cook for a few minutes on each side until golden.

This was excellent! However, I did make one alteration: I used bleu cheese instead of mozzarella. Absolutely scrumptious!

—KARLA

AMOUNT PER SERVING: CALORIES: 294 TOTAL FAT: 17.8 g CHOLESTEROL: 132 mg SODIUM: 397 mg
TOTAL CARBS:16 g DIETARY FIBER: 1.3 g PROTEIN: 17.5 g

AS SHOWN IN THE PICTURE

Spectacular Marsala Glazed Carrots with Hazelnuts

PREP TIME: 15 MINUTES
COOK IN: 20 MINUTES
READY IN: 35 MINUTES
SERVINGS: 6

Submitted by: **BARBARA M.**

1/2 cup coarsely chopped hazelnuts, toasted

1 pound baby carrots, halved

1 cup water

1/2 teaspoon salt

3 tablespoons unsalted butter

2 shallots, minced

1/2 cup dry Marsala wine

1/2 cup sugar

Preheat oven to 300°F (150°C).

Spread chopped hazelnuts in a single layer on a baking sheet. Bake in the preheated oven for 5 to 10 minutes, stirring once or twice, and watching very carefully as they will burn very easily. Remove from the oven when browned and fragrant.

Cut baby carrots in half cross-wise. In a saucepan over medium heat, bring water, carrots, salt, and 1 tablespoon of butter. Bring to a boil, and reduce heat to low. Cover, and simmer very lightly for 10 to 15 minutes, or until tender but firm. Drain and set aside.

Return pan to the stove over medium heat, and melt the remaining 2 tablespoons of butter. Cook shallots in the melted butter, stirring occasionally, until translucent. Add Marsala and sugar, and stir continually until sugar is completely dissolved. Continue simmering until sauce has thickened slightly.

Once thickened, toss carrots and hazelnuts with the sauce until well coated. Garnish with parsley, if desired. Serve immediately.

These were dreamy, plus the presentation is very nice and the tastes a unique combo. Nice for a fancy dinner at home, but a great compliment to a regular dinner too!
—**AMBERB**

This was delish! I didn't have hazelnuts but will get them for next time because I love them, but pecans worked well. I also didn't have shallots so I used Vidalia onion with a touch of garlic minced together and that worked out fine. Also, I didn't have unsalted, so I used salted butter. Total Yumfort Food!
—**RONAMAY**

AMOUNT PER SERVING: CALORIES: 258   TOTAL FAT: 13 g   CHOLESTEROL: 16 mg   SODIUM: 226 mg

TOTAL CARBS: 29.9 g   DIETARY FIBER: 2.6 g   PROTEIN: 2.8 g

Maple Dill Carrots

Submitted by: **LAURA SPIELMAN**

PREP TIME: 10 MINUTES
COOK IN: 10 MINUTES
READY IN: 20 MINUTES
SERVINGS: 4

3 cups peeled and sliced carrots
2 tablespoons butter
2 tablespoons brown sugar
1 1/2 tablespoons chopped fresh dill
1/2 teaspoon salt
1/2 teaspoon black pepper

Place carrots in a skillet and pour in just enough water to cover. Bring to a boil over medium heat; simmer until water has evaporated and the carrots are tender. Stir in butter, brown sugar, dill, salt, and pepper.

I was very skeptical about combining a sweet flavor with the dill, but try it! The title is little deceiving, the sugar merely enhances the natural sweetness of the carrots and is not the prominent flavor!

—GOURMETGIRLS3

AMOUNT PER SERVING: CALORIES: 119   TOTAL FAT: 6 g   CHOLESTEROL: 16 mg   SODIUM: 387 mg
TOTAL CARBS: 16.6 g   DIETARY FIBER: 3 g   PROTEIN: 1.1 g

Jacksonville Carrots

Submitted by: **TANYA**

PREP TIME: 15 MINUTES
COOK TIME: 20 MINUTES
READY IN: 35 MINUTES
SERVINGS: 4

4 large carrots, halved
2 tablespoons honey
1 tablespoon frozen apple juice concentrate, thawed
3 tablespoons minced fresh parsley
1/4 cup chopped toasted hazelnuts
1/4 teaspoon garlic powder
1/4 teaspoon ground nutmeg
1/2 teaspoon salt
1/4 teaspoon pepper
1/4 cup clarified butter

Steam the carrots in a steamer basket over 1 inch of boiling water for 7 to 10 minutes, or until tender but still firm. Cool, and grate with a large holed grater. Mix together the grated carrots, honey, apple juice concentrate, parsley, and hazelnuts. Season with garlic powder, nutmeg, salt and pepper.

Heat butter in a large skillet over medium-high heat. Fry the carrot mixture in the hot butter until heated through.

Terrific recipe. I used pre-cut matchstick carrots and cooked with apple juice and seasonings in the microwave for 3 minutes. Toasted pine nuts (didn't have hazelnuts) in a dry skillet while the carrots cooked. Added light butter, the carrots with juices, and honey (only 4 tsp). Warmed together in the skillet for about a minute. We loved this.

—THYMEFORME

AMOUNT PER SERVING: CALORIES: 229   TOTAL FAT: 17.4 g   CHOLESTEROL: 33 mg   SODIUM: 319 mg
TOTAL CARBS: 19.2 g   DIETARY FIBER: 3.1 g   PROTEIN: 2 g

Acorn Squash

Submitted by: TERRY

PREP TIME: 5 MINUTES
COOK IN: 1 HOUR
READY IN: 1 HOUR 5 MINUTES
SERVINGS: 2

1 medium acorn squash, halved and seeded
1 tablespoon butter
2 tablespoons brown sugar

Preheat oven to 350°F (175°C).

Turn acorn squash upside down onto a cookie sheet. Bake in a 350°F (175°C) oven until it begins to soften, approximately 30 to 45 minutes.

Remove squash from the oven and turn onto a plate so that the flesh is facing upwards. Place butter and brown sugar into the squash, and place remaining squash over the other piece. Place squash in a baking dish (so the squash won't slide around too much) while baking.

Place squash in the 350°F (175°C) oven and bake another 30 minutes.

AMOUNT PER SERVING: CALORIES: 188 TOTAL FAT: 6 g CHOLESTEROL: 16 mg SODIUM: 70 mg TOTAL CARBS: 35.7 g DIETARY FIBER: 3.2 g PROTEIN: 1.8 g

Provincial Tomatoes

Submitted by: SARAWILDER

PREP TIME: 10 MINUTES
COOK TIME: 5 MINUTES
READY IN: 15 MINUTES
SERVINGS: 4

2 large tomatoes, cut into quarter inch slices
Salt and pepper to taste
1 tablespoon olive oil, or as needed
1/2 cup grated Parmesan cheese
1/4 cup grated Asiago cheese
1/4 cup dry bread crumbs
2 tablespoons dried parsley

Preheat your oven's broiler.

Place tomato slices in a single layer on a baking sheet or in a baking dish, season with a little salt and pepper, and drizzle with olive oil. Mix together the Parmesan cheese, Asiago cheese, bread crumbs and parsley; sprinkle over the tomato slices. Drizzle a little bit more olive oil over the top.

Broil for 5 minutes, or until the top is golden and toasty.

I'm not a huge fan of tomatoes as a dish unto itself but wow, I absolutely loved these. And the next day I used the left over ones in BLT's... it really added some pizzazz to the sandwiches.

—ALIHEARTHIM

AMOUNT PER SERVING: CALORIES: 159 TOTAL FAT: 9.8 g CHOLESTEROL: 16 mg SODIUM: 385 mg TOTAL CARBS: 10.2 g DIETARY FIBER: 1.4 g PROTEIN: 8.7 g

AS SHOWN IN THE PICTURE

Corn and Zucchini Melody

Submitted by: **GAIL**

PREP TIME: 5 MINUTES
COOK IN: 25 MINUTES
READY IN: 30 MINUTES
SERVINGS: 5

4 slices bacon
2 cups chopped zucchini
1 1/2 cups fresh corn kernels
1 small onion, chopped
1 pinch pepper
1/4 cup shredded Monterey Jack cheese

Place bacon in a large, deep skillet. Cook over medium-high heat until evenly brown. Reserve 1 tablespoon of drippings. Drain bacon, chop, and set aside.

Heat the bacon drippings in the skillet over medium heat. Saute the zucchini, corn, and onion until tender but still crisp, about 10 minutes. Season with pepper. Spoon vegetables into a bowl, and sprinkle with chopped bacon and shredded cheese.

This is a quick, simple side dish that my whole family loved. A really good way to use up leftover corn and all the zucchini that comes with late summer. The bacon gives a wonderful subtle taste.

—ORCHARDGIRL

AMOUNT PER SERVING: CALORIES: 208   TOTAL FAT: 15.3 g   CHOLESTEROL: 20 mg   SODIUM: 204 mg
TOTAL CARBS: 14.4 g   DIETARY FIBER: 2.2 g   PROTEIN: 5.6 g

Corn Casserole

Submitted by: **PAM MIGNUOLO**

PREP TIME: 5 MINUTES
COOK TIME: 40 MINUTES
READY IN: 45 MINUTES
SERVINGS: 9

1 (8 ounce) container sour cream
1/2 cup unsalted butter, softened
1 (15 ounce) can creamed corn
1 (15 ounce) can whole kernel corn
1 (8.5 ounce) package corn bread mix

Preheat oven to 350°F (175°C).

In a mixing bowl, stir together the sour cream, butter, creamed corn, corn nibblets and corn muffin mix.

Pour into a 1 quart casserole dish and bake for 40 minutes.

I've been making this dish for years. It is a main staple at fall gatherings. The only difference between this recipe and mine is I melt my butter.

—SAMMYSWIMSTER

AMOUNT PER SERVING: CALORIES: 323   TOTAL FAT: 18.8 g   CHOLESTEROL: 39 mg   SODIUM: 693 mg
TOTAL CARBS: 37.1 g   DIETARY FIBER: 1.7 g   PROTEIN: 5.2 g

Sugar Snap Peas with Mint

Submitted by: **ORNERY**

PREP TIME: 6 MINUTES
COOK IN: 4 MINUTES
READY IN: 10 MINUTES
SERVINGS: 4

2 teaspoons olive oil
3/4 pound sugar snap peas, trimmed
3 green onions, chopped
1 clove garlic, chopped
1/8 teaspoon salt
1/8 teaspoon pepper
1 tablespoon chopped fresh mint

Heat oil in a large skillet over medium heat. Add the sugar snap peas, green onion, and garlic. Season with salt and pepper. Stir-fry for 4 minutes, then remove from heat and stir in the mint leaves.

This recipe is a wonderful summer side dish! I don't often cook with mint and was a tad skeptical, but tried it anyway. I'm glad I did! The mint isn't overpowering but gives the dish a very fresh summer taste. I didn't have green onions so I used fresh onion chives out of my garden. Lovely recipe!

—LAURENE29

AMOUNT PER SERVING: CALORIES: 65   TOTAL FAT: 2.6 g   CHOLESTEROL: 0 mg   SODIUM: 83 mg   TOTAL CARBS: 8.3 g
DIETARY FIBER: 2.6 g   PROTEIN: 2.6 g

Gonzo Garbanzos

Submitted by: **CLINTWILSON**

PREP TIME: 5 MINUTES
COOK TIME: 5 MINUTES
READY IN: 10 MINUTES
SERVINGS: 2

1 (15 ounce) can garbanzo beans
1 lemon, juiced
1 whole dried red chile peppers
1 clove garlic, quartered
2 tablespoons minced onion
1 tablespoon picante sauce
1 teaspoon ground black pepper
1/2 teaspoon Cajun seasoning
1/4 teaspoon sazon seasoning
1/4 teaspoon paprika

Drain off about half of the juice from the beans and put them into a saucepan. Mix in the lemon juice, chilies, garlic, onion, picante sauce, pepper, Cajun seasoning, sazon seasoning and paprika. Bring to a simmer over medium heat, and cook for about 7 minutes. Remove the chilies and garlic before serving.

Love, love, love this recipe; I used a tablespoon of bottled lemon juice, and doubled the Cajun seasoning in lieu of the sazon seasoning. I threw a little brown rice in and we had it for lunch; the kids loved it.

—LONGELEGANTLEGS

AMOUNT PER SERVING: CALORIES: 278   TOTAL FAT: 2.8 g   CHOLESTEROL: 0 mg   SODIUM: 822 mg   TOTAL CARBS: 57 g
DIETARY FIBER: 12.6 g   PROTEIN: 11.7 g

New Year's Day Black-Eyed Peas

PREP TIME: 15 MINUTES
COOK TIME: 3 HOURS
READY IN: 3 HOURS 15 MINUTES
SERVINGS: 16

Submitted by: **ROXANNA PARKS**

1 pound dry black-eyed peas
2 cups chopped cooked ham
Salt and pepper to taste
1 pinch garlic powder
2 onions, diced
1 (14.5 ounce) can whole tomatoes

Place black-eyed peas in 8 quart pot. Add enough water to fill pot 3/4 full. Stir in ham and diced onions, and season with salt, pepper, and garlic powder. Place tomatoes in a blender or food processor, and blend until the tomatoes are liquefied. Add tomatoes to pot. Bring all ingredients to boil. Cover the pot, and simmer on low heat for 2 1/2 to 3 hours, or until the peas are tender.

Why wait till new years? They're so good.

—AUTUMN

AMOUNT PER SERVING: CALORIES: 125   TOTAL FAT: 3.3 g   CHOLESTEROL: 16 mg   SODIUM: 79 mg   TOTAL CARBS: 16.8 g   DIETARY FIBER: 4.1 g   PROTEIN: 7.2 g

Ryan's Favorite Beans

PREP TIME: 30 MINUTES
COOK TIME: 1 HOUR
READY IN: 1 HOUR 30 MINUTES
SERVINGS: 20

Submitted by: **VALERIE'S KITCHEN**

6 slices bacon
1 pound ground beef
1 1/2 cups chopped onion
1 (31 ounce) can pork and beans, drained
1 (31 ounce) can pork and beans, with liquid
2 (15 ounce) cans kidney beans, drained
1 (15 ounce) can lima beans, drained
1 1/2 cups barbeque sauce
1/3 cup packed brown sugar
2 tablespoons cider vinegar
1 teaspoon liquid smoke flavoring (optional)
1 teaspoon salt
1/2 teaspoon ground black pepper

Preheat oven to 350°F (175°C).

Place bacon in a Dutch oven. Cook over medium high heat until evenly brown. Drain, crumble, and set aside. Place the ground beef and onion in the Dutch oven. Cook until beef is evenly brown and onion is tender.

Return bacon to the Dutch oven. Mix in the drained pork and beans, pork and beans with liquid, kidney beans, and lima beans. Stir in the barbeque sauce, brown sugar, vinegar, and liquid smoke. Season with salt and pepper.

Cover Dutch oven, and bake 1 hour in the preheated oven.

AMOUNT PER SERVING: CALORIES: 235   TOTAL FAT: 6.1 g   CHOLESTEROL: 22 mg   SODIUM: 906 mg   TOTAL CARBS: 34.1 g   DIETARY FIBER: 8.9 g   PROTEIN: 12.9 g

AS SHOWN IN THE PICTURE

Crispy Coated Cajun Fries

Submitted by: **SUNNYBC**

PREP TIME: 20 MINUTES
COOK IN: 10 MINUTES
READY IN: 30 MINUTES
SERVINGS: 6

2 pounds russet potatoes, cut into fries
1 cup corn flour
2 tablespoons cornmeal
2 tablespoons Cajun seasoning
1 quart oil for deep frying
Salt to taste

Place cut potatoes into a large bowl of cold water. Soak for 10 minutes. In a large resealable plastic bag, combine the corn flour, corn meal, and Cajun seasoning. Shake the bag to blend. Drain the potatoes, but leave them wet. Place the fries in the plastic bag with the seasoning, and shake to coat.

Heat the oil in a deep-fryer to 375°F (190°C).

Cook fries in hot oil for 7 to 10 minutes, or until golden brown. Remove from the fryer to paper towels to drain. Season with a small amount of salt.

AMOUNT PER SERVING: CALORIES: 345 TOTAL FAT: 15.1 g CHOLESTEROL: 0 mg SODIUM: 549 mg
TOTAL CARBS: 48 g DIETARY FIBER: 4.5 g PROTEIN: 4.6 g

Potato Chips

Submitted by: **JESSICA**

PREP TIME: 30 MINUTES
COOK IN: 5 MINUTES
READY IN: 35 MINUTES
SERVINGS: 4

1 tablespoon vegetable oil
1 potato, sliced paper thin (peel optional)
1/2 teaspoon salt, or to taste

Pour the vegetable oil into a plastic bag (a produce bag works well). Add the potato slices, and shake to coat.

Coat a large dinner plate lightly with oil or cooking spray. Arrange potato slices in a single layer on the dish.

Cook in the microwave for 3 to 5 minutes, or until lightly browned (if not browned, they will not become crisp). Times will vary depending on the power of your microwave. Remove chips from plate, and toss with salt (or other seasonings). Let cool. Repeat process with the remaining potato slices. You will not need to keep oiling the plate.

These were really good; they taste even better than my favorite chip brand. I used the popcorn flavor shakers (dill pickle, ketchup, salt & vinegar) and that made them even better.

—BRAVAN22

AMOUNT PER SERVING: CALORIES: 80 TOTAL FAT: 3.5 g CHOLESTEROL: 0 mg SODIUM: 295 mg TOTAL CARBS: 11.6 g
DIETARY FIBER: 1.1 g PROTEIN: 1.2 g

Oven Baked Potato Wedges

Submitted by: **SUE**

PREP TIME: 15 MINUTES
COOK IN: 45 MINUTES
READY IN: 1 HOUR
SERVINGS: 5

2 teaspoons olive oil
5 large russet potatoes, peeled and cut into wedges
1/2 cup melted butter
1 cup seasoned bread crumbs

Preheat oven to 350°F (175°C). Grease a baking sheet with the olive oil.

Brush potato wedges with butter, and roll in bread crumbs. Place wedges on prepared baking sheet.

Bake in preheated oven for 20 minutes. Remove from oven and turn wedges; cook for 10 to 15 minutes, or until tender.

I used this recipe as a base for Ranch Potato Wedges! I kept the breadcrumbs, but I added a packet of Ranch dressing seasoning. I also used olive oil for a healthier substitute. They were PERFECT! Awesome recipe!
—LARNBROWN

AMOUNT PER SERVING: CALORIES: 491 TOTAL FAT: 21.2 g CHOLESTEROL: 50 mg SODIUM: 853 mg
TOTAL CARBS: 68.6 g DIETARY FIBER: 4.6 g PROTEIN: 8.3 g

Fancy Potatoes

Submitted by: **JANET JONES**

PREP TIME: 15 MINUTES
COOK TIME: 35 MINUTES
READY IN: 50 MINUTES
SERVINGS: 6

5 large potatoes
1 cup sour cream
2 (8 ounce) packages cream cheese
1 pinch garlic salt
2 cups shredded Cheddar cheese

Preheat oven to 350°F (175°C).

Place potatoes in a large pot of salted boiling water, bring water back to a boil. Cook until potatoes are tender, approximately 15 to 20 minutes. Drain well. Let cool.

When potatoes are cooled, cut them into small chunks. Using an electric blender, whip potatoes with sour cream, cream cheese and garlic salt. Place mixture in a 9x13 inch casserole dish. Sprinkle with Cheddar cheese.

Bake for 20 minutes. Serve hot.

A wonderful potato dish. I did not whip the potatoes, but cut them into small cubes, just personal preference. Added some garlic powder, minced onion, parsley and some Cajun seasoning to spice it up. It was like a twice-baked potato casserole!
—TRIPLEJ28

AMOUNT PER SERVING: CALORIES: 737 TOTAL FAT: 46.6 g CHOLESTEROL: 139 mg SODIUM: 551 mg
TOTAL CARBS: 59.4 g DIETARY FIBER: 7.4 g PROTEIN: 22.4 g

Cheesy Sweet and Savory Spuds

Submitted by: **KAT**

PREP TIME: 35 MINUTES
COOK IN: 25 MINUTES
READY IN: 1 HOUR
SERVINGS: 8

6 Yukon Gold potatoes, peeled and cubed
2 sweet potatoes, peeled and cubed
2 tablespoons butter
1/2 cup heavy cream
1 tablespoon chicken bouillon granules
1 2/3 tablespoons brown sugar
2 teaspoons black pepper
2 cups shredded Monterey Jack cheese

Place the potatoes and sweet potatoes in a large pot with enough water to cover. Bring to a boil. Cook about 15 minutes, until tender but firm. Remove from heat, and drain.

Preheat the oven broiler.

In a large bowl, mash the potatoes. Gradually mix in butter, heavy cream, chicken bouillon, brown sugar, and pepper. Transfer the mixture to a medium baking dish, and top with Monterey Jack cheese.

Broil uncovered in the preheated oven 10 minutes, or until the cheese is melted and lightly browned.

AMOUNT PER SERVING: CALORIES: 303 TOTAL FAT: 17.2 g CHOLESTEROL: 53 mg SODIUM: 338 mg TOTAL CARBS: 28.2 g DIETARY FIBER: 2.2 g PROTEIN: 9.9 g

Garlic Mashed Potatoes Secret Recipe

Submitted by: **AUSTAD**

PREP TIME: 15 MINUTES
COOK TIME: 45 MINUTES
READY IN: 1 HOUR
SERVINGS: 6

3 pounds unpeeled red potatoes, quartered
1/2 pounds butter, room temperature
3 ounces Romano cheese, grated
3 tablespoons chopped garlic
1 1/2 teaspoons salt
1 1/2 teaspoons dried oregano

Bring a large pot of salted water to a boil. Add potatoes and cook until tender but still firm, about 45 minutes; drain. Stir in butter, cheese, garlic, salt and oregano. Mash with a potato masher or with an electric mixer.

Yummy! I've made this recipe several times now. No more instant potatoes at my house! Easy to make and delish. Great served with any meal.

—**LUCY**

AMOUNT PER SERVING: CALORIES: 498 TOTAL FAT: 33.4 g CHOLESTEROL: 94 mg SODIUM: 1,030 mg TOTAL CARBS: 43.2 g DIETARY FIBER: 3.9 g PROTEIN: 8.8 g

Fried Onion Rings

Submitted by: JILL

PREP TIME: 15 MINUTES
COOK TIME: 20 MINUTES
READY IN: 45 MINUTES
SERVINGS: 12

1 quart vegetable oil for frying
1 cup all-purpose flour
1 cup beer
1 pinch salt
1 pinch ground black pepper
4 onions, peeled and sliced into rings

In a large, deep skillet, heat oil to 365°F (180°C).

In a medium bowl, combine flour, beer, salt, and pepper. Mix until smooth. Dredge onion slices in the batter, until evenly coated. Deep fry in the hot oil until golden brown. Drain on paper towels.

I used Vidalia onions and tried some shrimp in the batter, as well. It coated the food beautifully and held together great, which is what I was looking for. Easy, easy. Good simple recipe for a batter. Season as you wish, before and after.

—LINDA

AMOUNT PER SERVING: CALORIES: 125 TOTAL FAT: 7.5 g CHOLESTEROL: 0 mg SODIUM: 35 mg TOTAL CARBS: 11.9 g DIETARY FIBER: 1 g PROTEIN: 1.6 g

Cajun Style Baked Sweet Potato

Submitted by: ELEANOR JOHNSON

PREP TIME: 10 MINUTES
COOK IN: 1 HOUR
READY IN: 1 HOUR 10 MINUTES
SERVINGS: 4

1 1/2 teaspoons paprika
1 teaspoon brown sugar
1/4 teaspoon black pepper
1/4 teaspoon onion powder
1/4 teaspoon dried thyme
1/4 teaspoon dried rosemary
1/4 teaspoon garlic powder
1/8 teaspoon cayenne pepper
2 large sweet potato, peeled and cubed
1 1/2 teaspoons olive oil

Preheat oven to 375°F (190°C).

In a small bowl, stir together paprika, brown sugar, black pepper, onion powder, thyme, rosemary, garlic powder, and cayenne pepper.

Slice the sweet potatoes in half lengthwise. Brush each half with olive oil. Rub the seasoning mix over the cut surface of each half. Place sweet potatoes on a baking sheet, or in a shallow pan.

Bake in preheated oven until tender, or about 1 hour.

If I could give this more than a 5, I would! We loved it! A great way to get in your sweet potatoes without the same boring casserole or just eating them with butter. I cut them into fry sized slices and baked them only 35 minutes. An AMAZING RECIPE!

—ILOVERIVERS

AMOUNT PER SERVING: CALORIES: 258 TOTAL FAT: 2.2 g CHOLESTEROL: 0 mg SODIUM: 24 mg TOTAL CARBS: 57.1 g DIETARY FIBER: 7.1 g PROTEIN: 4.1 g

Amanda's Potatoes

Submitted by: **AMANDA250**

PREP TIME: 20 MINUTES
COOK IN: 1 HOUR 45 MINUTES
READY IN: 2 HOURS 5 MINUTES
SERVINGS: 6

4 large onions, thinly sliced
1/2 cup light brown sugar
1/2 cup butter
6 large Yukon Gold potatoes, scrubbed and sliced with peel
1 cup heavy cream
2 sprigs fresh rosemary, chopped

Place onion, butter and brown sugar into a large skillet over low heat. Cook, stirring occasionally, until the onions have caramelized, about 45 minutes.

Preheat the oven to 350°F (175°C). Coat a 9x13 inch baking dish with cooking spray.

Place a single layer of potato slices in the bottom of the prepared baking dish. Cover with a thin layer of onions. Drizzle some of the cream, and sprinkle some of the rosemary over the layer. Repeat layers four times ending with onions, cream and rosemary.

Bake for 1 hour in the preheated oven, or until top potatoes are golden brown and sauce is bubbling.

AMOUNT PER SERVING: CALORIES: 525 TOTAL FAT: 30.4 g CHOLESTEROL: 96 mg SODIUM: 192 mg
TOTAL CARBS: 60.7 g DIETARY FIBER: 4.8 g PROTEIN: 6 g

Bleu Cheese Macaroni

Submitted by: **SARA**

PREP TIME: 5 MINUTES
COOK TIME: 20 MINUTES
READY IN: 25 MINUTES
SERVINGS: 6

2 cups uncooked elbow macaroni
2 tablespoons butter
1 teaspoon salt
1/2 teaspoon black pepper
1/2 cup sliced green bell pepper
1/2 cup sliced red bell pepper
3/4 cup heavy cream
1/3 cup all-purpose flour
1/2 cup plain yogurt
1 cup crumbled blue cheese
1/2 cup grated Parmesan cheese

Bring a large pot of lightly salted water to a boil. Add macaroni and cook for 8 to 10 minutes or until al dente; drain.

Meanwhile, in a medium saucepan over medium heat combine butter, salt, pepper and bell peppers. Simmer until heated through. Stir in cream, flour, yogurt, bleu cheese and Parmesan cheese.

Stir cooked macaroni into cheese mixture and serve hot.

Addictively yummy! I added fresh garlic. I made mine creamier by doubling the cream. Such great flavor – I'll be craving this one!

—DONNA K

AMOUNT PER SERVING: CALORIES: 420 TOTAL FAT: 24.8 g CHOLESTEROL: 76 mg SODIUM: 923 mg
TOTAL CARBS: 34.3 g DIETARY FIBER: 1.6 g PROTEIN: 15 g

Indian Style Basmati Rice

Submitted by: **DHANO923**

PREP TIME: 10 MINUTES
COOK TIME: 25 MINUTES
READY IN: 45 MINUTES
SERVINGS: 6

1 1/2 cups basmati rice
2 tablespoons vegetable oil
1 (2 inch) piece cinnamon stick
2 pods green cardamom
2 whole cloves
1 tablespoon cumin seed
1 small onion, thinly sliced
1 teaspoon salt, or to taste
2 1/2 cups water

Place rice into a bowl with enough water to cover. Set aside to soak for 20 minutes.

Heat the oil in a large pot or saucepan over medium heat. Add the cinnamon stick, cardamom pods, cloves, and cumin seed. Cook and stir for about a minute, then add the onion to the pot. Saute the onion until a rich golden brown, about 10 minutes. Drain the water from the rice, and stir into the pot. Cook and stir the rice for a few minutes, until lightly toasted. Add salt and water to the pot, and bring to a boil. Cover, and reduce heat to low. Simmer for about 15 minutes, or until all of the water has been absorbed. Let stand for 5 minutes, then fluff with a fork before serving.

AMOUNT PER SERVING: CALORIES: 234 TOTAL FAT: 5.5 g CHOLESTEROL: 0 mg SODIUM: 394 mg TOTAL CARBS: 42.8 g DIETARY FIBER: 1 g PROTEIN: 4.3 g

---

Garlic Grits

Submitted by: **MAGGIE**

PREP TIME: 10 MINUTES
COOK TIME: 25 MINUTES
READY IN: 35 MINUTES
SERVINGS: 5

1 quart water
1 teaspoon minced garlic
1 teaspoon salt
1 cup quick-cooking grits
1 1/2 cups diced processed cheese
1/4 cup butter
1 egg
1/4 cup milk

Preheat oven to 350°F (175°C). Grease a 2 quart casserole dish.

Bring water to a boil in a large saucepan with garlic and salt. Stir in grits, reduce heat to low, and cook until thick, about 5 minutes, stirring frequently. Remove from heat and stir in cheese and butter until melted. In a small bowl, whisk together egg and milk, then stir into grits. Pour grits mixture into greased casserole dish.

Bake in preheated oven for 20 to 25 minutes, until firm.

Very good recipe. The grits were very creamy with just a hint of garlic....just right. If you like a stronger garlic flavor, you will want to increase the amount of garlic. Being from the South and having cooked grits many times, the grits will be less lumpy if you put them into the water before you bring it to a boil.

—CHEFHENRY

AMOUNT PER SERVING: CALORIES: 378 TOTAL FAT: 24.2 g CHOLESTEROL: 101 mg SODIUM: 1,200 mg TOTAL CARBS: 26.5 g DIETARY FIBER: 0.5 g PROTEIN: 13.7 g

AS SHOWN IN THE PICTURE

Fried Rice with Ginger, Hoisin, and Sesame

Submitted by: **CARLYYY**

PREP TIME: 25 MINUTES
COOK IN: 10 MINUTES
READY IN: 35 MINUTES
SERVINGS: 6

1 tablespoon butter
1/2 cup uncooked white rice
1 cup water
1/2 cup hoisin sauce
1/2 cup barbeque sauce
1 tablespoon peanut butter
1 1/2 teaspoons soy sauce
1 clove garlic, minced
1 teaspoon grated fresh ginger
2 teaspoons sesame oil
1 cup chopped onion
1 cup grated carrot
2 cups frozen pea pods
2 cups frozen chopped broccoli, thawed
2 eggs
1/4 cup sesame seeds, lightly toasted

Melt the butter in a small saucepan over medium heat. Add the uncooked rice, and cook until toasted, stirring occasionally. Pour in the water and bring to a boil. Reduce heat to low, cover, and cook for about 15 minutes, or until tender.

While the rice is cooking, mix together the hoisin sauce, barbeque sauce, peanut butter, soy sauce, garlic, and ginger. Set aside.

When the rice is done cooking, heat the sesame oil in a wok or large skillet over medium-high heat. When it begins to smoke, add the onion and fry until clear. Add the carrot, and cook for about 1 minute, then add the rice, and stir fry for about 2 minutes. Add the broccoli and peas; cook and stir for about 1 minute. Push everything to the sides of the wok, and crack the eggs into the center. Scramble until cooked through, trying to keep the raw egg from mixing with everything else. When the eggs are cooked, stir them in with the rice.

Turn off the heat, and stir in about half of the sauce, tasting and adding more as desired. You may not need all of the sauce, but if you serve this with a meat it makes a good sauce for that too. Sprinkle with sesame seeds before serving.

Awesome combination of flavors! Only thing I added (because it's so incredible in dishes like this) is fresh chopped cilantro when it was done. Yum!
*—*SWEETPOTATO

This is so great! Unique twist on a traditional favorite. I'll definitely make this again. I love the sauce!
*—*GRANDIOSOO

I love all these flavors and was excited to try this recipe. My husband and I LOVED it! I made some substitutions, not out of "correction", but because I did not have the ingredients. Ran out of onion, used onion powder both in the sauce and while frying the rice. Used mixed stir-fry vegetables, and added some of last night's grilled chicken breast strips. WOW! The only addition I made was to add about a quarter teaspoon of Vietnamese chili sauce, making this dish a truly eclectic blend of Asian flavors! Marvelous, will make this AGAIN AND AGAIN! !

*—*SWEETPOTATO

AMOUNT PER SERVING: CALORIES: 285   TOTAL FAT: 11.2 g   CHOLESTEROL: 77 mg   SODIUM: 666 mg
TOTAL CARBS: 38.3 g   DIETARY FIBER: 6.2 g   PROTEIN: 9.7 g

AS SHOWN IN THE PICTURE

Roasted Garlic Bread

Submitted by: **AKERD**

PREP TIME: 15 MINUTES
COOK IN: 5 MINUTES
READY IN: 20 MINUTES
SERVINGS: 8

3 bulbs garlic
2 tablespoons olive oil
1 (1 pound) loaf Italian bread
1/2 cup butter
1 tablespoon chopped fresh parsley (optional)
2 tablespoons grated parmesan cheese (optional)

Preheat the oven to 350°F (175°C). Slice the tops off of the garlic bulbs so that the tip of each clove is exposed. Place the bulbs on a baking sheet, and drizzle with olive oil. Bake for 30 minutes, or until garlic is soft.

Set the oven to broil. Slice the loaf of bread in half horizontally, and place cut side up on a baking sheet.

Squeeze the cloves of garlic from their skins into a medium bowl. Stir in the butter, parsley, and Parmesan cheese until well blended. Spread onto the cut sides of the bread.

Broil for about 5 minutes, until toasted.

AMOUNT PER SERVING: CALORIES: 323   TOTAL FAT: 17.4 g   CHOLESTEROL: 32 mg   SODIUM: 476 mg
TOTAL CARBS. 35.4 g   DIETARY FIBER: 2 g   PROTEIN: 7 g

Sausage and Apple Stuffing

Submitted by: **LAURA**

PREP TIME: 30 MINUTES
COOK TIME: 30 MINUTES
READY IN: 1 HOUR
SERVINGS: 12

1/2 pound ground pork breakfast sausage
2 tablespoons butter
1/2 cup chopped celery
1/4 cup chopped onion
1 (4 ounce) can water chestnuts, drained and chopped
1 (12 ounce) package herb-seasoned dry bread stuffing mix
3 apples, peeled, cored and cubed
1 tablespoon chicken broth

Place ground pork breakfast sausage in a large, deep skillet. Cook over medium high heat until evenly brown. Drain and set aside.

Melt butter in a medium saucepan over medium heat. Stir in celery, onion and water chestnuts. Cook and stir until tender. Remove from heat.

Preheat oven to 325°F (165°C).

Prepare herb-seasoned dry bread stuffing mix according to package directions. Mix in sausage, celery mixture, apples and chicken broth.

Transfer mixture to a medium baking dish. Bake in the preheated oven 30 minutes, or until lightly browned.

AMOUNT PER SERVING: CALORIES: 223   TOTAL FAT: 10.6 g   CHOLESTEROL: 18 mg   SODIUM: 601 mg
TOTAL CARBS: 26.3 g   DIETARY FIBER: 1.8 g   PROTEIN: 5.5 g

DESSERTS

185

AS SHOWN IN THE PICTURE

Beth's Spicy Oatmeal Raisin Cookies

Submitted by: BETH SIGWORTH

PREP TIME: 15 MINUTES
COOK IN: 12 MINUTES
READY IN: 50 MINUTES
SERVINGS: 36

1/2 cup butter, softened
1/2 cup butter flavored shortening
1 cup packed light brown sugar
1/2 cup white sugar
2 eggs
1 teaspoon vanilla extract
1 1/2 cups all-purpose flour
1 teaspoon baking soda
1 teaspoon ground cinnamon
1/2 teaspoon ground cloves
1/2 teaspoon salt
3 cups rolled oats
1 cup raisins

Preheat oven to 350°F (175°C)

In a large bowl, cream together the butter, butter flavored shortening, brown sugar, white sugar, eggs, and vanilla until smooth. Combine the flour, baking soda, cinnamon, cloves, and salt; stir into the sugar mixture. Stir in the oats and raisins. Drop by rounded teaspoonfuls onto ungreased cookie sheets.

Bake 10 to 12 minutes until light and golden. Do not overbake. Let them cool for 2 minutes before removing from cookie sheets to cool completely. Store in airtight container. Make sure you get some, because they don't last long!

AMOUNT PER SERVING: CALORIES: 144 TOTAL FAT: 6.3 g CHOLESTEROL: 19 mg SODIUM: 100 mg
TOTAL CARBS: 20.5 g DIETARY FIBER: 1.1 g PROTEIN: 2.1 g

Lemon Pudding Cookies

Submitted by: ROBIN

PREP TIME: 15 MINUTES
COOK TIME: 12 MINUTES
READY IN: 50 MINUTES
SERVINGS: 6

1 cup buttermilk baking mix
1 (3 ounce) package instant lemon pudding mix
1 egg
1/4 cup vegetable oil
1/3 cup granulated sugar for decoration

Preheat oven to 350°F (180°C). Grease 2 large cookie sheets.

Mix baking mix, pudding, egg and oil in a large bowl until dough forms.

Roll dough into 1 inch balls. Place balls 2 inches apart on the cookie sheets. Dip flat bottom glass or cookie press into sugar. Press onto dough ball and flatten into 1/4 inch thick cookie. Bake until just golden brown on the edges, about 10 minutes. Transfer to racks and cool completely.

They are really great. For change I also made them with coconut or chocolate pudding and they turned out perfect.

—ZUZANA

AMOUNT PER SERVING: CALORIES: 265 TOTAL FAT: 10.4 g CHOLESTEROL: 35 mg SODIUM: 613 mg
TOTAL CARBS: 41.2 g DIETARY FIBER: 0 g PROTEIN: 2.7 g

Snickerdoodles

Submitted by: **LINDAK**

PREP TIME: 15 MINUTES
COOK IN: 10 MINUTES
READY IN: 30 MINUTES
SERVINGS: 36

1 cup shortening
1 1/2 cups white sugar
2 eggs
2 3/4 cups all-purpose flour
1 teaspoon baking soda
2 teaspoons cream of tartar
1/2 teaspoon salt
2 tablespoons white sugar
2 teaspoons ground cinnamon

Preheat oven to 375°F (190°C).

In a medium bowl, cream together the shortening and 1 1/2 cups sugar. Stir in the eggs. Sift together the flour, baking soda, cream of tartar, and salt; stir into the creamed mixture until well blended. In a small bowl, stir together the 2 tablespoons of sugar, and the cinnamon. Roll dough into walnut sized balls, then roll the balls in the cinnamon-sugar. Place them onto an unprepared cookie sheet, two inches apart.

Bake for 8 to 10 minutes in the preheated oven. Edges should be slightly brown. Remove from sheets to cool on wire racks.

AMOUNT PER SERVING: CALORIES: 125   TOTAL FAT: 6.1 g   CHOLESTEROL: 12 mg   SODIUM: 71 mg
TOTAL CARBS: 16.5 g   DIETARY FIBER: 0.3 g   PROTEIN: 1.3 g

Best Big, Fat, Chewy Chocolate Chip Cookie

Submitted by: **ELIZABETH**

PREP TIME: 10 MINUTES
COOK TIME: 15 MINUTES
READY IN: 40 MINUTES
SERVINGS: 18

2 cups all-purpose flour
1/2 teaspoon baking soda
1/2 teaspoon salt
3/4 cup unsalted butter, melted
1 cup packed brown sugar
1/2 cup white sugar
1 tablespoon vanilla extract
1 egg
1 egg yolk
2 cups semisweet chocolate chips

Preheat the oven to 325°F (165°C). Grease cookie sheets or line with parchment paper.

Sift together the flour, baking soda and salt; set aside.

In a medium bowl, cream together the melted butter, brown sugar and white sugar until well blended. Beat in the vanilla, egg, and egg yolk until light and creamy. Mix in the sifted ingredients until just blended. Stir in the chocolate chips by hand using a wooden spoon. Drop cookie dough 1/4 cup at a time onto the prepared cookie sheets. Cookies should be about 3 inches apart.

Bake for 15 to 17 minutes in the preheated oven, or until the edges are lightly toasted. Cool on baking sheets for a few minutes before transferring to wire racks to cool completely.

AMOUNT PER SERVING: CALORIES: 285   TOTAL FAT: 14 g   CHOLESTEROL: 44 mg   SODIUM: 112 mg   TOTAL CARBS: 40 g
DIETARY FIBER: 1.5 g   PROTEIN: 2.8 g

The Best Rolled Sugar Cookies

Submitted by: JILL SAUNDERS

PREP TIME: 20 MINUTES
COOK IN: 8 MINUTES
READY IN: 3 HOURS
SERVINGS: 60

1 1/2 cups butter, softened
2 cups white sugar
4 eggs
1 teaspoon vanilla extract
5 cups all-purpose flour
2 teaspoons baking powder
1 teaspoon salt

Lovely sugar cookie recipe! Very easy to roll out and made very tasty cookies that were not dry or crumbly at all. I chilled overnight and kept most of the dough in the fridge as I rolled out 8 or 10 at a time and that worked great.
—BRENAJST

In a large bowl, cream together butter and sugar until smooth. Beat in eggs and vanilla. Stir in the flour, baking powder, and salt. Cover, and chill dough for at least one hour (or overnight).

Preheat oven to 400°F (200°C). Roll out dough on floured surface 1/4 to 1/2 inch thick. Cut into shapes with any cookie cutter. Place cookies 1 inch apart on ungreased cookie sheets.

Bake 6 to 8 minutes in preheated oven. Cool completely.

AMOUNT PER SERVING: CALORIES: 110 TOTAL FAT: 5 g CHOLESTEROL: 27 mg SODIUM: 106 mg
TOTAL CARBS: 14.7 g DIETARY FIBER: 0.3 g PROTEIN: 1.5 g

Molasses Sugar Cookies

Submitted by: KARIN CHRISTIAN

PREP TIME: 20 MINUTES
COOK TIME: 12 MINUTES
READY IN: 3 HOURS 32 MINUTES
SERVINGS: 36

1 1/2 cups shortening
2 cups white sugar
1/2 cup molasses
2 eggs
4 cups all-purpose flour
4 teaspoons baking soda
2 teaspoons ground cinnamon
1 teaspoon salt
1 teaspoon ground cloves
1 teaspoon ground ginger

Melt shortening and cool. Add sugar, eggs and molasses; beat well.

Sift the flour, baking soda, cinnamon, salt, ground cloves and ginger. Add to the molasses mixture and stir until well combined. Chill dough for at least 3 hours or overnight.

Preheat oven to 375°F (190°C). Lightly grease a baking sheet.

Remove dough from the refrigerator and form into walnut sized balls. Roll balls in white sugar. Place balls about 2 inches apart on the prepared baking sheet.

Bake at 375°F (190°C) for 8 to 10 minutes for chewy cookies and 10 to 12 minutes for crisper cookies. Store cookies in an airtight container.

AMOUNT PER SERVING: CALORIES: 196 TOTAL FAT: 9 g CHOLESTEROL: 12 mg SODIUM: 210 mg TOTAL CARBS: 25 g
DIETARY FIBER: 0.5 g PROTEIN: 1.8 g

AS SHOWN IN THE PICTURE

Classic Peanut Butter Cookies

Submitted by: **SHIRLEY SADLER**

PREP TIME: 20 MINUTES
COOK TIME: 10 MINUTES
READY IN: 1 HOUR 30 MINUTES
SERVINGS: 24

1 cup unsalted butter
1 cup crunchy peanut butter
1 cup white sugar
1 cup packed brown sugar
2 eggs
2 1/2 cups all-purpose flour
1 teaspoon baking powder
1/2 teaspoon salt
1 1/2 teaspoons baking soda

Cream together butter, peanut butter and sugars. Beat in eggs. In a separate bowl, sift together flour, baking powder, baking soda, and salt. Stir into batter. Put batter in refrigerator for 1 hour.

Roll into 1 inch balls and put on baking sheets. Flatten each ball with a fork, making a criss-cross pattern. Bake in a preheated 375°F oven for about 10 minutes or until cookies begin to brown. Do not over-bake.

I love these cookies! I was out of crunchy PB, so I used creamy, also didn't have unsalted butter, so used the salted and left out the 1/2 tsp. salt.

—STEPHANIEUSREY

AMOUNT PER SERVING: CALORIES: 252   TOTAL FAT: 13.6 g   CHOLESTEROL: 38 mg   SODIUM: 210 mg
TOTAL CARBS: 29.6 g   DIETARY FIBER: 1.1 g   PROTEIN: 4.6 g

Pecan Filled Cookies

Submitted by: **LAURAL TAKASHIMA**

PREP TIME: 15 MINUTES
COOK TIME: 8 MINUTES
READY IN: 45 MINUTES
SERVINGS: 30

1/2 cup butter
1 cup light brown sugar
1 egg
1 teaspoon vanilla extract
2 cups all-purpose flour
1/2 teaspoon baking soda
1/4 teaspoon salt
1/2 cup chopped pecans
1/8 cup sour cream
1/4 cup brown sugar

Preheat oven to 350°F (175°C). Grease cookie sheets.

In a medium bowl, cream together the butter and 1 cup brown sugar until smooth. Beat in the egg and stir in the vanilla. Combine the flour, baking soda and salt, stir into the sugar mixture. Roll the dough into 1 inch balls and place them 2 inches apart onto the prepared cookie sheets. Make a depression in the center using the cap from the vanilla or the end of a wooden spoon. Mix together the pecans, sour cream and 1/4 cup brown sugar; fill each depression with the mixture.

Bake for 8 to 11 minutes in the preheated oven, or until light brown. Cool for a few minutes on the cookie sheets before removing to wire racks to cool completely.

AMOUNT PER SERVING: CALORIES: 99   TOTAL FAT: 4.9 g   CHOLESTEROL: 16 mg   SODIUM: 77 mg   TOTAL CARBS: 12.6 g
DIETARY FIBER: 0.4 g   PROTEIN: 1.3 g

Cranberry Hootycreeks

Submitted by: **SUSAN O'DELL**

PREP TIME: 25 MINUTES
READY IN: 25 MINUTES
SERVINGS: 4

5/8 cup all-purpose flour
1/2 cup rolled oats
1/2 cup all-purpose flour
1/2 teaspoon baking soda
1/2 teaspoon salt
1/3 cup packed brown sugar
1/3 cup white sugar
1/2 cup dried cranberries
1/2 cup white chocolate chips
1/2 cup chopped pecans

Layer the ingredients in a 1 quart or 1 liter jar, in the order listed. Attach a tag with the following instructions:

CRANBERRY HOOTYCREEKS

1. Preheat oven to 350°F (175°C). Grease a cookie sheet or line with parchment paper.

2. In a medium bowl, beat together 1/2 cup softened butter, 1 egg and 1 teaspoon of vanilla until fluffy. Add the entire jar of ingredients, and mix together by hand until well blended. Drop by heaping spoonfuls onto the prepared baking sheets.

3. Bake for 8 to 10 minutes, or until edges start to brown. Cool on baking sheets, or remove to cool on wire racks.

AMOUNT PER SERVING: CALORIES: 127 TOTAL FAT: 4.2 g CHOLESTEROL: 1 mg SODIUM: 106 mg

TOTAL CARBS: 20.9 g DIETARY FIBER: 1 g PROTEIN: 1.8 g

Oatmeal Peanut Butter Cookies

Submitted by: **JOANNE REANEY**

PREP TIME: 15 MINUTES
COOK TIME: 15 MINUTES
READY IN: 1 HOUR
SERVINGS: 12

1/2 cup shortening
1/2 cup margarine, softened
1 cup packed brown sugar
3/4 cup white sugar
1 cup peanut butter
2 eggs
1 1/2 cups all-purpose flour
2 teaspoons baking soda
1 teaspoon salt
1 cup quick-cooking oats

Preheat oven to 350°F (175°C).

In a large bowl, cream together shortening, margarine, brown sugar, white sugar, and peanut butter until smooth. Beat in the eggs one at a time until well blended. Combine the flour, baking soda, and salt; stir into the creamed mixture. Mix in the oats until just combined. Drop by teaspoonfuls onto ungreased cookie sheets.

Bake for 10 to 15 minutes in the preheated oven, or until just light brown. Don't over-bake. Cool and store in an airtight container.

AMOUNT PER SERVING: CALORIES: 399 TOTAL FAT: 23.6 g CHOLESTEROL: 50 mg SODIUM: 378 mg

TOTAL CARBS: 42 g DIETARY FIBER: 2.2 g PROTEIN: 8 g

AS SHOWN IN THE PICTURE

Raspberry Oatmeal Bars

Submitted by: **MEGAN**

PREP TIME: 15 MINUTES
COOK IN: 23 MINUTES
READY IN: 38 MINUTES
SERVINGS: 24

1 (18.5 ounce) package yellow cake mix
2 1/2 cups quick cooking oats
3/4 cup margarine, melted
1 cup raspberry jam
1 tablespoon water

Preheat the oven to 375°F (190°C). Grease a 9x13 inch pan.

In a large bowl, mix together oats, cake mix, and melted margarine so that it makes nice clumps and there is no dry mix left. Press 1/2 of the oats mixture evenly into the bottom the prepared pan. In a separate bowl, mix jam with water, and spread over the crust. Sprinkle the remaining oat mixture evenly over the top.

Bake in the preheated oven for **18** to **23** minutes, or until the top is lightly browned. Cool before cutting into bars

AMOUNT PER SERVING: CALORIES: 211 TOTAL FAT: 8.6 g CHOLESTEROL: <1 mg SODIUM: 208 mg
TOTAL CARBS: 31.7 g DIETARY FIBER: 1.1 g PROTEIN: 2.4 g

Raspberry and Almond Shortbread Thumbprints

Submitted by: **DEE**

PREP TIME: 30 MINUTES
COOK TIME: 18 MINUTES
READY IN: 1 HOUR 15 MINUTES
SERVINGS: 36

1 cup butter, softened
2/3 cup white sugar
1/2 teaspoon almond extract
2 cups all-purpose flour
1/2 cup seedless raspberry jam
1/2 cup confectioners' sugar
3/4 teaspoon almond extract
1 teaspoon milk

Preheat oven to 350°F (175°C).

In a medium bowl, cream together butter and white sugar until smooth. Mix in 1/2 teaspoon almond extract. Mix in flour until dough comes together. Roll dough into 1 1/2 inch balls, and place on ungreased cookie sheets. Make a small hole in the center of each ball, using your thumb and finger, and fill the hole with preserves.

Bake for 14 to 18 minutes in preheated oven, or until lightly browned. Let cool 1 minute on the cookie sheet.

In a medium bowl, mix together the confectioners' sugar, 3/4 teaspoon almond extract, and milk until smooth. Drizzle lightly over warm cookies.

AMOUNT PER SERVING: CALORIES: 104   TOTAL FAT: 5.2 g   CHOLESTEROL: 14 mg   SODIUM: 52 mg   TOTAL CARBS: 13.7 g
DIETARY FIBER: 0.2 g   PROTEIN: 0.8 g

AS SHOWN IN THE PICTURE

Chocolate Peanut Butter Bars

Submitted by: JUSTINE

PREP TIME: 20 MINUTES
READY IN: 25 MINUTES
SERVINGS: 24

2 1/2 cups graham cracker crumbs
1 cup peanut butter
1 cup butter, melted
2 cups semisweet chocolate chips
2 3/4 cups confectioners' sugar

In a medium bowl, stir together graham cracker crumbs, confectioners' sugar, peanut butter and melted butter. Press firmly into the bottom of a 9x13 inch pan. Melt chocolate chips over a double boiler or in the microwave, stirring occasionally. Spread melted chocolate over the crumb crust. Chill for about 5 minutes, then cut into bars before the chocolate is completely set, then chill until ready to serve.

Very easy to make if you have a food processor. The whole thing came together in under 10 minutes. Delicious! Very, very rich!

—MOM130

AMOUNT PER SERVING: CALORIES: 289 TOTAL FAT: 18.3 g CHOLESTEROL: 21 mg SODIUM: 183 mg
TOTAL CARBS: 31.3 g DIETARY FIBER: 17 g PROTEIN: 4 g

Best Brownies

Submitted by: ANGIE

PREP TIME: 25 MINUTES
COOK TIME: 35 MINUTES
READY IN: 1 HOUR
SERVINGS: 16

1/2 cup butter
1 cup white sugar
2 eggs
1 teaspoon vanilla extract
1/3 cup unsweetened cocoa powder
1/2 cup all-purpose flour
1/4 teaspoon salt
1/4 teaspoon baking powder
3 tablespoons butter, softened
3 tablespoons unsweetened cocoa powder
1 tablespoon honey
1 teaspoon vanilla extract
1 cup confectioners' sugar

Preheat oven to 350°F (175°C). Grease and flour an 8 inch square pan.

In a large saucepan, melt 1/2 cup butter. Remove from heat, and stir in sugar, eggs, and 1 teaspoon vanilla. Beat in 1/3 cup cocoa, 1/2 cup flour, salt, and baking powder. Spread batter into prepared pan.

Bake in preheated oven for 25 to 30 minutes. Do not overcook.

To Make Frosting: Combine 3 tablespoons butter, 3 tablespoons cocoa, 1 tablespoon honey, 1 teaspoon vanilla, and 1 cup confectioners' sugar. Frost brownies while they are still warm.

AMOUNT PER SERVING: CALORIES: 183 TOTAL FAT: 9 g CHOLESTEROL: 48 mg SODIUM: 133 mg TOTAL CARBS: 25.7 g
DIETARY FIBER: 1 g PROTEIN: 1.8 g

Crispy Rice Candy

Submitted by: **PATTY**

PREP TIME: 15 MINUTES
READY IN: 2 HOURS 15 MINUTES
SERVINGS: 84

2 cups crispy rice cereal
2 cups dry roasted peanuts
2 cups miniature marshmallows
1 cup crunchy peanut butter
2 pounds white chocolate, chopped

In a large bowl, combine cereal, peanuts, marshmallows and peanut butter. Stir until evenly mixed.

In a microwave-safe bowl, or in a double boiler, cook chocolate until melted. Stir occasionally until chocolate is smooth. Stir chocolate into cereal mixture. Mixture will be slightly runny.

Drop by tablespoons onto waxed paper. Let set until firm, 2 hours. Store in an airtight container.

Very sweet, but kind of addictive.... I used pretzels instead of peanuts, and the pretzels were really good in it.

—JULIANA

AMOUNT PER SERVING: CALORIES: 104   TOTAL FAT: 67 g   CHOLESTEROL: 2 mg   SODIUM: 31 mg   TOTAL CARBS: 9.6 g
DIETARY FIBER: 0.5 g   PROTEIN: 23 g

Peanut Butter Balls

Submitted by: **NANCY PUIG**

PREP TIME: 20 MINUTES
COOK TIME: 10 MINUTES
READY IN: 1 HOUR 20 MINUTES
SERVINGS: 24

2 cups creamy peanut butter
1/2 cup butter
4 cups confectioners' sugar
3 cups crisp rice cereal
2 cups semisweet chocolate chips

Melt peanut butter and butter in saucepan, over low heat. In large bowl, mix crispy rice cereal and confectioners' sugar well. Pour melted peanut butter and butter over cereal and sugar and blend together thoroughly.

Form into 1 inch or smaller balls, spread on cookie sheets, chill till firm in refrigerator (over night is okay).

Melt chocolate in double boiler and keep melted while working with balls. A teaspoon is best to use in dipping the balls in chocolate. Dip good and place on cookie sheet. As you dip them place them back on cookie sheet and keep chilled till firm.

AMOUNT PER SERVING: CALORIES: 320   TOTAL FAT: 19 g   CHOLESTEROL: 10 mg   SODIUM: 167 mg   TOTAL CARBS: 36 g
DIETARY FIBER: 21 g   PROTEIN: 63 g

Raspberry Truffle Fudge

Submitted by: **LEEZA**

PREP TIME: 10 MINUTES
COOK IN: 10 MINUTES
READY IN: 1 HOUR 20 MINUTES
SERVINGS: 40

3 cups semi-sweet chocolate chips
1 (14 ounce) can sweetened condensed milk
1 1/2 teaspoons vanilla extract
Salt to taste
1/4 cup heavy cream
1/4 cup raspberry flavored liqueur
2 cups semi-sweet chocolate chips

Spray a 9x9 inch pan with non-stick cooking spray, and line with wax paper.

In a microwave-safe bowl, combine 3 cups chocolate chips and sweetened condensed milk. Heat in microwave until chocolate melts, stirring occasionally. Be careful not to let it scorch. Stir in the vanilla and salt. Spread into pan, and cool to room temperature.

In a microwave-safe bowl, combine cream, liqueur, and 2 cups chocolate chips. Heat in microwave until the chocolate melts; stir until smooth. Cool to lukewarm, then pour over the fudge layer. Refrigerate until both layers are completely set, about 1 hour. Cut into 1 inch pieces.

AMOUNT PER SERVING: CALORIES: 149   TOTAL FAT: 7.5 g   CHOLESTEROL: 5 mg   SODIUM: 13 mg   TOTAL CARBS: 19.7 g   DIETARY FIBER: 1.1 g   PROTEIN: 2.3 g

World's Best Peanut Butter Fudge

Submitted by: **DEBBY**

PREP TIME: 5 MINUTES
COOK TIME: 20 MINUTES
READY IN: 1 HOUR 25 MINUTES
SERVINGS: 60

4 cups white sugar
1 cup milk
1/2 cup butter
1 (7 ounce) jar marshmallow creme
12 ounces peanut butter
2/3 cup all-purpose flour

Grease a 9x13 inch baking dish, set aside.

In a saucepan, combine sugar, milk, and butter. Bring to a boil, and cook 5 minutes. Remove from the heat. Stir in the marshmallow creme and peanut butter. Gradually stir in the flour. Spread into the prepared pan, and let cool.

This was wonderful!! By far the most popular fudge I made this holiday season. Next time I'm going to drizzle a little chocolate on the top and it will taste just like Reese's Pieces!

—**JENNIFER**

AMOUNT PER SERVING: CALORIES: 116   TOTAL FAT: 4.5 g   CHOLESTEROL: 4 mg   SODIUM: 46 mg   TOTAL CARBS: 18.2 g   DIETARY FIBER: 0.4 g   PROTEIN: 1.7 g

AS SHOWN IN THE PICTURE

Candy Bar Fudge

Submitted by: **PATTY STOCKTON**

PREP TIME: 20 MINUTES
COOK IN: 10 MINUTES
READY IN: 2 HOURS 30 MINUTES
SERVINGS: 32

1/2 cup butter
1/3 cup unsweetened cocoa powder
1/4 cup packed brown sugar
1/4 cup milk
3 1/2 cups confectioners' sugar
1 teaspoon vanilla extract
30 individually wrapped caramels, unwrapped
1 tablespoon water
2 cups salted peanuts
1/2 cup semisweet chocolate chips
1/2 cup milk chocolate chips

Grease an 8x8 inch square baking pan

In a microwave-safe bowl, combine butter, cocoa powder, brown sugar and milk. Microwave until mixture boils. Stir in confectioners' sugar and vanilla extract. Pour into prepared pan.

In a microwave-safe bowl, microwave caramels and water until caramels melt. Stir in peanuts. Spread mixture over chocolate layer.

In a small microwave-safe bowl, combine semisweet and milk chocolate chips; microwave until melted. Spread over caramel layer. Chill for 2 hours, or until firm.

AMOUNT PER SERVING: CALORIES: 204 TOTAL FAT: 9.9 g CHOLESTEROL: 9 mg SODIUM: 131 mg
TOTAL CARBS: 28.5 g DIETARY FIBER: 1.3 g PROTEIN: 3.2 g

Lemon Square Bars

Submitted by: **RALPH**

PREP TIME: 20 MINUTES
COOK IN: 50 MINUTES
READY IN: 1 HOUR 10 MINUTES
SERVINGS: 24

2 cups sifted all-purpose flour
1 cup confectioners' sugar
1 cup butter, melted
4 eggs
2 cups white sugar
1 teaspoon baking powder
1/4 cup all-purpose flour
5/8 cup lemon juice

Preheat oven to 350°F (175°C). Grease a 9x13 inch pan.

In a medium bowl, stir together 2 cups flour and confectioners' sugar. Blend in the melted butter. Press into the bottom of the prepared pan.

Bake in the preheated oven for 15 minutes, or until golden. In a large bowl, beat eggs until light. Combine the sugar, baking powder and 1/4 cup of flour so there will be no flour lumps. Stir the sugar mixture into the eggs. Finally, stir in the lemon juice. Pour over the prepared crust and return to the oven.

Bake for an additional 30 minutes or until bars are set. Allow to cool completely before cutting into bars.

AMOUNT PER SERVING: CALORIES: 209 TOTAL FAT: 8.6 g CHOLESTEROL: 56 mg SODIUM: 99 mg
TOTAL CARBS: 31.2 g DIETARY FIBER: 0.3 g PROTEIN: 2.4 g

Tiger Butter

Submitted by: ANN

PREP TIME: 1 MINUTE
COOK TIME: 3 MINUTES
READY IN: 30 MINUTES
SERVINGS: 12

1 pound white chocolate, chopped
1/4 cup semisweet chocolate chips
1/3 cup crunchy peanut butter
1/2 cup crispy rice cereal

Line a 9x9 inch dish with waxed paper.

Combine white chocolate, chocolate chips and peanut butter in a 2 quart microwave safe dish and microwave on low one minute. Stir until smooth. Stir in the rice cereal and spread into prepared pan. Let cool completely before cutting into squares.

Awesome & easy. Word to the wise: Pipe it into mini paper cups so you don't have to cut this stuff. It's pretty hard to cut into nice little pieces.

—JENYGYRL

AMOUNT PER SERVING: CALORIES: 267 TOTAL FAT: 16.7 g CHOLESTEROL: 8 mg SODIUM: 67 mg TOTAL CARBS: 27.2 g
DIETARY FIBER: 0.7 g PROTEIN: 4.1 g

German Chocolate Fudge

Submitted by: CATHY

PREP TIME: 15 MINUTES
COOK TIME: 6 MINUTES
READY IN: 2 HOURS 21 MINUTES
SERVINGS: 80

2 cups semisweet chocolate chips
12 (1 ounce) squares German sweet chocolate
1 (7 ounce) jar marshmallow creme
4 1/2 cups white sugar
2 tablespoons butter
1 (12 fluid ounce) can evaporated milk
1/8 teaspoon salt
2 cups chopped pecans

Combine chocolate chips, German sweet chocolate and marshmallow creme in large bowl.

Combine sugar, butter, evaporated milk and salt in heavy skillet. Bring to a boil over medium heat. Cook for 6 minutes, stirring constantly.

Pour hot syrup over chocolate mixture. Stir with wooden spoon until smooth. Stir in pecans.

Spread into buttered 10x15 inch pan. Let stand until firm; cut into squares.

This recipe is fabulous! I don't think I've ever received so many compliments on anything I've made. It was so easy, and it turned out perfectly. I followed the recipe exactly.

—KELLEY JO

AMOUNT PER SERVING: CALORIES: 135 TOTAL FAT: 5.9 g CHOLESTEROL: 2 mg SODIUM: 13 mg TOTAL CARBS: 20.7 g
DIETARY FIBER: 0.6 g PROTEIN: 1 g

Butternut Kisses

Submitted by: **CINDY CARNES**

PREP TIME: 20 MINUTES
COOK IN: 10 MINUTES
READY IN: 30 MINUTES
SERVINGS: 30 COOKIES

1 cup butter, softened
1 cup white sugar
2 eggs, beaten
2 tablespoons vanilla extract
2 1/2 cups all-purpose flour
1/2 teaspoon baking soda
1/4 teaspoon salt
1 cup ground walnuts
60 milk chocolate candy kisses, unwrapped

Preheat oven to 350°F (175°C).

Cream together the butter, sugar, eggs and vanilla.

Add the flour, baking soda and salt; mix well. Shape into 1 inch balls and roll in ground nuts.

Place on ungreased baking sheet and bake for 10 minutes or until set. Press kiss in center of each cookie. Cool on wire rack.

AMOUNT PER SERVING: CALORIES: 191 TOTAL FAT: 11.2 g CHOLESTEROL: 33 mg SODIUM: 115 mg
TOTAL CARBS: 20.7 g DIETARY FIBER: 0.9 g PROTEIN: 2.6 g

Best Toffee Ever - Super Easy

Submitted by: **FUNKYSEAMONKEY**

PREP TIME: 5 MINUTES
COOK TIME: 15 MINUTES
READY IN: 1 HOUR 20 MINUTES
SERVINGS: 32

2 cups butter
2 cups white sugar
1/4 teaspoon salt
2 cups semisweet chocolate chips
1 cup finely chopped almonds

In a large heavy bottomed saucepan, combine the butter, sugar and salt. Cook over medium heat, stirring until the butter is melted. Allow to come to a boil, and cook until the mixture becomes a dark amber color, and the temperature has reached 285°F (137°C). Stir occasionally.

While the toffee is cooking, cover a large baking sheet with aluminum foil or parchment paper.

As soon as the toffee reaches the proper temperature, pour it out onto the prepared baking sheet. Sprinkle the chocolate over the top, and let it set for a minute or two to soften. Spread the chocolate into a thin even layer once it is melted. Sprinkle the nuts over the chocolate, and press in slightly. Putting a plastic bag over your hand will minimize the mess.

Place the toffee in the refrigerator to chill until set. Break into pieces, and store in an airtight container.

AMOUNT PER SERVING: CALORIES: 22.6 TOTAL FAT: 16.9 g CHOLESTEROL: 3.1 mg SODIUM: 137 mg
TOTAL CARBS: 20 g DIETARY FIBER: 1.1 g PROTEIN: 1.5 g

AS SHOWN IN THE PICTURE

Elisa's Famous Fudge

Submitted by: **ELISA**

PREP TIME: 20 MINUTES
COOK IN: 10 MINUTES
READY IN: 2 HOURS 30 MINUTES
SERVINGS: 48

1 1/2 cups white sugar
2/3 cup evaporated milk
2 tablespoons butter
1/4 teaspoon salt
1 (7 ounce) jar marshmallow creme
3/4 cup semisweet chocolate chips
3/4 cup butterscotch chips
1/2 cup chopped pecans
1 teaspoon vanilla extract

Line an 8-inch square dish with foil.

In a heavy saucepan over medium heat, combine sugar, evaporated milk, butter and salt. Bring to a boil and let roll 5 minutes. Remove from heat and stir in marshmallow creme, chocolate chips, butterscotch chips, pecans and vanilla. Continue stirring until marshmallow creme is melted and all ingredients are thoroughly combined. Pour into prepared dish.

Refrigerate for 2 hours, until firm. Lift from dish, remove foil, and cut into pieces.

I substituted peanut butter chips for the chocolate chips & peanuts for the pecans. Delicious! Very smooth and rich!!

— **DEBBB**

AMOUNT PER SERVING: CALORIES: 83   TOTAL FAT: 3.2 g   CHOLESTEROL: 2 mg   SODIUM: 26 mg   TOTAL CARBS: 13.4 g
DIETARY FIBER: 0.3 g   PROTEIN: 0.5 g

Mom's Best Peanut Brittle

Submitted by: **AMANDA**

PREP TIME: 10 MINUTES
COOK TIME: VARIES
READY IN: VARIES
SERVINGS: 16

1 cup white sugar
1/2 cup light corn syrup
1/4 teaspoon salt
1/4 cup water
1 cup peanuts
2 tablespoons butter, softened
1 teaspoon baking soda

Grease a large cookie sheet. Set aside.
In a heavy 2 quart saucepan, over medium heat, bring to a boil, sugar, corn syrup, salt, and water. Stir until sugar is dissolved. Stir in peanuts. Set candy thermometer in place and continue cooking. Stir frequently until temperature reaches 300°F (120°C), or until a small amount of mixture dropped into very cold water separates into hard and brittle threads.

Remove from heat; immediately stir in butter or margarine and baking soda; pour at once onto cookie sheet. With 2 forks, lift and pull peanut mixture into rectangle about 14x12 inches; cool. Snap candy into pieces.

Buttery and beautiful. Cashews ok to use too. Great recipe.

— **CATERERJ**

AMOUNT PER SERVING: CALORIES: 143   TOTAL FAT: 6 g   CHOLESTEROL: 4 mg   SODIUM: 143 mg   TOTAL CARBS: 22.3 g
DIETARY FIBER: 0.7 g   PROTEIN: 2.2 g

AS SHOWN IN THE PICTURE

Peppermint Brittle

Submitted by: BRENDA MOORE

PREP TIME: 5 MINUTES
COOK IN: 5 MINUTES
READY IN: 1 HOUR 10 MINUTES
SERVINGS: 36

2 pounds white chocolate

30 small peppermint candy canes

I have been making this recipe during the Holiday season for years! I call it "Holiday Cheer" and once you taste it, you'll understand why! It goes perfect with a cup of home-made cocoa.
—JULES214

Line a large jellyroll pan with heavy-duty foil.

Place white chocolate in a microwave-safe bowl. Heat in microwave on medium setting for 5 to 6 minutes. Stir occasionally, until chocolate is melted and smooth.

Place candy canes in a plastic bag, or between two pieces of waxed paper. Using a mallet or rolling pin, break the candy canes into chunks. Stir peppermint into melted white chocolate. Spread evenly in pan, and chill until set, about 1 hour. Break into pieces by slamming pan on counter.

AMOUNT PER SERVING: CALORIES: 159 TOTAL FAT: 8.9 g CHOLESTEROL: 5 mg SODIUM: 28 mg TOTAL CARBS: 18.3 g DIETARY FIBER: 0 g PROTEIN: 1.8 g

White Chocolate Party Mix

Submitted by: ALTHEA

PREP TIME: 15 MINUTES
COOK IN: 1 HOUR
READY IN: 1 HOUR 15 MINUTES
SERVINGS: 28

1 pound white chocolate

3 cups crispy rice cereal squares

3 cups crispy corn cereal squares

3 cups toasted oat cereal

2 cups thin pretzel sticks

2 cups peanuts

1 (12 ounce) package mini candy-coated chocolate pieces

In the top of a double boiler over simmering water, slowly melt the white chocolate.

In a large bowl, combine cereals, pretzels, peanuts and slowly pour the chocolate over the cereal mixture and stir to evenly coat.

Spread the mixture onto wax paper and cool. Break into small pieces, store in an air-tight container and refrigerate to keep fresh.

I make this and order special color M&M's for the occasion. This is excellent.

—JRBETH

AMOUNT PER SERVING: CALORIES: 262 TOTAL FAT: 14.2 g CHOLESTEROL: 4 mg SODIUM: 191 mg TOTAL CARBS: 29.5 g DIETARY FIBER: 2.1 g PROTEIN: 5.2 g

Caramel Popcorn

Submitted by: **BRIAN**

PREP TIME: 30 MINUTES
COOK TIME: 1 HOUR
READY IN: 1 HOUR 30 MINUTES
SERVINGS: 20

1 cup butter
2 cups brown sugar
1/2 cup corn syrup
1 teaspoon salt
1/2 teaspoon baking soda
1 teaspoon vanilla extract
5 quarts popped popcorn

To make cleanup a breeze, simply put some hot water in the pans and put them back in the warm oven. Come back about an hour later, and the pans are practically clean.
—**ATTTT**

Preheat oven to 250°F (95°C). Place popcorn in a very large bowl.

In a medium saucepan over medium heat, melt butter. Stir in brown sugar, corn syrup and salt. Bring to a boil, stirring constantly. Boil without stirring 4 minutes. Remove from heat and stir in soda and vanilla. Pour in a thin stream over popcorn, stirring to coat.

Place in two large shallow baking dishes and bake in preheated oven, stirring every 15 minutes, for 1 hour. Remove from oven and let cool completely before breaking into pieces.

AMOUNT PER SERVING: CALORIES: 243   TOTAL FAT: 12.3 g   CHOLESTEROL: 25 mg   SODIUM: 357 mg
TOTAL CARBS: 34 g   DIETARY FIBER: 1.1 g   PROTEIN: 1.1 g

AS SHOWN IN THE PICTURE

Caramel Apples

Submitted by: **SUZIE**

PREP TIME: 8 MINUTES
COOK IN: 2 MINUTES
READY IN: 25 MINUTES
SERVINGS: 6

6 apples
1 (14 ounce) package individually wrapped caramels, unwrapped
2 tablespoons milk

Remove the stem from each apple and press a craft stick into the top. Butter a baking sheet.

Place caramels and milk in a microwave safe bowl, and microwave 2 minutes, stirring once. Allow to cool briefly.

Roll each apple quickly in caramel sauce until well coated. Place on prepared sheet to set.

I melt the caramels in a 4 C Pyrex cup, so that the apple fits down in the cup. This is the easiest way to dip that I have found (no wasted caramel). I give each child a square of wax paper and have them butter the square. Then with adult help (the caramel needs to cool a little) I let them decorate the apples from a selection of toppings; candy corn, M&M's, Halloween sprinkles, cookie crumbs and any other small candies.
—**DANA**

AMOUNT PER SERVING: CALORIES: 334   TOTAL FAT: 5.9 g   CHOLESTEROL: 5 mg   SODIUM: 163 mg
TOTAL CARBS: 71.6 g   DIETARY FIBER: 4.5 g   PROTEIN: 3.4 g

AS SHOWN IN THE PICTURE

Strawberry Trifle

Submitted by: **T'S MOM**

PREP TIME: 15 MINUTES
COOK IN: 25 MINUTES
READY IN: 4 HOURS 40 MINUTES
SERVINGS: 18

1 (5 ounce) package instant
vanilla pudding mix
3 cups cold milk
1 (9 inch) angel food cake, cut in cubes
4 bananas, sliced
1 (10 ounce) package frozen
strawberries, thawed
1 (12 ounce) container frozen
whipped topping, thawed

Prepare pudding with milk according to package directions. In a trifle bowl or other glass serving dish, layer half the cake pieces, half the pudding, half the bananas, half the strawberries and half the whipped topping. Repeat layers. Cover and chill in refrigerator 4 hours before serving.

This was very good and made a beautiful dessert. I used fresh strawberries and blueberries since they are in season, and I used pound cake instead of angel food cake. Great dessert for the summer!

—SFORD1024

AMOUNT PER SERVING: CALORIES: 162 TOTAL FAT: 4.3 g CHOLESTEROL: 4 mg SODIUM: 185 mg

TOTAL CARBS: 27 g DIETARY FIBER: 1.4 g PROTEIN: 3.1 g

Strawberries with Balsamic Vinegar

Submitted by: **HOOLIE**

PREP TIME: 10 MINUTES
READY IN: 1 HOUR 10 MINUTES
SERVINGS: 6

16 ounces fresh strawberries, hulled
and large berries cut in half
2 tablespoons balsamic vinegar
1/4 cup white sugar
1/4 teaspoon freshly ground black
pepper, or to taste

Place strawberries in a bowl. Drizzle vinegar over strawberries, and sprinkle with sugar. Stir gently to combine. Cover, and let sit at room temperature for at least 1 hour but not more than 4 hours. Just before serving, grind pepper over berries.

This was great over vanilla ice cream. I didn't expect the balsamic vinegar and pepper to taste so great.

—BOOG

AMOUNT PER SERVING: CALORIES: 58 TOTAL FAT: 0.3 g CHOLESTEROL: 0 mg SODIUM: 2 mg TOTAL CARBS: 14.4 g

DIETARY FIBER: 1.7 g PROTEIN: 0.5 g

AS SHOWN IN THE PICTURE

Old Fashioned Peach Cobbler

Submitted by: **ELETA**

PREP TIME: 30 MINUTES
COOK IN: 1 HOUR 10 MINUTES
READY IN: 2 HOURS 10 MINUTES
SERVINGS: 18

2 1/2 cups all-purpose flour
3 tablespoons white sugar
1 teaspoon salt
1 cup shortening
1 egg
1/4 cup cold water
3 pounds fresh peaches, peeled, pitted, and sliced
1/4 cup lemon juice
3/4 cup orange juice
1/2 cup butter
2 cups white sugar
1/2 teaspoon ground nutmeg
1 teaspoon ground cinnamon
1 tablespoon cornstarch
1 tablespoon white sugar
1 tablespoon butter, melted

I can eat this whole cobbler! I have made this three times, and always use frozen peaches, however, I let them cook on low along with the butter, juices, sugar and spices for an hour
—AMY

In a medium bowl, sift together the flour, 3 tablespoons sugar, and salt. Work in the shortening with a pastry blender until the mixture resembles coarse crumbs. In a small bowl, whisk together the egg and cold water. Sprinkle over flour mixture, and work with hands to form dough into a ball. Chill 30 minutes.

Preheat oven to 350°F (175°C). Roll out half of dough to 1/8 inch thickness. Place in a 9x13 inch baking dish, covering bottom and halfway up sides. Bake for 20 minutes, or until golden brown.

In a large saucepan, mix the peaches, lemon juice, and orange juice. Add 1/2 cup butter, and cook over medium-low heat until butter is melted. In a mixing bowl, stir together 2 cups sugar, nutmeg, cinnamon, and cornstarch; mix into peach mixture. Remove from heat, and pour into baked crust.

Roll remaining dough to a thickness of 1/4 inch. Cut into half-inch-wide strips. Weave strips into a lattice over peaches. Sprinkle with 1 tablespoon sugar, and drizzle with 1 tablespoon melted butter.

Bake in preheated oven for 35 to 40 minutes, or until top crust is golden brown.

This is so delicious! I have never made cobbler like this before, but this is the only way I will make it from now on. I used only 1/4 cup orange juice, cut the sugar down to 1 c. and used 3 T. cornstarch, and only used 1/4 tsp nutmeg. I ended up with a very velvety filling with excellent peach flavor! Yummy!

—TERESA S

Great recipe!! Flavor is exceptional! Despite my other culinary skills, pie crust is not something I make well and this crust was light and delicious. This is a definite keeper.

—VJD

AMOUNT PER SERVING: CALORIES: 338   TOTAL FAT: 17.6 g   CHOLESTEROL: 27 mg   SODIUM: 194 mg

TOTAL CARBS: 43.7 g   DIETARY FIBER: 0.6 g   PROTEIN: 2.3 g

Zucchini Apple Bread

Submitted by: ROSE PUTMAN

PREP TIME: 20 MINUTES
COOK IN: 1 HOUR
READY IN: 1 HOUR 20 MINUTES
SERVINGS: 24

4 eggs
1 cup white sugar
1 cup brown sugar
1/2 cup vegetable oil
1 teaspoon vanilla extract
3 1/2 cups all-purpose flour
1 1/2 teaspoons baking soda
1/2 teaspoon salt
2 teaspoons ground cinnamon
1/2 cup chopped walnuts
2 cups peeled, chopped zucchini
1 cup chopped, peeled apple

Preheat oven to 350°F (175°C). Grease 2 - 9x5 inch loaf pans.

In a large bowl, combine eggs, white sugar, brown sugar, oil and vanilla until well blended. In a separate bowl, combine flour, baking soda, salt and cinnamon. Stir flour mixture into egg mixture. Fold in walnuts, zucchini and apple. Pour into prepared pans.

Bake 1 hour, or until top springs back when touched lightly in center. Let cool in pans 10 minutes before removing to wire rack to cool completely.

AMOUNT PER SERVING: CALORIES: 208 TOTAL FAT: 7.2 g CHOLESTEROL: 35 mg SODIUM: 142 mg
TOTAL CARBS: 32.9 g DIETARY FIBER: 1 g PROTEIN: 3.4 g

Rum Raisin Bread

Submitted by: JILL M.

PREP TIME: 15 MINUTES
COOK TIME: 40 MINUTES
READY IN: 2 HOURS 55 MINUTES
SERVINGS: 10

2 tablespoons rum
1/2 cup raisins
1/2 cup water
2 cups bread flour
1 tablespoon dry milk powder
2 teaspoons brown sugar
1 teaspoon salt
2 teaspoons butter
2 tablespoons heavy whipping cream
1/2 teaspoon rum flavored extract
1 egg
1 teaspoon olive oil
1 1/2 teaspoons active dry yeast

Use your bread machine for this easy and tasty bread. In a small bowl, pour rum over raisins. Let stand for 30 minutes and drain.

Place ingredients in pan in the order recommended by the manufacturer. Use the regular setting for a 1 pound loaf.

If your machine has a fruit setting, add the raisins at the signal, or about 5 minutes before the kneading cycle has finished.

This was a great bread. It was very moist but not too sweet. I substituted currents for the raisins, they worked very well.

—ISADORE

AMOUNT PER SERVING: CALORIES: 165 TOTAL FAT: 3.4 g CHOLESTEROL: 28 mg SODIUM: 255 mg
TOTAL CARBS: 27.3 g DIETARY FIBER: 1.1 g PROTEIN: 4.7 g

Banana Nut Bread

Submitted by: **GWYNNE COMSTOCK**

PREP TIME: 10 MINUTES
COOK IN: 1 HOUR
READY IN: 1 HOUR 10 MINUTES
SERVINGS: 24

2 1/2 cups white sugar
1 cup shortening
3 eggs
1 1/2 cups mashed bananas
3 cups all-purpose flour
1 1/4 cups buttermilk
1 1/2 teaspoons baking soda
1 1/2 teaspoons baking powder
1 teaspoon vanilla extract
1/2 cup chopped walnuts

Preheat oven to 350°F (175°C).

Cream together shortening and sugar. Add eggs one at a time, beating well after each addition. Mix in bananas, buttermilk, and vanilla. Mix in flour, baking powder, and soda. Stir in nuts if desired. Pour batter into two greased 9x5 inch pans.

Bake for 50 to 60 minutes in the preheated oven, or until a toothpick inserted into the center of the loaf comes out clean.

This recipe is great. I added more bananas and 1/2 cup more walnuts. Be sure to cut the slices thick, it does tend to 'break' easily.

—SKYBLUE

AMOUNT PER SERVING: CALORIES: 257   TOTAL FAT: 11.1 g   CHOLESTEROL: 27 mg   SODIUM: 131 mg
TOTAL CARBS. 37.2 g   DIETARY FIBER. 0.9 g   PROTEIN. 3.3 g

Cranberry Nut Bread

Submitted by: **KARIN CHRISTIAN**

PREP TIME: 15 MINUTES
COOK TIME: 50 MINUTES
READY IN: 1 HOUR 5 MINUTES
SERVINGS: 12

2 cups all-purpose flour
3/4 cup white sugar
3/4 teaspoon salt
1 1/2 teaspoons baking powder
1/2 teaspoon baking soda
1 cup chopped cranberries
1/2 cup chopped nuts
1 tablespoon orange zest
1 egg
2 tablespoons vegetable oil
3/4 cup orange juice

Preheat oven to 350°F (175°C). Grease one 9x5 inch loaf pan.

Combine the flour, sugar, salt, baking powder and baking soda. Add the cranberries and chopped nuts, stir to coat with flour.

Combine the egg, oil, orange juice and grated orange peel. Add the egg mixture to the flour mixture and stir until just combined. Spoon the batter into the prepared pan.

Bake at 350°F (175°C) for 50 minutes or until a toothpick comes out clean. Let bread sit for 10 minutes and then remove from the pan and place on a cooling rack. Let cool completely before slicing.

AMOUNT PER SERVING: CALORIES: 196   TOTAL FAT: 6.2 g   CHOLESTEROL: 18 mg   SODIUM: 265 mg
TOTAL CARBS. 32.2 g   DIETARY FIBER: 1.4 g   PROTEIN: 3.6 g

AS SHOWN IN THE PICTURE

Pumpkin Gingerbread

Submitted by: TERRI

PREP TIME: 15 MINUTES
COOK IN: 45 MINUTES
READY IN: 1 HOUR
SERVINGS: 24

3 cups sugar
1 cup vegetable oil
4 eggs
2/3 cup water
1 (15 ounce) can pumpkin puree
2 teaspoons ground ginger
1 teaspoon ground allspice
1 teaspoon ground cinnamon
1 teaspoon ground cloves
3 1/2 cups all-purpose flour
2 teaspoons baking soda
1 1/2 teaspoons salt
1/2 teaspoon baking powder

Preheat oven to 350°F (175°C). Lightly grease two 9x5 inch loaf pans.

In a large mixing, combine sugar, oil and eggs; beat until smooth. Add water and beat until well blended. Stir in pumpkin, ginger, allspice and cinnamon.

In medium bowl, combine flour, soda, salt, and baking powder. Add dry ingredients to pumpkin mixture and blend just until all ingredients are mixed. Divide batter between prepared pans.

Bake in preheated oven until toothpick comes out clean, about 1 hour.

AMOUNT PER SERVING: CALORIES: 263 TOTAL FAT: 10.2 g CHOLESTEROL: 35 mg SODIUM: 310 mg
TOTAL CARBS: 40.7 g DIETARY FIBER: 1.1 g PROTEIN: 3.1 g

Lemon Poppy Seed Bread

Submitted by: MARGIE

PREP TIME: 20 MINUTES
COOK TIME: 1 HOUR
READY IN: 1 HOUR 20 MINUTES
SERVINGS: 20

3 cups all-purpose flour
1 1/2 teaspoons salt
1 1/2 teaspoons baking powder
1 1/2 tablespoons poppy seeds
2 1/2 cups white sugar
1 1/8 cups vegetable oil
3 eggs
1 1/2 cups milk
1 1/2 teaspoons vanilla extract
1 1/2 teaspoons lemon extract
1/4 cup orange juice
3/4 cup white sugar
1/2 teaspoon lemon extract

Preheat oven to 350°F (175°C). Grease three 8x4 inch bread pans.

In a large mixing bowl, stir together the flour, salt, baking powder, poppy seeds and 2 1/2 cups white sugar. Add the eggs, milk, oil, vanilla and lemon extract; mix until smooth, about 1 minute. Pour batter evenly into the prepared pans.

Bake at 350°F (175°C) for 50 to 55 minutes, or until a toothpick inserted into the center of the loaves comes out clean. Cool loaves in the pans for 10 minutes before removing to a wire rack.

Combine orange juice with remaining 3/4 cup sugar and desired flavor of extract; stir well. Pour this mixture over the loaf while it is still hot. Allow loaf to cool completely before serving.

AMOUNT PER SERVING: CALORIES: 330 TOTAL FAT: 13.9 g CHOLESTEROL: 33 mg SODIUM: 230 mg
TOTAL CARBS: 48.4 g DIETARY FIBER: 0.6 g PROTEIN: 3.6 g

AS SHOWN IN THE PICTURE

Butterscotch Bread Pudding

Submitted by: MARGARET BURGER

PREP TIME: 10 MINUTES
COOK IN: 1 HOUR
READY IN: 1 HOUR 10 MINUTES
SERVINGS: 8

1 (10.75 ounce) loaf day-old
bread, torn into small pieces
4 cups milk
2 cups brown sugar
1/2 cup butter, melted
3 eggs, beaten
2 teaspoons vanilla extract
1 cup butterscotch chips

Preheat oven to 350°F (175 °C). Butter a 9x13 inch
baking dish.

In a large bowl, combine bread, milk, sugar, butter,
eggs, vanilla and butterscotch chips; mixture should
be the consistency of oatmeal. Pour into prepared pan.

Bake in preheated oven 1 hour, until nearly set.
(It should have a "thigh wiggle" or wiggle as much
as a well endowed thigh.) Serve warm or cold.

This is the best bread pudding I have ever tasted.
Easy to make and turns out perfect every time.
—LISA1973

AMOUNT PER SERVING: CALORIES: 622 TOTAL FAT: 23.1 g CHOLESTEROL: 121 mg SODIUM: 448 mg
TOTAL CARBS: 92 g DIETARY FIBER: 0.9 g PROTEIN: 9.6 g

Creamy Rice Pudding

Submitted by: ERICA G.

PREP TIME: 25 MINUTES
COOK TIME: 20 MINUTES
READY IN: 45 MINUTES
SERVINGS: 4

3/4 cup uncooked white rice
2 cups milk, divided
1/3 cup white sugar
1/4 teaspoon salt
1 egg, beaten
2/3 cup golden raisins
1 tablespoon butter
1/2 teaspoon vanilla extract

In a medium saucepan, bring 1 1/2 cups water to a
boil. Add rice and stir. Reduce heat, cover and simmer
for 20 minutes.

In another saucepan, combine 1 1/2 cups cooked rice,
1 1/2 cups milk, sugar and salt. Cook over medium heat
until thick and creamy, 15 to 20 minutes. Stir in
remaining 1/2 cup milk, beaten egg and raisins. Cook 2
minutes more, stirring constantly. Remove from heat, and
stir in butter and vanilla. Serve warm.

Absolutely perfect. I haven't had much success with
other recipes but the taste and consistency was just
right. Taste just like my grandmother's. I served it with
blueberry sauce on top.
—ENLOVEI7

AMOUNT PER SERVING: CALORIES: 367 TOTAL FAT: 6.8 g CHOLESTEROL: 71 mg SODIUM: 255 mg
TOTAL CARBS: 67.8 g DIETARY FIBER: 0.9 g PROTEIN: 8.9 g

Pineapple and Pistachio Pudding

Submitted by: **TANYA**

PREP TIME: 10 MINUTES
COOK IN: 30 MINUTES
READY IN: 40 MINUTES
SERVINGS: 6

1 (1 ounce) package instant sugar-free pistachio pudding mix

1 (8 ounce) container plain low-fat yogurt

1 (8 ounce) container vanilla low-fat yogurt

1 (8 ounce) can unsweetened crushed pineapple, undrained

1 cup frozen whipped topping, thawed

In a large bowl, combine pistachio pudding mix, plain yogurt, vanilla yogurt and crushed pineapple. Mix until smooth. Fold in whipped topping. Cover, and refrigerate until chilled

It's so easy to find the ingredients and to make – just have a mixer ready. I took it to a dinner party and it was a hit with everyone! I added a few ground pistachios, to it.

—ELENA32

AMOUNT PER SERVING: CALORIES: 132   TOTAL FAT: 4.2 g   CHOLESTEROL: 4 mg   SODIUM: 247 mg
TOTAL CARBS: 18.7 g   DIETARY FIBER: 0.6 g   PROTEIN: 4.3 g

Panna Cotta

Submitted by: **CHERYLA33**

PREP TIME: 5 MINUTES
COOK TIME: 10 MINUTES
READY IN: 4 HOURS 15 MINUTES
SERVINGS: 6

1/3 cup skim milk

1 (.25 ounce) envelope unflavored gelatin

2 1/2 cups heavy cream

1/2 cup white sugar

1 1/2 teaspoons vanilla extract

Pour milk into a small bowl, and stir in the gelatin powder. Set aside.

In a saucepan, stir together the heavy cream and sugar, and set over medium heat. Bring to a full boil, watching carefully, as the cream will quickly rise to the top of the pan. Pour the gelatin and milk into the cream, stirring until completely dissolved. Cook for one minute, stirring constantly. Remove from heat, stir in the vanilla and pour into six individual ramekin dishes.

Cool the ramekins uncovered at room temperature. When cool, cover with plastic wrap, and refrigerate for at least 4 hours, but preferably overnight before serving

AMOUNT PER SERVING: CALORIES: 418   TOTAL FAT: 36.7 g   CHOLESTEROL: 136 mg   SODIUM: 47 mg
TOTAL CARBS: 20.2 g   DIETARY FIBER: 0 g   PROTEIN: 3.5 g

Banana Pudding

Submitted by: **BARBARA**

PREP TIME: 20 MINUTES
READY IN: 40 MINUTES
SERVINGS: 12

**1 (14 ounce) can sweetened
condensed milk**
1 1/2 cups cold water
**1 (3.4 ounce) package instant
vanilla pudding mix**
2 cups heavy cream
3 bananas, sliced
1/2 cup lemon juice
36 vanilla wafers

In a medium bowl, stir together condensed milk and water. Beat in pudding mix until smooth. Chill in refrigerator 5 minutes.

In a separate bowl, whip cream until stiff peaks form. Fold whipped cream into chilled pudding mixture.

Dip sliced bananas in lemon juice. Shake off excess.

In a 2 1/2 quart serving bowl, spoon 1 cup pudding mixture. Top with one-third each of the wafers, bananas and remaining pudding. Repeat layers twice. Chill until serving.

AMOUNT PER SERVING: CALORIES: 386 TOTAL FAT: 21.2 g CHOLESTEROL: 65 mg SODIUM: 227 mg
TOTAL CARBS: 46.8 g DIETARY FIBER: 1.1 g PROTEIN: 4.5 g

Cherry Dump Pudding

Submitted by: **STEPHANIE AULD**

PREP TIME: 15 MINUTES
COOK TIME: 45 MINUTES
READY IN: 1 HOUR
SERVINGS: 12

2 cups all-purpose flour
1/2 teaspoon salt
2 teaspoons baking powder
1 cup white sugar
1/2 cup butter
1 cup milk
1 teaspoon vanilla extract
4 cups pitted sour cherries
1/2 cup white sugar
1 1/4 cups cherry juice

Preheat oven to 375°F (190°C). Grease a 10x10-inch baking dish.

In large bowl, combine flour, salt, baking powder and 1 cup sugar; stir. Add butter, milk and vanilla; beat with electric mixer for 2 minutes, or until smooth. Pour mixture into pan and cover evenly with cherries.

Heat cherry juice in microwave or in small saucepan, until just simmering. Sprinkle 1/2 cup of sugar over cherries, and pour hot cherry juice on top. Bake 40 to 45 minutes, or until pick inserted in center comes out clean.

This recipe was incredibly easy and delicious. We used a jar of pitted sour cherries, as fresh cherries were not in season.

—**KUNGFUKAREN**

AMOUNT PER SERVING: CALORIES: 294 TOTAL FAT: 8.4 g CHOLESTEROL: 22 mg SODIUM: 232 mg
TOTAL CARBS: 52.3 g DIETARY FIBER: 1.4 g PROTEIN: 3.4 g

AS SHOWN IN THE PICTURE

Totally Groovy Chocolate Fondue

Submitted by: STACI MONDELL

PREP TIME: 5 MINUTES
COOK IN: 10 MINUTES
READY IN: 15 MINUTES
SERVINGS: 6

2 cups milk chocolate chips
3 tablespoons heavy cream
2 tablespoons cherry brandy
1 tablespoon strong brewed coffee
1/8 teaspoon ground cinnamon

Combine chocolate, cream, brandy, coffee and cinnamon in a fondue pot over a low flame (or in a saucepan over low heat). Heat until melted, stirring occasionally. Serve at once.

All I can say is Mmmmmmmmmmmmmm!! This was great! I added coffee liqueur instead of the coffee, Baileys instead of Cherry brandy and a little more cream to help smooth it out. If you can't find milk chocolate chips (my grocery store was out) just buy a milk chocolate bar and chop it to make 2 cups. Angel food cake, strawberries and banana were our favorites for dipping!

—MELN31

AMOUNT PER SERVING: CALORIES: 317   TOTAL FAT: 18.6 g   CHOLESTEROL: 10 mg   SODIUM: 42 mg   TOTAL CARBS: 35.8 g   DIETARY FIBER: 0 g   PROTEIN: 4.1 g

---

Butterscotch Fondue

Submitted by: SHARON MENSING

PREP TIME: 5 MINUTES
COOK TIME: 15 MINUTES
READY IN: 20 MINUTES
SERVINGS: 8

1/2 cup packed brown sugar
1/3 cup light corn syrup
1/4 cup heavy whipping cream
2 tablespoons butter or margarine
1/2 teaspoon vanilla extract
Fresh fruit

In a small saucepan, combine the brown sugar, corn syrup, cream and butter. Bring to a boil over medium heat, stirring occasionally. Reduce heat to medium-low; cook for 5 minutes. Remove from heat; stir in vanilla. Transfer to a fondue pot and keep warm. Serve with fruit.

This was delicious and so easy to make. Terrific with apples.

—BRUNETTE

AMOUNT PER SERVING: CALORIES: 317   TOTAL FAT: 18.6 g   CHOLESTEROL: 10 mg   SODIUM: 42 mg   TOTAL CARBS: 35.8 g   DIETARY FIBER: 0 g   PROTEIN: 41 g

AS SHOWN IN THE PICTURE

Old Fashioned Coconut Cream Pie

Submitted by: **CAROL H.**

PREP TIME: 20 MINUTES
COOK IN: 30 MINUTES
READY IN: 4 HOURS 50 MINUTES
SERVINGS: 8

3 cups half-and-half
2 eggs
3/4 cup white sugar
1/2 cup all-purpose flour
1/4 teaspoon salt
1 cup flaked coconut, toasted
1 teaspoon vanilla extract
1 (9 inch) pie shell, baked
1 cup frozen whipped topping, thawed

In a medium saucepan, combine half-and-half, eggs, sugar, flour and salt. Bring to a boil over low heat, stirring constantly. Remove from heat, and stir in 3/4 cup of the coconut and the vanilla extract. Pour into pie shell and chill 2 to 4 hours, or until firm.

Top with whipped topping, and with remaining 1/4 cup of coconut.

Note: To toast coconut, spread it in an ungreased pan and bake in a 350 degree F (175 degrees C) oven for 5 to 7 minutes, or until golden brown, stirring occasionally.

AMOUNT PER SERVING: CALORIES: 425 TOTAL FAT: 23.9 g CHOLESTEROL: 87 mg SODIUM: 272 mg
TOTAL CARBS: 45.8 g DIETARY FIBER: 1 g PROTEIN: 68 g

Chocolate Mocha Pie

Submitted by: **CALI**

PREP TIME: 10 MINUTES
COOK TIME: 10 MINUTES
READY IN: 2 HOURS 10 MINUTES
SERVINGS: 8

1 (9 inch) prepared chocolate cookie crumb crust
1 (3.5 ounce) package non-instant chocolate pudding mix
2 1/2 cups milk
2 teaspoons instant coffee granules
2 tablespoons white sugar
1 (1.3 ounce) envelope whipped topping mix
1/2 teaspoon vanilla extract
1 (1.75 ounce) package chocolate Sprinkles (optional)

Prepare pie filling using the directions on the package, using 2 cups milk.

In a small bowl, combine 1 cup hot filling, instant coffee, and sugar. Stir to dissolve and blend. Chill

Cool remaining filling 5 minutes, stirring several times. Pour into crust, and chill.

Prepare whipped topping mix as directed on package, using remaining 1/2 cup milk and vanilla. Beat chilled cup of pudding until smooth, and then fold into whipped topping. Pile lightly over filling in crust, spreading evenly. Chill several hours before serving. Top with chocolate sprinkles if desired.

AMOUNT PER SERVING: CALORIES: 295 TOTAL FAT: 12.6 g CHOLESTEROL: 7 mg SODIUM: 270 mg
TOTAL CARBS: 41.4 g DIETARY FIBER: 0.6 g PROTEIN: 44 g

AS SHOWN IN THE PICTURE

Kentucky Pecan Pie

Submitted by: LAURIE NANNI

PREP TIME: 15 MINUTES
COOK IN: 1 HOUR
READY IN: 1 HOUR 15 MINUTES
SERVINGS: 8

1 cup white corn syrup
1 cup packed brown sugar
1/3 teaspoon salt
1/3 cup butter, melted
3 eggs
1 cup chopped pecans
1 recipe pastry for a 9 inch single crust pie

Combine syrup, sugar, salt, and melted butter or margarine. Slightly beat the eggs, and add to sugar mixture. Beat well, and pour into uncooked pie shell. Sprinkle pecans on top.

Bake at 350°F (175°C) for 50 to 60 minutes.

This makes a very good pecan pie! Nice and rich, the way pecan pie should be! I added a touch of vanilla, but otherwise made it per the recipe and it turned out great. Will definitely use this recipe again!

—AJDRAKESTER

AMOUNT PER SERVING: CALORIES: 531   TOTAL FAT: 27.7 g   CHOLESTEROL: 100 mg   SODIUM: 376 mg
TOTAL CARBS: 70.7 g   DIETARY FIBER: 2.3 g   PROTEIN: 5.2 g

Apple Maple Crumble Pie

Submitted by: HELENE

PREP TIME: 15 MINUTES
COOK TIME: 35 MINUTES
READY IN: 50 MINUTES
SERVINGS: 9

5 apples, peeled, cored and sliced
2/3 cup maple syrup
1/2 cup butter
1/2 cup brown sugar
3/4 cup all-purpose flour
1 pinch salt
3/4 cup rolled oats

Preheat oven to 375°F (190°C).

Place the apples in an 8x8 inch baking dish. Pour the maple syrup over the apples. In a bowl, cream together the butter and brown sugar. Stir in the flour, salt and oats. Sprinkle the oat mixture over the apples.

Bake in preheated oven 35 minutes, until golden and bubbly and apples are tender.

Excellent! I used 3 Granny Smith Apples and 2 Golden Delicious. The combination was perfect. The guests begged to take the leftovers.

——WHENSLEY

AMOUNT PER SERVING: CALORIES: 306   TOTAL FAT: 11.1 g   CHOLESTEROL: 28 mg   SODIUM: 155 mg
TOTAL CARBS: 51.6 g   DIETARY FIBER: 3.1 g   PROTEIN: 2.4 g

Pear Pie

Submitted by: NANCY MARTIN

PREP TIME: 15 MINUTES
COOK IN: 50 MINUTES
READY IN: 1 HOUR 5 MINUTES
SERVINGS: 6

1 (9 inch) unbaked pie crust
3 eggs
1/3 cup all-purpose flour
1 cup white sugar
1 teaspoon almond extract
1/4 cup melted butter
3 pears, peeled, cored and sliced

Preheat oven to 375°F (190°C.)

In a large bowl, combine eggs, flour, sugar, almond extract and melted butter. Pour into unbaked pie crust. Arrange sliced pears in spokes radiating from center.

Bake in the preheated oven for 15 minutes, then reduce temperature to 350°F (175°C) and bake for 25 to 35 minutes, or until custard is firm. Cool completely before serving.

This is a delicious pie! I never thought of combining pears with a custard pie, but it is perfect.
—STACEY10LYNN

AMOUNT PER SERVING: CALORIES: 477 TOTAL FAT: 20.6 g CHOLESTEROL: 127 mg SODIUM: 266 mg
TOTAL CARBS: 68.4 g DIETARY FIBER: 3.8 g PROTEIN: 6.2 g

Crustless Cranberry Pie

Submitted by: JEAN

PREP TIME: 15 MINUTES
COOK TIME: 40 MINUTES
READY IN: 55 MINUTES
SERVINGS: 8

1 cup all-purpose flour
1 cup white sugar
1/4 teaspoon salt
2 cups cranberries
1/2 cup chopped walnuts
1/2 cup butter, melted
2 eggs
1 teaspoon almond extract

Preheat oven to 350°F (175°C). Grease one 9 inch pie pan.

Combine the flour, sugar and salt. Stir in the cranberries and the walnuts and toss to coat. Stir in the butter, beaten eggs and almond extract. If you are using frozen cranberries the mixture will be very thick. Spread the batter into the prepared pan.

Bake at 350°F (175°C) for 40 minutes or until a wooden pick inserted near the center comes out clean. Serve warm with whipped cream or ice cream. Makes about 8 servings.

I have made this many times - each time delicious. The first time I made it cranberries were out of season, so I used canned cranberry sauce. It turned out sweet and moist, although I did extend its time in the oven.
—ROCKY

AMOUNT PER SERVING: CALORIES: 339 TOTAL FAT: 17.9 g CHOLESTEROL: 84 mg SODIUM: 207 mg
TOTAL CARBS: 41.6 g DIETARY FIBER: 2.1 g PROTEIN: 4.5 g

Grandma's Egg Custard Pie

Submitted by: MARLES RIESSLAND

PREP TIME: 15 MINUTES
COOK TIME: 35 MINUTES
READY IN: 50 MINUTES
SERVINGS: 8

1 (9 inch) unbaked pie crust
3 eggs, beaten
3/4 cup white sugar
1/4 teaspoon salt
1 teaspoon vanilla extract
1 egg white
2 1/2 cups scalded milk
1/4 teaspoon ground nutmeg
3 drops yellow food coloring (optional)

Preheat oven to 400°F (205°C).

Mix together eggs, sugar, salt and vanilla. Stir well. Blend in the scalded milk. For more yellow color, add few drops yellow food coloring.

Line pie pan with pastry and brush inside bottom and sides of shell with egg white to help prevent a soggy crust. Pour custard mixture into piecrust. Sprinkle with nutmeg.

Bake for 30 to 35 minutes or until a knife inserted near center comes out clean. Cool on rack.

I've made this pie three or four times now and it's always the favorite wherever I take it!

—JRIL

AMOUNT PER SERVING: CALORIES: 254   TOTAL FAT: 10.5 g   CHOLESTEROL: 86 mg   SODIUM: 281 mg
TOTAL CARBS: 33.5 g   DIETARY FIBER: 0.2 g   PROTEIN: 6.3 g

Mississippi Mud Cake

Submitted by: CAROL

PREP TIME: 30 MINUTES
COOK TIME: 45 MINUTES
READY IN: 1 HOUR 15 MINUTES
SERVINGS: 14

1 3/4 cups strong brewed coffee
1/4 cup dark rum
5 (1 ounce) squares unsweetened chocolate
1 cup butter
2 eggs
2 cups white sugar
1 teaspoon vanilla extract
2 cups all purpose flour
1 teaspoon baking soda
1/8 teaspoon salt

Place coffee and rum in a saucepan and heat to simmer. Add the chocolate and the butter or margarine. Cook, stirring, occasionally, until both are melted. Remove from the heat.

In a large bowl, beat the eggs. Gradually beat in the sugar until the mixture is thick. Beat in the vanilla and the chocolate mixture. In another bowl, stir together the flour, baking soda, and salt. Beat into the chocolate mixture.

Turn the batter into a greased and floured tube pan. Bake in a preheated 275°F (135°C) oven for 1 1/2 hours, or until the cake tests done with a toothpick. Transfer to a rack to cool. Makes 16 servings.

AMOUNT PER SERVING: CALORIES: 366   TOTAL FAT: 19.6 g   CHOLESTEROL: 66 mg   SODIUM: 256 mg
TOTAL CARBS: 45.3 g   DIETARY FIBER: 2 g   PROTEIN: 3.9 g

AS SHOWN IN THE PICTURE

Cranberry Upside-Down Coffee Cake

Submitted by: **MARJORITA WHYTE**

PREP TIME: 30 MINUTES
COOK IN: 1 HOUR
READY IN: 1 HOUR 30 MINUTES
SERVINGS: 12

1 1/2 cups all-purpose flour
1 1/2 teaspoons baking powder
1 teaspoon baking soda
1/2 teaspoon ground cinnamon
1/4 teaspoon salt
2/3 cup packed brown sugar
1/3 cup butter
1 1/4 cups cranberries
1/2 cup chopped pecans
1/2 cup butter, room temperature
3/4 cup white sugar
2 eggs
1 teaspoon vanilla extract
1 cup sour cream

Preheat oven to 350°F (175°C). Wrap the outside of a 9 inch springform pan with aluminum foil to prevent leaking. Sift together the flour, baking powder, baking soda, cinnamon and salt. Set aside.

In a saucepan over medium heat, combine brown sugar and 1/3 cup butter. Bring to a boil, then pour into bottom of springform pan. Sprinkle with cranberries and pecans.

In a large bowl, cream together the butter and 3/4 cup sugar until light and fluffy. Beat in the eggs one at a time, then stir in the vanilla. Beat in the flour mixture alternately with the sour cream. Pour batter into prepared pan.

Bake in the preheated oven for 60 minutes, or until a toothpick inserted into the center of the cake comes out clean. Cool in pan for 10 minutes, then invert onto serving platter and carefully remove pan. Serve warm.

I found this recipe right before Christmas last year, and it was such a hit at our Christmas Eve party that I've had requests to bring it again. I switched it up with blueberries for a baby shower, and made it with cherries and almonds for a summer barbeque.......this is one of my favorite recipes ever!

—FAIRUZAH

Wonderful!! This is such a delicious cake. I made it for breakfast, and measured out all of the ingredients last night to make things easy this morning and it was just amazing. I used walnuts for the topping instead of pecans, I had extra cranberries, so I added them into the batter (this was nice - they 'popped' and gave lovely pinkish-red patches, like you get in muffins. This is an amazing recipe - the cake is so soft and delicious! I'll be making this again and again!!

—PULCHERRIMA

AMOUNT PER SERVING: CALORIES: 358   TOTAL FAT: 21.4 g   CHOLESTEROL: 78 mg   SODIUM: 340 mg
TOTAL CARBS: 39.4 g   DIETARY FIBER: 1.4 g   PROTEIN: 3.9 g

Lemon Poppy Seed Bundt Cake

PREP TIME: 10 MINUTES
COOK IN: 1 HOUR
READY IN: 1 HOUR 30 MINUTES
SERVINGS: 16

Submitted by: **SHANNA FENTON**

1/4 cup poppy seeds
1/4 cup milk
1 (18.25 ounce) package lemon cake mix
1 (3.4 ounce) package instant vanilla pudding mix
1 cup water
1/2 cup vegetable oil
4 eggs

Soak poppy seeds in milk for 2 hours. Preheat oven to 350°F (175°C). Grease and flour a 10 inch Bundt pan.

In a large bowl, stir together cake mix and pudding mix. Make a well in the center and pour in water, oil, and eggs. Beat on low speed until blended. Scrape bowl, and beat 4 minutes on medium speed. Blend in poppy seed mixture. Pour batter into prepared pan.

Bake in the preheated oven for 60 minutes, or until a toothpick inserted into the center of the cake comes out clean. Let cool in pan for 10 minutes, then turn out onto a wire rack and cool completely.

AMOUNT PER SERVING: CALORIES: 250 TOTAL FAT: 12.9 g CHOLESTEROL: 62 mg SODIUM: 336 mg
TOTAL CARBS: 30 g DIETARY FIBER: 0.5 g PROTEIN: 4 g

AS SHOW IN THE PICTURE

Pecan Sour Cream Pound Cake

PREP TIME: 30 MINUTES
COOK TIME: 1 HOUR 30 MINUTES
READY IN: 2 HOURS 20 MINUTES
SERVINGS: 12

Submitted by: **CAROLE RESNICK**

1/4 cup chopped pecans
3 cups cake flour
1/2 teaspoon salt
1/4 teaspoon baking soda
1 cup unsalted butter
3 cups white sugar
6 eggs
1 teaspoon vanilla extract
1 cup sour cream
1 cup confectioners' sugar
3 tablespoons orange juice
1 teaspoon vanilla extract

Preheat oven to 300 °F (150°C). Grease and flour a 10 inch Bundt or tube pan. Sprinkle pecans on bottom of pan; set aside. Sift together flour, salt, and baking soda into a medium bowl; set aside.

In a large bowl, cream butter and white sugar until light and fluffy. Beat in eggs one at a time, then stir in vanilla. Add flour mixture alternately with sour cream. Pour batter over pecans in prepared pan.

Bake in the preheated oven for 75 to 90 minutes, or until a toothpick inserted into the center of the cake comes out clean. Let cool in pan for 20 minutes, then turn out onto a wire rack and cool completely.

To prepare the glaze: In a small bowl, combine confectioners' sugar, orange juice and 1 teaspoon vanilla. Drizzle over cake while still warm.

AMOUNT PER SERVING: CALORIES: 597 TOTAL FAT: 24 g CHOLESTEROL: 156 mg SODIUM: 168 mg
TOTAL CARBS: 89.8 g DIETARY FIBER: 0.9 g PROTEIN: 7.1 g

AS SHOWN IN THE PICTURE

Tiramisu Layer Cake

Submitted by: BETTINA BRYANT

PREP TIME: 5 MINUTES
COOK IN: 20 MINUTES
READY IN: 2 HOURS
SERVINGS: 12

CAKE:

1 (18.25 ounce) package moist white cake mix

1 teaspoon instant coffee powder

1/4 cup coffee

1 tablespoon coffee flavored liqueur

FILLING:

1 (8 ounce) container mascarpone cheese

1/2 cup confectioners' sugar

2 tablespoons coffee flavored liqueur

FROSTING:

2 cups heavy cream

1/4 cup confectioners' sugar

2 tablespoons coffee flavored liqueur

GARNISH:

2 tablespoons unsweetened cocoa powder

1 (1 ounce) square semisweet chocolate

Usually I won't even consider making a dessert with a cake mix. This one is well worth making an exception. I've served it at a couple parties and everyone loved it.
—J U N I

Preheat oven to 350°F (175°C). Grease and flour 3 (9 inch) pans.

Prepare the cake mix according to package directions. Divide two thirds of batter between 2 pans. Stir instant coffee into remaining batter; pour into remaining pan.

Bake in the preheated oven for 20 to 25 minutes, or until a toothpick inserted into the center of the cake comes out clean. Let cool in pan for 10 minutes, then turn out onto a wire rack and cool completely. In a measuring cup, combine brewed coffee and 1 tablespoon coffee liqueur; set aside.

To make the filling: In a small bowl, using an electric mixer set on low speed, combine mascarpone, 1/2 cup confectioners' sugar and 2 tablespoons coffee liqueur; beat just until smooth. Cover with plastic wrap and refrigerate.

To make the frosting: In a medium bowl, using an electric mixer set on medium-high speed, beat the cream, 1/4 cup confectioners' sugar and 2 tablespoons coffee liqueur until stiff. Fold 1/2 cup of cream mixture into filling mixture.

To assemble the cake: Place one plain cake layer on a serving plate. Using a thin skewer, poke holes in cake, about 1 inch apart. Pour one third of reserved coffee mixture over cake, then spread with half of the filling mixture. Top with coffee-flavored cake layer; poke holes in cake. Pour another third of the coffee mixture over the second layer and spread with the remaining filling. Top with remaining cake layer; poke holes in cake. Pour remaining coffee mixture on top. Spread sides and top of cake with frosting. Place cocoa in a sieve and lightly dust top of cake. Garnish with chocolate curls. Refrigerate at least 30 minutes before serving.

To make the chocolate curls, use a vegetable peeler and run it down the edge of the chocolate bar.

AMOUNT PER SERVING: CALORIES: 468   TOTAL FAT: 28.9 g   CHOLESTEROL: 78 mg   SODIUM: 309 mg
TOTAL CARBS: 46.7 g   DIETARY FIBER: 0.8 g   PROTEIN: 44 g

Easy Mint Chocolate Chip Ice Cream

Submitted by: DARRYN M. BRIGGS

PREP TIME: 5 MINUTES
COOK IN: 40 MINUTES
READY IN: 2 HOUR 45 MINUTES
SERVINGS: 8

2 cups 2% milk
2 cups heavy cream
1 cup sugar
1/2 teaspoon salt
1 teaspoon vanilla extract
1 teaspoon peppermint extract
3 drops green food coloring (optional)
1 cup miniature semisweet chocolate chips

In a large bowl, stir together the milk, cream, sugar, salt, vanilla extract and peppermint extract until the sugar has dissolved. Color to your liking with the green food coloring.

Pour the mixture into an ice cream maker, and freeze according to the manufacturer's instructions. After about 10 minutes into the freezing, add the chocolate chips. After the ice cream has thickened, about 30 minutes later, spoon into a container, and freeze for 2 hours.

AMOUNT PER SERVING: CALORIES: 455   TOTAL FAT: 30.7 g   CHOLESTEROL: 86 mg   SODIUM: 201 mg
TOTAL CARBS: 45.4 g   DIETARY FIBER: 1.5 g   PROTEIN: 4.3 g

Cinnamon Ice Cream

Submitted by: ELIZABETH

PREP TIME: 5 MINUTES
COOK TIME: 15 MINUTES
READY IN: 1 HOUR 50 MINUTES
SERVINGS: 8

1 cup white sugar
1 1/2 cups half-and-half cream
2 eggs, beaten
1 cup heavy cream
1 teaspoon vanilla extract
2 teaspoons ground cinnamon

In a saucepan over medium-low heat, stir together the sugar and half-and-half. When the mixture begins to simmer, remove from heat, and whisk half of the mixture into the eggs. Whisk quickly so that the eggs do not scramble. Pour the egg mixture back into the saucepan, and stir in the heavy cream. Continue cooking over medium-low heat, stirring constantly, until the mixture is thick enough to coat the back of a metal spoon. Remove from heat, and whisk in vanilla and cinnamon. Set aside to cool.

Pour cooled mixture into an ice cream maker, and freeze according to the manufacturer's instructions.

AMOUNT PER SERVING: CALORIES: 280   TOTAL FAT: 17.5 g   CHOLESTEROL: 111 mg   SODIUM: 46 mg
TOTAL CARBS: 28.4 g   DIETARY FIBER: 0.3 g   PROTEIN: 3.5 g

German Chocolate Cake

Submitted by: **DEAN**

PREP TIME: 30 MINUTES
COOK IN: 30 MINUTES
READY IN: 1 HOUR
SERVINGS: 12

1/2 cup water
4 (1 ounce) squares German sweet chocolate
1 cup butter, softened
2 cups white sugar
4 egg yolks
1 teaspoon vanilla extract
1 cup buttermilk
2 1/2 cups cake flour
1 teaspoon baking soda
1/2 teaspoon salt
4 egg whites
1 cup white sugar
1 cup evaporated milk
1/2 cup butter
3 egg yolks, beaten
1 1/3 cups flaked coconut
1 cup chopped pecans
1 teaspoon vanilla extract
1/2 teaspoon shortening
1 (1 ounce) square semisweet chocolate

Preheat oven to 350°F (175°C). Grease and flour three - 9 inch round pans. Sift together the flour, baking soda and salt. Set aside. In a small saucepan, heat water and 4 ounces chocolate until melted. Remove from heat and allow to cool.

In a large bowl, cream 1 cup butter and 2 cups sugar until light and fluffy. Beat in 4 egg yolks one at a time. Blend in the melted chocolate mixture and vanilla. Beat in the flour mixture alternately with the buttermilk, mixing just until incorporated.

In a large glass or metal mixing bowl, beat egg whites until stiff peaks form. Fold 1/3 of the whites into the batter, then quickly fold in remaining whites until no streaks remain.

Pour into 3 - 9 inch pans. Bake in the preheated oven for 30 minutes, or until a toothpick inserted into the center of the cake comes out clean. Allow to cool for 10 minutes in the pan, then turn out onto wire rack.

To make the filling: In a saucepan combine 1 cup sugar, evaporated milk, 1/2 cup butter, and 3 egg yolks. Cook over low heat, stirring constantly until thickened. Remove from heat. Stir in coconut, pecans and vanilla. Cool until thick enough to spread.

Spread filling between layers and on top of cake. In a small saucepan, melt shortening and 1 ounce of chocolate. Stir until smooth and drizzle down the sides of the cake.

Delicious! I used six semisweet chocolate squares. Nice, moist and light. I made it for a birthday celebration and it disappeared in no time. I made it one night and served it the next; the frosting mellowed well, and was a big spoonful of creamy goodness. Thanks for a great recipe!
—**COUNTESS**

AMOUNT PER SERVING: CALORIES: 749   TOTAL FAT: 42 g   CHOLESTEROL: 194 mg   SODIUM: 528 mg   TOTAL CARBS: 88 g
DIETARY FIBER: 2.5 g   PROTEIN: 9.3 g

Hot Fudge Ice Cream Bar Dessert

Submitted by: CONNIE WEST

PREP TIME: 30 MINUTES
COOK IN: 4 MINUTES
READY IN: 1 HOUR 35 MINUTES
SERVINGS: 18

1 (16 ounce) can chocolate syrup
3/4 cup peanut butter
19 ice cream sandwiches
1 (12 ounce) container frozen whipped topping, thawed
1 cup salted peanuts

Pour the chocolate syrup into a medium microwave safe bowl and microwave 2 minutes on high. Do not allow to boil. Stir peanut butter into hot chocolate until smooth. Allow to cool to room temperature.

Line the bottom of a 9x13 inch dish with a layer of ice cream sandwiches. Spread half the whipped topping over the sandwiches. Spoon half the chocolate mixture over that. Top with half the peanuts. Repeat layers. Freeze until firm, 1 hour. Cut into squares to serve.

Amazing dessert! I omitted the nuts and crunched up a whole bag of mini Butterfingers. I recommend making this the night before and letting it freeze over night. YUM!

—KELLI

AMOUNT PER SERVING: CALORIES: 384 TOTAL FAT: 18.8 g CHOLESTEROL: 21 mg SODIUM: 172 mg
TOTAL CARBS: 47.1 g DIETARY FIBER: 2.3 g PROTEIN: 7.9 g

Chocolate Chip Cookie Ice Cream Cake

Submitted by: ARVILLA

PREP TIME: 15 MINUTES
READY IN: 1 HOUR 15 MINUTES
SERVINGS: 16

1 (18 ounce) package small chocolate chip cookies
1/4 cup margarine, melted
1 cup hot fudge topping
2 quarts vanilla ice cream
1 cup whipped cream
12 cherries

Crush half the cookies (about 20) to make crumbs. Combine crumbs with melted margarine and press into the bottom of a 9-inch springform pan or pie plate. Stand remaining cookies around edge of pan. Spread 3/4 cup fudge topping over crust. Freeze 15 minutes.

Meanwhile, soften 1 quart of ice cream in microwave or on countertop. After crust has chilled, spread softened ice cream over fudge layer. Freeze 30 minutes.

I used moose tracks ice cream, a whole box of Famous Amos chocolate chip cookies, Reddy Whip, and hot fudge (not chocolate syrup). This dessert is amazing!

—LISA R

AMOUNT PER SERVING: CALORIES: 529 TOTAL FAT: 27.3 g CHOLESTEROL: 43 mg SODIUM: 324 mg
TOTAL CARBS: 67.6 g DIETARY FIBER: 1.9 g PROTEIN: 6.3 g

Easy Dump Cake

Submitted by: MEREDITH

PREP TIME: 25 MINUTES
COOK IN: 55 MINUTES
READY IN: 1 HOUR 20 MINUTES
SERVINGS: 12

1 (18.25 ounce) package yellow cake mix
1 (5.9 ounce) package instant chocolate pudding mix
4 eggs, beaten
2/3 cup vegetable oil
2/3 cup white sugar
1/3 cup water
1 (8 ounce) container sour cream
1 cup semisweet chocolate chips

Preheat oven to 350°F (175°C). Grease and flour a Bundt pan.

In a bowl, mix the yellow cake mix, pudding mix, eggs, vegetable oil, sugar, and water. Gently fold in the sour cream and chocolate chips. Pour batter into the prepared Bundt pan.

Bake in the preheated oven for 55 minutes. Cool in pan for 10 minutes before transferring to cooling racks.

Very good and moist cake. I used a chocolate cake mix, vanilla pudding and peanut butter chips. It turned out great and the family loved it.

—JOANN

AMOUNT PER SERVING: CALORIES: 518   TOTAL FAT: 27.3 g   CHOLESTEROL: 80 mg
SODIUM: 513 mg   TOTAL CARBS: 66.7 g   DIETARY FIBER: 1.6 g   PROTEIN: 5.5 g

Gooey Butter Cake

Submitted by: TAMMY

PREP TIME: 15 MINUTES
COOK TIME: 45 MINUTES
READY IN: 1 HOUR
SERVINGS: 24

1 (18.5 ounce) package yellow cake mix
4 eggs
1 cup butter
2 cups confectioners' sugar
8 ounces cream cheese

Preheat oven to 350°F (175°C). Butter one 9x13 inch cake pan.

Melt the butter slightly. Mix it with 2 of the eggs and cake mix. Pour batter into prepared pan.

Mix the remaining 2 eggs with the cream cheese, and the confectioner's sugar. Pour this mixture evenly over the first mixture. Do not stir.

Bake at 350°F (175°C) for 45 minutes

This is one of my absolutely, most favorite indulgences!! True, it's not an attractive cake ... sides get brown and wrinkle inward... but the taste!!! I can't stop eating and always end up with a stomach ache!!! Very much like a cream cheese cake. YUM!!!!!!!!!!

—TORTUGAS2X

AMOUNT PER SERVING: CALORIES: 245   TOTAL FAT: 14.3 g   CHOLESTEROL: 67 mg   SODIUM: 258 mg
TOTAL CARBS: 27.1 g   DIETARY FIBER: 0.2 g   PROTEIN: 2.8 g

Chocolate Cavity Maker Cake

Submitted by: **CAITLIN KOCH**

PREP TIME: 30 MINUTES
COOK TIME: 1 HOUR
READY IN: 2 HOURS
SERVINGS: 12

1 (18.25 ounce) package dark chocolate cake mix

1 (3.9 ounce) package instant chocolate pudding mix

1 (16 ounce) container sour cream

3 eggs

1/3 cup vegetable oil

1/2 cup coffee flavored liqueur

2 cups semisweet chocolate chips

Preheat oven to 350°F (175°C). Grease and flour a 10 inch Bundt pan.

In a large bowl, combine cake mix, pudding mix, sour cream, eggs, oil and coffee liqueur. Beat until ingredients are well blended. Fold in chocolate chips. Batter will be thick. Spoon into prepared pan.

Bake in preheated oven for 1 hour, or until cake springs back when lightly tapped. Cool 10 minutes in pan, then turn out and cool completely on wire rack.

It's a heavenly chocolate cake. I used Kahlua liquor for this recipe and I sprinkled powder sugar on top.

—OLIVECHEVELLE

AMOUNT PER SERVING: CALORIES: 536   TOTAL FAT: 27.9 g   CHOLESTEROL: 70 mg   SODIUM: 487 mg

TOTAL CARBS: 65 g   DIETARY FIBER: 2.9 g   PROTEIN: 6.1 g

Million Dollar Cake

Submitted by: **GLENDA**

PREP TIME: 30 MINUTES
COOK TIME: 25 MINUTES
READY IN: 9 HOURS 55 MINUTES
SERVINGS: 12

1 (18.5 ounce) package yellow cake mix

8 ounces cream cheese

1 1/2 cups confectioners' sugar

1 (20 ounce) can crushed pineapple with juice

2 (8 ounce) cans mandarin oranges, drained

1 (3.5 ounce) package instant vanilla pudding mix

1 (8 ounce) container frozen whipped topping, thawed

Mix and bake cake mix as per package instruction for two 8 or 9 inch round layers. Let layers cool then split each layer in half so as to have 4 layers.

Whip cream cheese until soft, add the confectioners' sugar and thoroughly mix. Stir in the pineapple (juice also) and the drained mandarin oranges (Reserve about 5 mandarin orange slices to decorate the top of cake.), breaking up the oranges with back of a spoon. Stir in the dry pudding mix. Mix well until you feel the pudding mix has been dissolved. Fold in the whipped topping. Place one cake layer on a cake plate cut side up; spread with frosting. Place another layer cut side down on the first one. Again spread with frosting. Repeat until all layers are used spreading last bit of frosting on top and sides of cake. Keep refrigerated. It is best if refrigerated overnight before serving.

AMOUNT PER SERVING: CALORIES: 452   TOTAL FAT: 16.4 g   CHOLESTEROL: 22 mg   SODIUM: 465 mg

TOTAL CARBS: 73.9 g   DIETARY FIBER: 0.9 g   PROTEIN: 3.8 g

AS SHOWN IN THE PICTURE

Amaretto Divine

Submitted by: **JANET AYERS**

PREP TIME: 30 MINUTES
COOK IN: 15 MINUTES
READY IN: 45 MINUTES
SERVINGS: 10

1 (18.25 ounce) package yellow cake mix

1 cup non dairy amaretto flavored creamer

1 cup amaretto liqueur

3 eggs

1/3 cup vegetable oil

1 (3.5 ounce) package instant vanilla pudding mix

1 cup non dairy amaretto flavored creamer

1/4 cup amaretto liqueur

2 cups heavy cream, whipped

4 (1.4 ounce) bars chocolate covered toffee bars, chopped

1 (1.5 ounce) bar chocolate candy bar, melted

1/2 cup sliced almonds

Preheat oven to 325°F (165°C). Grease and flour three 8- inch pans.

Mix together the cake mix, 1 cup amaretto flavored creamer, 1 cup amaretto liqueur, eggs and oil until blended. Distribute cake batter evenly between the cake pans. Bake in the preheated oven for 15 minutes, making certain the cake layers do not overbake. Allow to cool completely before filling.

To make the amaretto whipped cream filling: Combine pudding mix, 1/4 cup amaretto liqueur and 1 cup amaretto flavored creamer. Set aside for 5 minutes until thickened. Fold the whipped cream into the amaretto mixture, then stir in the crushed chocolate covered toffee bars. Use to fill and frost top of the cake (do not frost sides). Drizzle cake with melted chocolate candy bar and sprinkle with sliced almonds. Refrigerate until ready to serve.

Divine is certainly the word for it! It is the most wonderful cake I have ever eaten! Filling is light and tasty and cake is so good! I was afraid I had used too much amaretto but, once baked, it was a subtle flavor.
—**TOBSCHOLARLY**

What a delightful cake! I turned it into a Death by Chocolate Cake; I used a chocolate cake, Kaluha, hazelnut creamer and chocolate pudding. I left the candy bars the same in the filling but went with just hazelnuts on top. I used real whipped cream - wonderfully rich!
—**MOTHERNYTE**

AMOUNT PER SERVING: CALORIES: 892   TOTAL FAT: 48.4 g   CHOLESTEROL: 139 mg   SODIUM: 580 mg
TOTAL CARBS: 93 g   DIETARY FIBER: 17 g   PROTEIN: 76 g

AS SHOWN IN THE PICTURE

White Chocolate Raspberry Cheesecake

Submitted by: CINDY

PREP TIME: 1 HOUR
COOK IN: 1 HOUR
READY IN: 10 HOURS
SERVINGS: 16

1 cup chocolate cookie crumbs
3 tablespoons white sugar
1/4 cup butter, melted
1 (10 ounce) package frozen raspberries
2 tablespoons white sugar
2 teaspoons cornstarch
1/2 cup water
2 cups white chocolate chips
1/2 cup half-and-half cream
3 (8 ounce) packages cream cheese, softened
1/2 cup white sugar
3 eggs
1 teaspoon vanilla extract

Very good. I used graham cracker crumbs instead of chocolate for a more traditional taste. I also drop quarter size circles of sauce on top the cheesecake (pre-baking) and drew a toothpick through them to make hearts.

—JEAN MARIE

In a medium bowl, mix together cookie crumbs, 3 tablespoons sugar, and melted butter. Press mixture into the bottom of a 9 inch springform pan.

In a saucepan, combine raspberries, 2 tablespoons sugar, cornstarch, and water. Bring to boil, and continue boiling 5 minutes, or until sauce is thick. Strain sauce through a mesh strainer to remove seeds.

Preheat oven to 325°F (165°C). In a metal bowl over a pan of simmering water, melt white chocolate chips with half-and-half, stirring occasionally until smooth.

In a large bowl, mix together cream cheese and 1/2 cup sugar until smooth. Beat in eggs one at a time. Blend in vanilla and melted white chocolate. Pour half of batter over crust. Spoon 3 tablespoons raspberry sauce over batter. Pour remaining cheesecake batter into pan, and again spoon 3 tablespoons raspberry sauce over the top. Swirl batter with the tip of a knife to create a marbled effect.

Bake for 55 to 60 minutes, or until filling is set. Cool, cover with plastic wrap, and refrigerate for 8 hours before removing from pan. Serve with remaining raspberry sauce.

I used 2 cups of Oreo crumbs (I put them in my food processor, cream and all) , 1 Tablespoon sugar and 1/4 cup butter for the crust in a 10 in spring form pan. I also used seedless raspberry preserves and that significantly decreased the time I spent making this cheesecake. Heating the preserves up slightly in the microwave (10-15 seconds) makes it very easy to drop in the batter. I was very easy and it came out very pretty and delicious.

—LATTINACOOK

Excellent cheesecake! I used a vegetable peeler on a white chocolate bar and a dark chocolate bar to make chocolate curls. BEAUTIFUL!

ALLICAT2U

AMOUNT PER SERVING: CALORIES: 407   TOTAL FAT: 27.6 g   CHOLESTEROL: 101 mg   SODIUM: 230 mg
TOTAL CARBS: 35.1 g   DIETARY FIBER: 1 g   PROTEIN: 65 g

Cheesecake Bars

Submitted by: FRANCES MANN

PREP TIME: 20 MINUTES
COOK IN: 40 MINUTES
READY IN: 1 HOUR
SERVINGS: 36

1/3 cup butter, softened
1/3 cup packed brown sugar
1/3 cup chopped walnuts
1 cup sifted all-purpose flour
1/4 cup white sugar
8 ounces cream cheese
1 tablespoon lemon juice
2 tablespoons milk
1 egg
1/2 teaspoon vanilla extract

Preheat oven to 350°F(175°C).

To make pastry: Cream together the butter and brown sugar until light and fluffy. Add in the flour and chopped nuts and stir until mixture becomes crumbly. Set aside 1/4 cup to use as a topping. Press pastry mixture into 8-inch square pan and bake for 12 to 15 minutes. Let cool on rack.

To make filling: Beat together the white sugar, and cream cheese until smooth. Stir in the egg, milk, lemon juice, and vanilla and mix well. Spread filling mixture over baked crust. Sprinkle reserved mixture on as a topping.

Bake for 25 to 30 minutes. Let cool on wire rack and refrigerate. Serve with fruit.

AMOUNT PER SERVING: CALORIES: 73 TOTAL FAT: 4.8 g CHOLESTEROL: 18 mg SODIUM: 39 mg TOTAL CARBS: 6.4 g DIETARY FIBER: 0.2 g PROTEIN: 1.2 g

---

AS SHOWN IN THE PICTURE

Chocolate Turtle Cheesecake

Submitted by: STEPHANIE

PREP TIME: 30 MINUTES
COOK TIME: 55 MINUTES
READY IN: 5 HOURS 25 MINUTES
SERVINGS: 12

2 cups vanilla wafer crumbs
2 tablespoons unsalted butter, melted
1 (14 ounce) package individually wrapped caramels
1 (5 ounce) can evaporated milk
1 cup chopped pecans
2 (8 ounce) packages cream cheese, softened
1/2 cup white sugar
1 teaspoon vanilla extract
2 eggs
1/2 cup semisweet chocolate chips

Preheat oven to 350°F (175°C). In a large bowl, mix together the cookie crumbs and melted butter. Press into the bottom of a 9 inch springform pan.

In a heavy saucepan over low heat, melt the caramels with the evaporated milk. Heat and stir frequently until smooth. Pour caramel sauce into crust, and top with pecans.

In a large bowl, combine cream cheese, sugar and vanilla; beat well until smooth. Add eggs one at a time, mixing well after each addition. Melt the chocolate, and blend into cream cheese mixture. Pour chocolate batter over pecans.

Bake in preheated oven for 40 to 50 minutes, or until filling is set. Loosen cake from the edges of pan, but do not remove rim until cooled to prevent the top from cracking. Chill in refrigerator for 4 hours, or overnight.

AMOUNT PER SERVING: CALORIES: 433 TOTAL FAT: 25.8 g CHOLESTEROL: 66 mg SODIUM: 230 mg TOTAL CARBS: 47.2 g DIETARY FIBER: 1.8 g PROTEIN: 6.5 g

Paul's Pumpkin Bars

Submitted by: DEB MARTIN

PREP TIME: 15 MINUTES
COOK IN: 30 MINUTES
READY IN: 45 MINUTES
SERVINGS: 24

4 eggs
1 2/3 cups white sugar
1 cup vegetable oil
1 (15 ounce) can pumpkin puree
2 cups all-purpose flour
2 teaspoons baking powder
1 teaspoon baking soda
2 teaspoons ground cinnamon
1 teaspoon salt
1 (3 ounce) package cream cheese, softened
1/2 cup butter, softened
1 teaspoon vanilla extract
2 cups sifted confectioners' sugar

Preheat oven to 350°F (175°C).

In a medium bowl, mix the eggs, sugar, oil, and pumpkin with an electric mixer until light and fluffy. Sift together the flour, baking powder, baking soda, cinnamon and salt. Stir into the pumpkin mixture until thoroughly combined.

Spread the batter evenly into an ungreased 10x15 inch jellyroll pan. Bake for 25 to 30 minutes in preheated oven. Cool before frosting.

To make the frosting, cream together the cream cheese and butter. Stir in vanilla. Add confectioners' sugar a little at a time, beating until mixture is smooth. Spread evenly on top of the cooled bars. Cut into squares.

AMOUNT PER SERVING: CALORIES: 279 TOTAL FAT: 15.2 g CHOLESTEROL: 50 mg SODIUM: 293 mg
TOTAL CARBS: 34.1 g DIETARY FIBER: 0.9 g PROTEIN: 2.6 g

AS SHOWN IN THE PICTURE

Frozen Peanut Butter Cheesecake

Submitted by: ANGEL SHEPHARD

PREP TIME: 10 MINUTES
COOK TIME: 30 MINUTES
READY IN: 40 MINUTES
SERVINGS: 8

1/3 cup butter
1 cup semisweet chocolate chips
2 1/2 cups crispy rice cereal
1 (8 ounce) package cream cheese, softened
2 (5 ounce) cans sweetened condensed milk
3/4 cup peanut butter
2 tablespoons lemon juice
1 teaspoon vanilla extract
1 cup whipped cream
1/2 cup chocolate fudge sauce

In a heavy sauce pan over low heat, melt the butter and chocolate chips. Remove from heat and gently stir in rice cereal until coated. Press into the bottom and sides of a 9 inch pie plate. Chill 30 minutes.

In a large bowl, beat cream cheese until fluffy. Gradually beat in condensed milk and peanut butter until smooth. Stir in lemon juice and vanilla. Fold in whipped cream. Pour into prepared crust. Drizzle chocolate topping over pie and freeze for 4 hours or until firm. Keep in freezer until ready to serve, and return leftovers to the freezer as well.

AMOUNT PER SERVING: CALORIES: 645 TOTAL FAT: 42.5 g CHOLESTEROL: 69 mg SODIUM: 461 mg
TOTAL CARBS: 58.7 g DIETARY FIBER: 3.3 g PROTEIN: 13.6 g

A

Acorn Squash, 167
African Peanut Soup, 64
Amanda's Potatoes, 178
Amaretto Divine, 242
Amy's Barbecue Chicken Salad, 46
Annie's Fruit Salsa and Cinnamon Chips, 26
Apples(s)
 Apple Bread, 214
 Avocado Salad with Tangerine Dressing, 55
 Caramel, 209
 Cole Slaw, 156
 Maple Crumble Pie, 227
 Zucchini Sausage and, Stuffing, 183
 Zucchini Apple Bread, 214
Artichoke
 Spinach Dip, Hot, 15
 Spinach Lasagna, 120
 Pasta, Chicken, 90
Asian Chicken Noodle Salad, 53
Asparagus
 Baked with Balsamic Butter Sauce, 153
 Lasagna, 127
 Pan-Fried, 152
Aussie Chicken, 79
Avocado
 Apple, Salad with Tangerine Dressing, 55
 Tomato and Mango Salsa, 17

B

Bacon
 Cheddar Stuffed Mushrooms, 34
 Penne Pasta with Spinach, 127
 Tomato, Grilled Cheese, 139
 Water Chestnut Rolls, 36
 Warm Blue Cheese Dip with Garlic, 12
Baked Apricot Chicken, 91
Baked Asparagus with Balsamic Butter Sauce, 153
Baked Dijon Salmon, 110
Baked Fennel with Parmesan, 160
Baked Onion Dip, 24
Baked Potato Dip, 25
Banana Nut Bread, 215
Banana Pudding, 221
Bars
 Best Brownies, 197
 Candy Bar Fudge, 201
 Cheesecake Bars, 247
 Chocolate Peanut Bars, 197
 Hot Fudge Ice Cream, Dessert, 239
 Lemon Square Bars, 201
 Paul's Pumpkin, 249
 Raspberry Oatmeal, 195
Basmati Rice, Indian Style, 179

BBQ Pork for Sandwiches, 139
Best Big, Fat, Chewy Chocolate Chip Cookie, 188
Best Brownies, 197
Best Ever Jalapeno Poppers, 31
Best Hot Crab Dip, 16
Best Toffee Ever – Super Easy, 203
Beth's Spicy Oatmeal Raisin Cookies, 187
Black Bean Salsa, 23
Black Bean and Corn Salad, 59
Blackened Tuna, 98
B.L.T. Salad with Basil and Mayo Dressing, 39
Bleu Cheese Dip with Garlic and Bacon, Warm, 12
Bleu Cheese Macaroni, 178
Bourbon Pecan Chicken, 85
Bread
 Banana Nut, 215
 Cranberry Nut, 215
 Lemon Poppy Seed, 217
 Roasted Garlic, 183
 Rum Raisin Bread, 214
 Zucchini Apple, 214
Broccoli
 Excellent Cheese Soup, 64
 Fresh Salad, 39
 Garlic Butter and Cashews, with, 149
Burgers
 Summer Chicken, 86
 Mexican Turkey, 97
 Mom's Big, 133
Brussels Sprouts, Shredded, 152
Butternut Kisses, 203
Butterscotch Bread Pudding, 218
Butterscotch Fondue, 223

C

Cabbage, Fried, 157
Caesar Salad Supreme, 51
Cajun Chicken Pasta, 89
Cajun Style Baked Sweet Potato, 177
Cake. See also Cheesecake
 Chocolate Cavity Maker Cake, 241
 Chocolate Chip Cookie Ice Cream, 239
 Cranberry Upside-Down Coffee Cake, 231
 Easy Dump Cake, 240
 German Chocolate, 237
 Lemon Poppy Seed Bundt, 232
 Million Dollar Cake, 241
 Mississippi Mud Cake, 229
 Pecan Sour Cream Pound, 232
 Tiramisu Layer, 235
Candy Bar Fudge, 201
Cannelloni, Vegetable Stuffed, 117
Caramel
 Apples, 209
 Popcorn, 209

Carrots
    Jacksonville, 166
    Maple Dill, 166
    Spectacular Marsala Glazed, with Hazelnuts, 164
Cashews, Broccoli with Garlic Butter and, 149
Cheese
    Bacon, Tomato Grilled, 139
    Baked Fennel with Parmesan, 160
    Cheddar, Stuffed Mushrooms, Bacon and, 34
    Mushroom, and Chicken, 90
    Oven Fried, Chicken, 81
    Pork Chops with Fresh Tomato, Onion, Garlic, and, 141
    Salsa Bowls Dip, 15
Cheesecake
    Bars, 247
    Chocolate Turtle, 247
    Frozen Peanut Butter, 249
    White Chocolate Raspberry, 245
Cheesy Salmon Pasta, 114
Cheesy Sweet and Savory Spuds, 175
Cherry Chicken Salad, 47
Cherry Dump Pudding, 221
Cherry Tomatoes, Green Beans with, 149
Chicken
    Amy's Barbecue Salad, 46
    Asian Chicken Noodle, 53
    Aussie, 79
    Baked Apricot, 91
    Bourbon Pecan, 85
    Cajun Pasta, 89
    Cherry Chicken Salad, 47
    Chutney, Salad, 46
    Chinese, Salad, 49
    Cranberry I, 91
    Easier Marsala, 72
    Easy Grilled Teriyaki, 82
    Enchiladas Suisas, 93
    Garlic Chicken Fried, 74
    Garlic, Basil and Parsley, 81
    Ginger Orange Glazed Chicken Wrap, 33
    Grams, Pot Pie, 94
    Grilled, Salad with Seasonal Fruit, 44
    Hawaiian Chicken, 76
    Hot and Sour Soup, 67
    Irish, Dumplings, 83
    Focaccia Sandwiches, 73
    Lemon Butter, 72
    Marinated Chicken Kabobs, 71
    Mushroom and Swiss, 90
    Old-Fashioned, and Noodles, 95
    Oven Fried Parmesan, 81
    Pasta, and Artichokes, 90
    Pecan Crusted, Salad, 47
    Pesto, Florentine, 83

    Quesadillas, 34
    Santa Fe Chicken Salad, 49
    Spinach Stuffed, Breast, 76
    Spicy Garlic Lime, 73
    Summer Burgers, 86
    Tangy Fajitas, 74
    Tomato Curry, 82
    Tortilla Soup, 63
    Wing Dip, 25
    Wild Rice, and Soup, 65
Chinese Chicken Salad, 49
Chocolate
    Cavity Maker Cake, 241
    Fondue, Totally Groovy Chocolate, 223
    Fudge, German, 202
    German, Cake, 237
    Mocha Pie, 225
    Peanut Butter Bars, 197
    Turtle Cheesecake, 247
    White, Chocolate Party Mix, 207
    Raspberry Cheesecake, White, 245
Chocolate Chip
    Best Big, Fat, Chewy Chocolate Chip Cookie, 188
    Cookie Ice Cream Cake, 239
    Easy Mint, Ice Cream, 236
Chutney Chicken Salad, 46
Cinnamon Ice Cream, 236
Cioppino, 107
Classic Peanut Butter Cookies, 191
Cobbler, Old Fashioned Peach, 212
Cocktail Meatballs, 33
Coconut Cream Pie, Old Fashioned, 225
Coffee Cake, Cranberry Upside-Down, 231
Cookies. see also Bars
    Best Big, Fat, Chewy Chocolate Chip Cookie, 188
    Best Rolled Sugar Cookies, 189
    Beth's Spicy Oatmeal Raisin, 187
    Cranberry Hootycreeks, 192
    Classic Peanut Butter Cookies, 191
    Lemon Pudding Cookies, 187
    Molasses Sugar Cookies, 189
    Oatmeal Peanut Butter Cookies, 192
    Pecan Filled Cookies, 191
    Snickerdoodles, 188
Collard Greens, Kickin', 153
Corn
    Black Bean, Hot, Dip, 20
    Casserole, 169
    Kettle, 28
    Zucchini Melody, 169
Crab
    Best Hot Dip, 16
    Cakes, 105

Cranberries
Hootycreeks, 192
Cranberry Chicken, I, 91
Cranberry Nut Bread, 215
Crustless Pie, 228
Upside-Down Coffee Cake, 231
Creamy Pesto Shrimp, 105
Creamy Rice Pudding, 218
Creamy Tomato-Basil Soup, 65
Crispy Coated Cajun Fries, 173
Crispy Rice Candy, 198
Crispy Vegetables Pakoras, 36
Crustless Cranberry Dip, 228
Curry, Potato, 115

D

Dill Dip, 19
Dip. see also Salsa
Annie's Fruit Salsa and Cinnamon Chips, 26
Artichoke and Spinach, Hot, 15
Baked Onion, 24
Baked Potato, 25
Black Bean Salsa, 23
Blue Cheese Dip with Garlic and Bacon, Warm, 12
Chicken Wing, 25
Crab, Best, 16
Dill Dip, 19
For the Stars, 24
Hot Corn, 20
Hummus, Spicy Three Pepper, 11
Mexican Layered Dip, 20
Salsa Cheese Boule, 13
Salsa De Tomatillo, 15
Sun-Dried Tomato Dip, 19

E

Easier Chicken Marsala, 72
Easy Arugula Salad, 44
Easy Dump Cake, 240
Easy Grilled Chicken Teriyaki, 82
Easy Mint Chocolate Chip Ice Cream, 236
Elisa's Famous Fudge, 205
Enchiladas
Potato and Bean, 128
Spinach, 128
Suisas, 93
Excellent Broccoli Cheese Soup, 64

F

Fancy Potatoes, 174
Fennel and Watercress Salad, and, 41
Festive Onions, 160
Fettuccine, Seafood, 99
Fig and Olive Tapenade, 13
Florentine, Pesto Chicken, 83
Focaccia Chicken Sandwiches, 73

Fondue
Butterscotch, 223
Totally Groovy Chocolate, 223
Four Cheese Vegetarian Lasagna, 122
Fried Cabbage, 157
Fried Green Tomatoes, 159
Fried Onion Rings, 177
Fried Rice with Ginger, Hoisin, and Sesame, 181
Fresh Broccoli Salad, 39
Fresh Salsa, 17
Frozen Peanut Butter Cheesecake, 249
Fudge
Candy Bar, 201
Elisa's Famous Fudge, 205
Hot, Ice Cream Bar Dessert, 239
German Chocolate, 202
Raspberry Truffle, 199
World's Best Peanut Butter, 199

G

Garlic
Broccoli with, Butter and Cashews, 149
Chicken with Basil, and Parsley, 81
Chicken Fried Chicken, 74
Feta Pate, To Die For, 12
Grilled Halibut with Cilantro, Butter 98
Grits, 179
Mashed Potatoes Secret Recipe, 175
Pasta with Prawns, 125
Pork Chops with Fresh Tomato, Onion, Garlic, and Feta, 141
Roasted, Bread, 183
German Chocolate Cake, 237
German Chocolate Fudge, 202
Ginger Orange Glazed Chicken Wings, 33
Gingerbread, Pumpkin 217
Glazed Carrots with Hazelnuts, Spectacular Marsala, 164
Glazed Meatloaf, 135
Gonzo Garbanzos, 170
Gooey Butter Cake, 240
Gram's Chicken Pot Pie, 95
Grandma's Egg Custard Pie, 229
Greek Veggie Salad, 42
Green Beans with Cherry Tomatoes, 149
Grilled
Chicken Salad with Seasonal Fruit, 44
Easy, Chicken Teriyaki, 82
Halibut with Cilantro Garlic Butter, 98
Marinated Shrimp, 103
Mediterranean Vegetable Sandwich, 131
Rock Lobster Tails, 109
Salmon, 112
Salmon Skewers, 31
Tomato Bacon, Cheese, 139
Grits, Garlic, 179

H

Harvest Salad, 41
Hawaiian Chicken, 76
Herbed Mushrooms with White Wine, 163
Hoisin, and Sesame, Fried Rice with Ginger, 181
Honey Glazed Ham, 143
Honey Ribs, 143
Honey Mustard Chicken, 71
Honeyed Pork Chops, 142
Hot Artichoke and Spinach Dip, 15
Hot Corn Dip, 20
Hot Fudge Ice Cream Bar Dessert, 239
Hot and Sour Chicken Soup, 67
Hummus, Spicy Three Pepper, 11

I

Ice cream
    Chocolate Chip Cookie Ice Cream Cake, 239
    Cinnamon Ice Cream, 236
    Easy Mint Chocolate Chip, 236
    Hot Fudge Ice Cream Bar Dessert, 239
Indian Style Basmati Rice, 179
Irish Chicken Dumplings, 83

J

Jacksonville Carrots, 166
Jalapeño, Best Ever, Poppers, 31
Jambalaya, Oven Baked, 101

K

Kabobs, Marinated Chicken, 71
Kentucky Pecan Pie, 227
Kettle Corn, 28
Kickin' Collard Greens, 153

L

Lasagna
    Artichoke Spinach, 120
    Asparagus, 127
    Vegetarian Four Cheese, 122
Laurie's Stuffed Peppers, 136
Layered Mexican Dip, 20
Lemon
    Butter Chicken, 72
    Pasta Sauce, 114
    Poppy Seed Bread, 217
    Poppy Seed Bundt Cake, 232
    Pudding Cookies, 187
    Square Bars, 201
Lemongrass and Citrus Poached Salmon, 112
Lobster Tails, Grilled Rock, 109

M

Mama's Potato Salad, 51

Maple Dill Carrots, 100
Maple Salmon, 109
Marie's Easy Slow Cooker Pot Roast, 135
Marinated Chicken Kabobs, 71
Marinated Turkey Breast, 86
Meatballs, Cocktail, 33
Meatloaf, Glazed, 135
Mediterranean
    Greek Salad, 57
    Grilled, Vegetable Sandwich, 131
    Summer Tomatoes, 159
MeMa Rie's Zippy Zucchini, 151
Mexican Layered Dip, 20
Mexican Turkey Burgers, 97
Million Dollar Cake, 241
Mint, Chocolate Chip Ice Cream, Easy, 236
Mississippi Mud Cake, 229
Molasses Sugar Cookies, 189
Mom's Big Burgers, 133
Mom's Best Peanut Brittle, 205
Mushroom(s)
    Bacon and Cheddar Stuffed, 34
    Herbed, with White Wine, 163
    Swiss Chicken, 90

N

New Year's Day Black-Eyed Peas, 171
Noodle(s)
    Asian Chicken, Salad, 53
    Old-Fashioned, and Chicken, 95

O

Oatmeal
    Peanut Butter Cookies, 192
    Raisin Cookies, Beth's Spicy, 187
    Raspberry Bars, 195
Okra and Tomatoes, 157
Old-Fashioned Chicken and Noodles, 95
Old Fashioned Coconut Cream Pie, 225
Old Fashioned Peach Cobbler, 212
Onion(s)
    Baked, Dip 24
    Festive, 160
    Fried Rings, 177
    Pork Chops with Fresh Tomato, Garlic, and Feta, 141
Open-Faced Broiled Roast Beef Sandwich, 133
Orange Glazed Chicken Wings, Ginger, 33
Oven Baked Jambalaya, 101
Oven Baked Potato Wedges, 174
Oven Fried Parmesan Chicken, 81

P

Pan-Fried Asparagus, 152
Panna Cotta, 220

Papaya Bruschetta, 23
Parsley, Chicken with Garlic, Basil, and, 81
Pasta
    Bleu Cheese Macaroni, 178
    Cajun Chicken, 89
    Cheesy Salmon, 114
    Chicken and Artichokes, 90
    Fresh Tomatoes and Corn, 124
    Garlic Pasta with Prawns, 125
    Lemon Sauce, 114
    Penne and Vodka Sauce, 118
    Pomodoro, 118
    Scallops, Zucchini, and Tomatoes, 124
    Twelve Minute, Toss, 125
    Vegetable Stuffed Cannelloni, 117
Paul's Pumpkin Bars, 249
Peach Cobbler, Old Fashioned, 212
Peanut Brittle, Mom's Best, 205
Peanut Butter
    Balls, 198
    Chocolate, Bars, 197
    Classic, Cookies, 191
    Cheesecake, Frozen, 249
    Fudge, World's Best, 199
    Oatmeal, Cookies, 192
Pear Pie, 228
Pecan(s)
    Bourbon Chicken, 85
    Crusted, Chicken Salad, 47
    Filled Cookies, 191
    Kentucky, Pie, 227
    Snack, 28
    Sour Cream Pound Cake, 232
Penne and Vodka Sauce, 118
Penne Pasta with Spinach and Bacon, 127
Peppermint Brittle, 207
Peppers, Laurie's Stuffed, 136
Pepper Jelly Dressing, Spinach Salad with, 42
Pesto
    Chicken Florentine, 83
    Creamy, Shrimp, 105
Pie
    Apple Maple Crumble, 227
    Chocolate Mocha, 225
    Crustless Cranberry, 228
    Grandma's Egg Custard, 229
    Grams Chicken Pot, 95
    Kentucky Pecan, 227
    Old Fashioned Coconut Cream, 225
    Pear, 228
Pineapple and Pistachio Pudding, 220
Poached Salmon, Lemongrass and Citrus, 112
Pleasant Pork Chops, 141
Pomodora Pasta, 118

Poppy Seed Bundt Cake, Lemon, 232
Pork
    Chops, with Fresh Tomato, Onion, Garlic, and Feta, 141
    Honeyed Chops, 142
    Honey Glazed Ham, 143
    Honey Ribs, 143
    Roast, with Maple and Mustard Glaze, 142
    Pleasant Chops, 141
    Sweet and Sour, 145
Pot Roast, Cooker, Marie's Easy Slow, 135
Potato(es)
    Bean Enchiladas, 128
    Cajun Style Baked Sweet, 177
    Chips, 173
    Curry, 115
    Garlic Mashed Potatoes Secret Recipe, 175
    Fancy, 174
    Mama's, Salad, 51
    Oven Baked, Wedges, 174
    Sweet and Savory Spuds, 175
Provincial Tomatoes, 167
Pudding
    Banana, 221
    Butterscotch Bread, 218
    Cherry Dump, 221
    Creamy Rice, 218
    Lemon, Cookies, 187
    Pineapple and Pistachio, 220
Pumpkin
    Gingerbread, 217
    Paul's Pumpkin Bars, 249

Q

Quesadillas, Chicken, 34
Quinoa and Black Beans, 115

R

Raisin Cookies, Beth's Spicy Oatmeal, 187
Raisin Rum Bread, 214
Raspberry
    Almond Shortbread Thumbprints, 195
    Oatmeal Bars, 195
    Truffle Fudge, 199
    Cheesecake, White Chocolate Raspberry, 245
Raw Vegetable Salad, 55
Rice
    Creamy, Pudding, 218
    Crispy, Candy, 198
    Fried Rice with Ginger, Hoisin, and Sesame, 181
    Indian Style Basmati, 179
    Spinach, and (Spanakorizo), 156
Roast Pork with Maple and Mustard Glaze, 142
Roasted Beets and Sautéed Beet Greens, 161
Roasted Garlic Bread, 183

Roasted Vegetables, 161
Rum Raisin Bread, 214
Ryan's Favorite Beans, 171

S

Salad
   Amy's Barbecue Chicken, 46
   Apple Avocado, with Tangerine Dressing, 55
   Asian Chicken Noodle, 53
   B.L.T. with Basil Mayo Dressing, 39
   Black Bean and Corn, 59
   Caesar Salad Supreme, 51
   Cherry Chicken, 47
   Chinese Chicken, 49
   Chutney Chicken, 46
   Easy Arugula Salad, 44
   Fennel and Watercress, 41
   Fresh Broccoli, 39
   Greek Veggie, 42
   Grilled Chicken, with Seasonal Fruit, 44
   Harvest, 41
   Mama's Potato, 51
   Mediterranean Greek Salad, 57
   Pecan Crusted Chicken, 47
   Raw Vegetable Salad, 55
   Santa Fe Chicken, 49
   Spinach with Pepper Jelly Dressing, 42
   Wild Rice, 59
Salmon
   Baked Dijon, 110
   Cheesy, Pasta, 114
   Grilled, 112
   Grilled, Skewers, 31
   Lemongrass and Citrus Poached, 112
   Maple, 109
   Smoked Sushi Roll, 37
Salsa
   Annie's Fruit and Cinnamon Chips, 26
   Avocado, Tomato and Mango, 17
   Black Bean, 23
   Cheese Boule Dip, 13
   De Tomatillo, 15
   Fresh, 17
Santa Fe Chicken Salad, 49
Sandwiches
   BBQ Pork for, 139
   Focaccia Chicken, 73
   Grilled Mediterranean Vegetable, 131
   Open-Faced Broiled Roast Beef, 133
Sausage and Apple Stuffing, 183
Seafood
   Baked Dijon Salmon, 110
   Blackened Tuna, 98
   Crab Cakes, 105

   Creamy Pesto Shrimp, 105
   Fettuccine, 99
   Garlic Pasta with Prawns, 125
   Grilled Halibut, 98
   Grilled Salmon Skewers, 31
   Grilled Marinated Shrimp, 103
   Grilled Rock Lobster Tails, 109
   Lemongrass and Citrus Poached Salmon, 112
   Maple Salmon, 109
   Scallops, Zucchini, and Tomatoes, Pasta with, 124
   Spicy Creole Shrimp, 99
   Thai Spiced Barbecue Shrimp, 103
   Trout Amandine, 110
Shredded Brussels Sprouts, 152
Shrimp
   Creamy Pesto, 105
   Grilled Marinated, 103
   Spicy, Creole, 99
   Thai Spiced Barbecue, 103
Shortbread Thumbprints, Raspberry and Almond, 195
Smoked Salmon Sushi Rolls, 37
Snickerdoodles, 188
Soup
   African Peanut, 64
   Chicken Tortilla, 63
   Creamy Tomato-Basil, 65
   Excellent Broccoli Cheese, 64
   Hot Sour Chicken, 67
   Wild Rice and Chicken, 65
Sour Cream Pound Cake, Pecan, 232
Spectacular Marsala Glazed Carrots with Hazelnuts, 164
Spicy Garlic Lime Chicken, 73
Spicy Shrimp Creole, 99
Spicy Three Pepper Hummus, 11
Spinach
   Artichoke, Hot, 15
   Artichoke Lasagna, 120
   Bars, 155
   Enchiladas, 128
   Penne Pasta with Bacon, 127
   Rice (Spanakorizo), 156
   Salad with Pepper Jelly Dressing, 42
   Stuffed Chicken Breast, 76
   With a Twist, 155
Spread(s)
   Fig and Olive Tapenade, 13
   To Die For Garlic Feta Pate, 12
Strawberries with Balsamic Vinegar, 211
Strawberry Trifle, 211
Stuffed Acorn Squash Supreme, 151
Sugar Snap Peas with Mint, 170
Summer Chicken Burgers, 86
Sun-Dried Tomato Dip, 19
Sweet and Sour Pork, 145

T

Tabbouleh, 57
Tangy Chicken Fajitas, 74
Thai Spiced Barbecue Shrimp, 103
The Best Rolled Sugar Cookie, 189
The Ultimate Pasta Salad, 61
Tiger Butter, 202
Tiramisu Layer Cake, 235
To Die For Garlic Feta Pate, 12
Tomato(es)
    Avocado and Mango Salsa, 17
    Bacon Grilled Cheese, 139
    Curry Chicken, 82
    Fried Green Tomatoes, 159
    Mediterranean Summer Tomatoes, 159
    Pasta with Scallops, Zucchini, and, 124
    Pork Chops with Fresh Tomato, Onion, Garlic, and Feta, 141
    Provincial, 167
Totally Groovy Chocolate Fondue, 223
Trifle, Strawberry, 211
Trout Amandine, 110
Tuna
    Blackened, 98
Turkey
    Marinated Breast, 86
    Mexican, Burgers, 97
Twelve Minute Pasta Toss, 125

V

Vegetables
    Acorn Squash, 167
    Apple Cole Slaw, 156
    Amanda's Potatoes, 178
    Baked Asparagus with Balsamic Butter Sauce, 153
    Baked Fennel with Parmesan, 160
    Cajun Style Baked Sweet Potato, 177
    Corn and Zucchini Melody, 169
    Crispy Coated Cajun Fries, 173
    Crispy Pakoras, 36
    Festive Onions, 160
    Fried Cabbage, 157
    Fried Onion Rings, 177
    Gonzo Garbanzos, 170
    Greek Veggie Salad, 42
    Green Beans with Cherry Tomatoes, 149
    Grilled Mediterranean, Sandwich, 131
    Herbed Mushrooms with White Wine, 163
    Jacksonville Carrots, 166
    Kickin' Collard Greens, 153
    Maple Dill Carrots, 166
    New Year's Day Black-Eyed Peas, 171
    Okra and Tomatoes, 157
    Oven Baked Potato Wedges, 174
    Pan-Fried Asparagus, 152
    Potato Chips, 173
    Provincial Tomatoes, 167
    Raw Vegetable Salad, 55
    Roasted. 161
    Roasted ⌐et and Sautéed Greens, 161
    Ryan's Favorite Beans, 171
    Shredded Brussels Sprouts, 152
    Spectacular Marsala Glazed Carrots with Hazelnuts, 164
    Spinach and Rice (Spanakorizo), 156
    Spinach bars, 155
    Spinach with a Twist, 155
    Stuffed Acorn Squash Supreme, 151
    Stuffed Cannelloni, 117
    Sugar Snap Peas with Mint, 170
    Zucchini Patties, 163
Vegetarian Four Cheese Lasagna, 122

W

Warm Cheese Dip with Garlic and Bacon, 12
White Chocolate Party Mix, 207
White Chocolate Raspberry Cheesecake, 245
Wild Rice
    Chicken Soup, 65
    Salad, 59
Wing(s)
    Chicken Dip, 25
    Ginger Orange Glazed Chicken, 33
World's Best Peanut Butter Fudge, 199

Z

Zucchini
    Apple Bread, 214
    Melody, Corn and, 169
    MeMa Rie's Zippy, 151
    Pasta with Scallops, and Tomatoes, 124
    Patties, 163